A DIGEST

OF

THE LAW OF

MARITIME CAPTURES

AND

PRIZES.

BY HENRY WHEATON,

COUNSELLOR AT LAW AND ADVOCATE.

THE LAWBOOK EXCHANGE, LTD.
Clark, New Jersey
2007

ISBN-13: 978-1-58477-854-7
ISBN-10: 1-58477-854-7

The quality of this reprint is equivalent to the quality of the original work.

THE LAWBOOK EXCHANGE, LTD.
33 Terminal Avenue
Clark, New Jersey 07066-1321

Please see our website for a selection of our other publications and fine facsimile reprints of classic works of legal history:
www.lawbookexchange.com

Library of Congress Cataloging-in-Publication Data

Wheaton, Henry, 1785-1848.
A digest of the law of maritime captures and prizes / by Henry Wheaton.
p. cm.
Originally pubished: R. McDermut & D. D. Arden, 1815.
Includes bibliographical references and index.
ISBN-13: 978-1-58477-854-7 (cloth : alk. paper)
ISBN-10: 1-58477-854-7 (cloth : alk. paper)
1. Capture at sea. 2. Prize law. I. Title.
KZ6580.W49 2007
341.6'3--dc22 2007029257

Printed in the United States of America on acid-free paper

A DIGEST

OF

THE LAW OF

MARITIME CAPTURES

AND

PRIZES.

BY HENRY WHEATON,

COUNSELLOR AT LAW AND ADVOCATE.

NEW-YORK:

PUBLISHED BY R. M'DERMUT & D. D. ARDEN,

NO. 1 CITY-HOTEL, BROADWAY.

Forbes & Co. Printers,

78 Gold-street.

1815.

PREFACE.

The law of prize is the most important practical branch of the law of nations. The utility of a work detailing its principles cannot be questioned; and had the United States continued a belligerent power, it would have been indispensably necessary to the statesman, the lawyer, and the merchant. Nor is it conceived that its importance is materially diminished by the restoration of peace, since this country cannot, hereafter, when the flames of war are spread throughout the rest of the civilized world, hope for an exemption from its calamities. But even should it be our unexpected felicity to enjoy the blessings of peace, while other nations are involved in war, the rights and the duties of neutrality must always form an interesting subject of enquiry; while the principles of public law reflect a strong and useful light on many questions of private and municipal jurisprudence.

Ample materials for such a work are to be found in the learned writers upon the law of nations, and in the adjudications of those courts which administer that law. If the former are not always reconcileable with each other, nor the latter consistent with themselves, or capable of being harmonized into a system of perfect symmetry and order, the knowledge of both is not the less necessary; and this defect arises from the imperfect sanctions by which this species of law is guarded. The object of our enquiry is not, *What the law* OUGHT TO BE; but, *What it* PRACTICALLY IS: since it is the latter which furnishes the rule of conduct for those who are governed by it. As public, unlike municipal law, is sanctioned not by the power of a single sovereign or state, but by a resort to force among independent sovereigns or states, it is necessarily imperfect in practice, however just and beautiful in theory. The law of nations is adapted to a state of war, and is intended to mitigate its violence. It is, however, frequently compelled to yield to the very violence it was designed to restrain, and becomes the victim of innovations made and enforced by the edicts of particular states and the adjudications of their tribunals. The purity and simplicity of the primitive law of nations, which is nothing more than the law of nature applied to the conduct of nations and states, has thus been corrupted. It is no longer that law of which Cicero speaks with such eloquent sublimity. *Huic legi nec abrogari fas est, nec derogari ex hac aliquid licet, nec tota abrogari potest. Nec vero aut per senatum, aut per populum solvi hac lege possumus. Neque est querendus explanator, aut interpres ejus alius. Nec erit alia lex Romæ, alia Athenis; alia nunc, alia posthac: sed et omnes gentes, et omni tempore, una lex, et sempiterna, et immortalis continebit; unusque erit communis quasi magister et imperator omnium deus.*

We are therefore compelled to extract from a mass of contradictory decisions, usages, and conventions, those rules which are sanctioned by the justest principles and the most general practice. This task is not less difficult in the law of prize than in any other branch of the *jus gentium*. The author of the present work is not insensible of its imperfections, but may claim some indulgence for his errors on account of the novelty and difficulty of the undertaking.

In a digest of laws, nothing should be sacrificed to the merit of originality. I have therefore freely copied from the elementary writers and the reporters every thing which seemed material to my design, and have interwoven such illustrative observations as were thought necessary. In the customary or *unwritten* law of nations, to borrow an analogous distinction from our municipal law, it is frequently of as much importance to give the very words of the legislator (for the elementary writer or the judge, who make law by their authority and precedents, must be so considered) as it is to transcribe the articles of a treaty or an ordinance, which, by the same analogy, form the *written* or statute law of nations. And who would presume to correct and amend the style of a Bynkershoek, a Pothier, a Scott, or a Marshall? If a fastidious, or even a good taste, would condemn a work constructed of such various materials, this defect is at least palliated by the beauty of utility.

The decisions of the present judge of the high court of admiralty in England are entitled to great respect and attention, and being the adjudications of a court of the law of nations, are of binding authority in that law, except upon those questions in regard to which certain peculiar doctrines have been maintained by the British government. Whatever reason our country may have to complain of the injurious application of those doctrines to us as a neutral nation, it must in candour be admitted that on every other head the decisions of Sir William Scott merit the highest consideration, on account of their intrinsic value and the judicial eloquence by which they are adorned, I have therefore made a liberal, though cautious use of them, in the compilation of this digest. Had that great man followed the example of his illustrious countryman, Sir James Mackintosh, in refusing to be bound by the instructions and rescripts of his government, where they infringed the law of nations and abridged the rights of neutrals, the authority of his adjudications would have been entitled to still more respect with foreign nations and with future ages.

The decisions of the prize courts of other countries have not been reported with the same regularity and correctness as those of Great Britain. I have collected such of them as are to be found in the books accessible in this country, and have inserted them in their appropriate divisions of the work. The adjudications in prize causes which had taken place in the courts of the United States previous to the late war with Great Britain, together with the rich materials afforded by the decisions of the supreme court during that war, have also been incorporated. To these I have added several cases determined in the Circuit Courts by a learned judge, whose attainments in this branch of law, it may be said without injustice to others, are unrivalled in a tribunal whose decisions both on questions of municipal and public law do so much honour to the jurisprudence of this country.

In the multiplicity of elementary books with which the profession is inundated, it becomes important that every distinct work should be circumscribed within the narrowest possible limits. I have consequently aimed at conciseness so far as was consistent with my object. I have sketched a rude outline which some abler hand must hereafter fill up and adorn. *Quam vero ego in aliorum sententiis, ac scriptis dijudicandis mihi sumpsi libertatem ; eandem sibi in me sumant, omnes eos oro, atque obtestor, quorum in manus ista veniant. Non illi promptius me monebunt errantem, quam ego monentes sequar.* GROTIUS de J. B. ac P. Prolegom.

ANALYTICAL INDEX.

CHAPTER I.

CHAPTER II.

CHAPTER III.

CHAPTER IV.

CHAPTER V.

CHAPTER VI.

CHAPTER VII.

CHAPTER VIII.

CHAPTER IX.

CHAPTER X.

APPENDIX.

LAW

OF

MARITIME CAPTURES AND PRIZES.

CHAPTER I.

Of the commencement of war; and of captures made before the declaration of war, or by non-commissioned captors.

1. WHETHER a declaration of war to the enemy is necessary to legalize hostilities, is a preliminary question of the first importance in the law of prize. It was formerly considered essential, and practised. Such was the usage of the antient nations, which was observed in modern Europe until the seventeenth century. The present custom is to publish the declaration, or a manifesto, explaining the motives for commencing hostilities, within the territory of the belligerent state. This publication is necessary for the instruction and direction of the subjects or citizens of the nation declaring war, in order to fix the date of the rights belonging to them from the moment of this declaration, and regarding certain effects which the law of nations attributes to a war in form. Without such a public declaration of war, it would be difficult to distinguish in a treaty of peace, those acts which are to be accounted lawful effects of the war, from those which either nation may consider as

wrongs, and for which they may claim reparation.([a]) The only difference, therefore, between a modern declaration of war and that practised by the Romans under their *Fecial* law, is, that the former is published within the territory of the belligerent state, and communicated every where by means of the invention of the art of printing and the establishment of posts, which rapidly diffuse the information, and supersede the necessity of a particular notice to the enemy by heralds as in antient times.

2. But though by the modern customary law of nations, a formal declaration of war to the enemy is not considered necessary, nor generally practised; letters of marque and reprisal are issued as the first step which is generally taken at the commencement of a war, and which is considered as equivalent to a declaration of it.

Reprisals are either *general* or *special.* They are *general*, when a sovereign or state, who have, or think they have received an injury from another, issue orders to their military and naval officers, and deliver commissions to their subjects or citizens, to take the persons and property of the subjects of the other nation, wherever they may be found.([b])

3. From the moment a sovereign or state is at war with another nation they have a right, strictly speaking, to act as an enemy not only in respect to the persons and property of the enemy found in his territory or on the high seas, but also with respect to the enemy's subjects and their property which may happen to be found in the territory of the belligerent state at the breaking out of the war. They have a right then, to seize on the ships of the enemy found

([a]) *Vattel*, L. 3. c 4. § 56. *Martens*, L. 8. c. 2. § 4. *Bynkershoek*, Q. J. P. L. 1. c. 2. *Ut bellum legitimum sit indictionem belli non videri necessarium.*

([b]) *Du Ponceau's Bynkershoek*, L. 1. c. 24. *In Notis.*

in their ports, and on all their other property.[c] Even sacred things are not exempt by the law of nations from this general liability to capture; and there is a remarkable observation of Cicero on this subject in his fourth oration against Verres, that, *Victory made all the* SACRED *things of the Syracusans* PROFANE. But by the modern law and usage of nations, the temples of religion, public edifices devoted to civil purposes only, and the monuments of the arts and repositories of science, are exempted from the operations of war. Christianity, chivalry, colonization, commerce, and civilization in general, have successively combined to soften the extreme severity of these operations. The generality of the above mentioned rule still applies, however, to cases of *maritime* capture. Some late writers have attempted to extend this relaxation to maritime warfare, upon the ground that private property is exempt from spoliation in land wars, and therefore ought not to be liable to capture and confiscation by sea. But besides the usage of considering such property, when captured in cities taken by storm, as booty; it is well known that contributions are levied upon territories occupied by a hostile army in lieu of a general confiscation of the property belonging to the inhabitants, and that the object of wars by land being conquest, or the acquisition of territory to be exchanged as an equivalent for the restoration of other territory lost, the regard of the victor for those who are to be, or have been, his subjects, will naturally restrain him from the exercise of his extreme rights in this particular: whereas the object of maritime wars is the destruction of the enemy's commerce and navigation, the sources and sinews of his naval power, which object can only be attained by the capture and confiscation of private property. Nor is any notice of the existence of the war to the party necessary in

(c) *Grotius, de J. B. ac P.* L.3. c.21. § 9. *Puffendorf,* L. 8. c. 6. § 19.20. *Wolf, Jus, Gent.* § 1184. 1198. *Martens,* L. 8. c. 2. § 5. *Bynkershoek,* *Q. J. Pub.* L. 1. c. 2.

order to legalize the capture of his property; for it is sufficient that actual hostilities existed at the time when the capture was made, and that those hostilities were authorised by the proper authority. If no general declaration of war to the enemy be essential, no particular notice to his subjects or citizens can be necessary, to render the capture of their property lawful. The declaration is every where operative from its date upon all the persons and property of the enemy. It operates every where from its date to legalize captures precisely as a treaty of peace operates from its date (unless otherwise provided) to annul them. But in order to induce the confiscation of enemy's property, found within the territory of the belligerent state at the declaration of war, some act of the government, other than the declaration itself is essential.

Previous to the late war between the United States and Great Britain, a vessel, owned by citizens of the belligerent state, was chartered to a house of trade in the enemy's country, one of whom was also a citizen, for the purpose of carrying a cargo from Savannah to Plymouth. After the cargo was put on board, the vessel was stopped by an embargo. It was afterwards agreed between the master of the ship and the agent of the shipper, that she should proceed with her cargo to New-Bedford where her owner resided, and there remain without prejudice to the charter party. In pursuance of this agreement, the vessel proceeded to New-Bedford, where she continued until after the declaration of war in 1812. In the month of October or November of that year, the ship was unloaded, and the cargo, except a part of it consisting of pine timber, was landed. The pine timber was floated up a salt water creek, where, at low tide, the ends of the timber rested on the mud, and where it was secured from floating out with the tide, by impediments fastened in the entrance of the creek. In November the cargo was sold by the agent of the owners, who was a citizen, to the claimant, also a citizen. A libel was afterwards filed by the United States Attorney for the district against the cargo, as well for the United States as for and in behalf of a noncommissioned captor and all other persons concerned. It did not appear that this seizure was made under any instructions from the President of the United States, nor was there any evidence of its having his sanction, unless the libel being filed and prosecuted by the law officer who represents the Government might imply that sanction. On the contrary, it was admitted that the seizure was made by an individual, and the libel filed at his instance, by the District Attorney, who acted from his own impression of what appertained to his duty. The property was claimed under the purchase made in the preceding November.

Could the pine timber, even admitting the property not to be changed by the sale, be condemned as prize of war?

The cargo having been legally acquired and put on board the vessel, having been detained by an embargo not intended to act on foreign property; the vessel having sailed before the war from Savannah under a stipulation to reland the cargo in some other port of the belligerent state; the relanding having been made with respect to the residue of the cargo; and the pine timber having been floated into shallow water where it was secured, and in the custody of the owner of the ship, a citizen, the court could not perceive any solid distinction (so far as respects confiscation) between this property and other enemy's property found on land at the commencement of hostilities. It was therefore considered as a question relating to such property generally, and to be governed by the same rule.

Respecting the power of government no doubt was entertained. That war gives to the sovereign full right to take the persons and confiscate the property of the enemy wherever found, was conceded. The mitigations of this rigid rule, which the humanity and wise policy of modern times has introduced into practice, will more or less affect the exercise of this right, but cannot impair the right itself. That remains undiminished; and whenever the sovereign authority shall choose to bring it into operation, the judicial department must give effect to its will. But until that will shall be expressed, no power of condemnation could exist in the court.

The questions to be decided were,

1st, May enemy's property found on land at the commencement of hostilities be seized and condemned as a necessary consequence of the declaration of war?

2ndly, Was there any legislative act which authorized such seizure and condemnation?

Since in this country, from the structure of the government, proceedings to condemn the property of an enemy found within the territory at the declaration of war, can be sustained only upon the principle that they are instituted in the execution of some existing law, we are led to ask,

Is the declaration of war such a law? Does that declaration, by its own operation, so vest the property of the enemy in the government, as to support a proceeding for its seizure and confiscation; or does it vest only a right, the assertion of which depends on the will of the sovereign power?

The universal practice of forbearing to seize and confiscate debts and credits; the principle universally received that the right to them revives on the restoration of peace, would seem to prove that war is not an absolute confiscation of this property, but simply confers the right of confiscation.

Between debts contracted under the faith of laws, and property acquired in the course of trade, on the faith of the same laws, reason draws no distinction, and although, in practice, vessels with their cargoes, found in port at the declaration of war, may have been seized, it was not believed that modern usage would sanction the seizure of the goods of an enemy on land, which were acquired in peace in the course of trade. Such a proceeding is rare, and would be deemed a harsh exercise of the rights of war. But although the practice in this respect may not be uniform, that circumstance does not essentially affect the question. The enquiry is, whether such property vests in the sovereign by the mere declaration of war, or remains subject to a right of confiscation, the exercise of which depends on the national will: and the rule which applies to one case, so far as respects the operation of the declaration of war on the thing itself, must apply to all others over which war gives an equal right. The right of the sovereign to confiscate debts being precisely the same with the right to confiscate other property found in the country, the operation of a declaration of war on debts and other property found within the country must be the same. What then is the operation?

Even Bynkershoek, who maintains the broad principle that in war every thing done against an enemy is lawful; that he may be destroyed, though unarmed and defenceless; that fraud or even poison may be employed against him; that a most unlimited right is acquired to his person and property; admits that war does not transfer to the sovereign a debt due to his enemy; and, therefore, if payment of such debt be not exacted, peace revives the former right of the creditor; because, says he, the occupation which is had by war consists more in fact than in law. He adds—Let it not, however, be supposed that it is only true of actions, that they are not condemned, *ipso jure*, for other things also belonging to the enemy may be concealed and escape condemnation.

Vattel says—The sovereign can neither detain the persons nor the property of those subjects of the enemy who are within his dominions at the time of the declaration.

It is true that this rule is, in terms, applied by Vattel to the property of those only who are personally within the territory at the commencement of hostilities; but it applies equally to things in action and to things in possession: and, if war did, of itself, without any further exercise of the sovereign will, vest the property of the enemy in the sovereign, his presence could not exempt it from this operation of war. Nor can a reason be perceived for maintaining that the public faith is more entirely pledged for the security of property trusted in the territory of the nation in time of peace, if it be accompanied by its owner, than if it be confided to the care of others.

The modern rule then would seem to be, that tangible property belonging to an enemy and found in the country at the commencement of war, ought not to be immediately confiscated; and in almost every commercial treaty an article is inserted stipulating for the right to withdraw such property.

This rule appears to be totally incompatible with the idea that war does of itself vest the property in the belligerent government. It may be considered as the opinion of all who have written on the *jura belli*, that war gives the right to confiscate, but does not itself confiscate the property of the enemy; and their rules go to the exercise of this right.

The constitution of the United States was framed at a time when this rule, introduced by commerce, in favour of moderation and humanity, was received throughout the civilized world. In expounding that constitution, a construction ought not lightly to be admitted which would give to a declaration of war an effect in this country, it does not possess elsewhere, and which would fetter that exercise of entire discretion respecting enemy property, which may enable the government to apply to the enemy the rule that he applies to us.

If we look to the constitution itself, we find this reasoning much strengthened by the words of that instrument.

That the declaration of war has only the effect of placing the two nations in a state of hostility, of producing a state of war, of giving those rights which war confers; but not of operating by its own force any of those results (such as a transfer of property) which are usually produced by ulterior measures of government, is fairly deducible from the enumeration of powers which accompanies that of declaring war. *Congress shall have power—to declare war, grant letters of marque and reprisal, and make rules concerning captures on land and water.*

It would be restraining this clause within narrower limits than the words themselves import, to say that the power to make rules concerning captures on land and water, is to be confined to captures which are extra-territorial. If it extends to rules respecting enemy property found within the territory, then we perceive an express grant to Congress of the power in question, as an independent, substantive power, not included in that of declaring war.

The acts of Congress furnish many instances of legislative opinion that the declaration of war does not, of itself, authorise proceedings against the persons or property of the enemy found, at the time, within the territory.

War gives an equal right over persons and property; and if its declaration is not considered as prescribing a law respecting the person of an enemy found in our country, neither does it prescribe a law for his property. The act concerning alien enemies, which confers on the President very great discretionary powers respecting their persons, affords a strong implication that he did not possess those powers by virtue of the declaration of war.

The Act for the Safe Keeping and Accommodation of Prisoners of War, is of the same character.

The Act Prohibiting Trade with the Enemy, contains the following clause: That the President be and he hereby is authorized to give, at any time within six months after the passage of this act, passports for the safe transportation of any ship or other property belonging to British subjects, and which is now within the limits of the United States. The phraseology of this law shows that the property of a British subject was not considered by the legislature as being vested in the United States by the declaration of war; and the authority which the act confers on the President, is manifestly considered as one which he did not previously possess.

The proposition that a declaration of war does not, in itself, enact a confiscation of the property of the enemy within the territory of the belligerent state, is believed to be entirely free from doubt. Is there in the act of Congress of June, 1812, by which war is declared against Great Britain, any expression which would indicate such an intention?

This act, after placing the two nations in a state of war, authorizes the President to use the whole land and naval force of the United States to carry the war into effect, and to issue to private armed vessels of the United States commissions or letters of marque and general reprisal against the vessels, goods and effects of the government of the United Kingdom of Great Britain and Ireland, and the subjects thereof.

That reprisals may be made on enemy property found within the United States at the declaration of war, if such be the will of the nation, had been admitted; but it was not admitted that, in the declaration of war, the nation had expressed its will to that effect.

It cannot be necessary to employ argument in shewing that when the Attorney for the United States institutes proceedings at law for the confiscation of enemy property found on land, or floating in a river in the care and custody of a citizen, he is not acting under authority of letters of marque and reprisal, still less under the authority of such letters issued to a private armed vessel.

The act concerning Letters of Marque Prizes, and Prize Goods, certainly contains nothing to authorize this seizure.

There being no other act of Congress which bears upon the subject, it was considered as proved, that the legislature had not confiscated enemy property which was within the United States at the declaration of war.

One view, however, has been taken of this subject which deserves to be further considered.

It was urged, that, in executing the laws of war, the executive may seize, and the courts condemn all property, which, according to the modern law of nations, is subject to confiscation, although it might require an act of the legislature to justify the condemnation of that property which, according to the modern usage, ought not to be confiscated.

The argument must assume for its basis the position that modern usage constitutes a rule which acts upon the thing itself by its own force, and not through the sovereign power. This position was not allowed. This usage is a guide which the sovereign follows or abandons at his will. The rule, like other precepts of morality, of humanity, and even of wisdom, is addressed to the judgment of the sovereign; and although it cannot be disregarded by him without obloquy, yet it may be disregarded.

The rule is in its nature flexible. It is subject to infinite modification. It is not an immutable rule of law, but depends on political considerations which may continually vary.

Commercial nations in the situation of the United States have always a considerable quantity of property in the possession of their neighbours. When war breaks out, the question, what shall be done with the enemy property in our country, is a question rather of policy than of law. The rule which we apply to the property of our enemy, will be applied by him to the property of our citizens. Like all other questions of policy, it is proper for the consideration of a department which can modify it at will; not for the consideration of a department which can pursue only the law as it is written. It is proper for the consideration of the legislature, not of the executive or judiciary. It appears to the court that the power of confiscating enemy property is in the legislature, and that the legislature had not declared its will to confiscate property which was within our territory at the declaration of war.[d]

In the above case the inferior court of prize had condemned the property, and two of the judges of the supreme court dissented from the above decision, remarking, that it seemed to have been taken for granted that the opinion of the court below proceeded, in some degree, upon a supposition that a declaration of war operates, *per se*, an *actual confiscation* of enemy's property found within our territory. On the contrary, it was admitted that a declaration of war does not, of itself, import a confiscation of enemy's property, within or without the country, on the land or on the high seas. The title of the enemy is not by war divested, but remains in *proprio vigore*, until a hostile seizure and possession has impaired his title. But a declaration of war gives a right to confiscate enemy's property, and enables the power to whom the execution of the laws and the prosecution of the war are confided, to enforce that right. If, indeed, there be a limit imposed as to the extent to which hostilities may be carried by the executive, the executive cannot lawfully transcend that limit; but if no such limit exists, the war may be carried on according to the principles of the modern law of nations, and enforced when, and where, and on what property the executive chooses. In no act whatsoever had Congress declared the confiscation of enemy's property. They had authorized the President to grant letters of marque and general reprisal, which he might revoke and annul at his pleasure: and even as to captures actually made under such commissions, no absolute title by confiscation vested in the captors, until a sentence of condemnation. If, therefore, enemy's property had come into the ports of the United States after the war, and the President had declined to issue letters of marque and reprisal, there was no act of Congress which, in terms,

([d]) Per Marshall, C. J. *Brown vs. the United States*, Supreme Court of the U. S. February Term, 1814, M. S.

declared it confiscated and subjected it to condemnation. If, nevertheless, it was confiscable, the right of confiscation resulted not from the express provisions of any statute, but from the very state of war, which subjects the hostile property to the disposal of the government. But until the title should have been divested by some overt act of the government and some judicial sentence, the property would unquestionably remain in the enemy owner; and if a peace had intervened, it would have been completely beyond the reach of subsequent condemnation. There was, then, no distinction recognized by any act of Congress, between enemy's property which was within the ports of the United States at the commencement of the war, and enemy's property found elsewhere. Neither were declared *ipso facto*, confiscated; and both were merely confiscable.

The act of June 18th, 1812, the Prize act of June 26th, 1812, the act of July 6th, 1812, and the act of March 3d, 1813, were all the acts which conferred powers on the President, or make provisions touching the management of the war. In no one of them was there the slightest limitation upon the executive powers growing out of a state of war; and they existed, therefore, in their full and perfect vigour. By the constitution the executive is charged with the faithful execution of the laws; and the language of the act of June 18th, 1812, declaring war, authorized him to carry it into effect. In what manner, and to what extent should he carry it into effect? There was no act of the legislature defining the powers, objects, or mode of warfare: By what rules, then, must he have been governed? The only rational answer is, by the law of nations as applied to a state of war. Whatever act is approved by that law, in hostilities among civilized nations, such act he might in his discretion, adopt and exercise; for with him the sovereignty of the nation rests as to the execution of the laws. If any of such acts are disapproved by the legislature, it is in their power to narrow and limit the extent to which the rights of war shall be exercised ; but until such limit is assigned, the executive must have all the rights of modern warfare vested in him, to be exercised in his sound discretion, or he can have none. Upon what principle can he have an *implied* authority to adopt one and not another? The best manner of annoying the enemy must, from the nature of things, vary under different circumstances ; and the executive is responsible to the nation for the faithful discharge of his duty, under all the changes of hostilities.

But it was said that a declaration of war does not, of itself, import a right to confiscate enemy's property found within the country at the commencement of war. This proposition could not be admitted in the extent in which it is laid down. Nothing is more clear from authority than the right to seize hostile property afloat in ports at the commencement of war. It is the settled practice of nations, and the modern rule of Great Britain herself applied to American property in the present war; applied, also, to property not merely on board of ships, but, as it appeared by an affidavit in this case, to spars floating along side of them. It was also said that a declaration of war does not carry with it the right to confiscate property found in the country at the commencement of war, because the constitution itself, in giving congress the power, *to declare war, grant letters of marque and reprisal, and make rules concerning captures by land and water*,—has clearly evinced that the power to declare war did not, *ex vi terminorum*, include a right to capture property every where, and that the power to make rules concerning captures on land and water, may well be considered as a substantive power as to captures of property *within the territory*. But if the power to make rules respecting captures, &c. be a substantive power, it is equally applicable to all captures, wherever made, on land or on water. The terms of the grant import no limitation as to place. Upon the same construction the power to grant letters of marque and reprisal is a substantive power; and a declaration of war could not, of itself, authorize any seizure whatsoever of hostile property, unless this power was called into exercise. The power to declare war includes all the powers incident to war, and necessary to carry it into effect. If the constitution had been silent as to letters of marque and captures, it would not have narrowed the authority of congress. The authority to grant letters of marque and reprisal, and to regulate captures are ordinary and necessary incidents to the power of declaring war. It would be utterly ineffectual without them. The expression, therefore, of that which is implied in the very nature of the grant, cannot weaken the force of the grant itself. The words are merely explanatory, and introduced *ex abundanti cautela*.—The above decision seems to admit that the effect of hostilities is to confer all the rights which war confers; and it seems tacitly to concede, that, by virtue of the declaration of war, the executive would have a right to seize enemy's property which should actually come within the territory during the war. Certainly no such power was given directly by any statute: and if the argument be correct, that the power to make captures on land or water must be expressly called into exercise by the legislature, before the executive can, even after war, enforce a capture and condemnation, it will be very difficult to support the concession. Suppose an enemy's ship of war or merchant ship should have come within our ports, there was no statute declaring such ship actually confiscated. There was no express authority either for the navy or army to make a capture of her: and although the executive might authorize a private armed vessel so to do, yet it would depend altogether upon the will of the vessel's owner whether they would so do or not. Can it be possible that the executive has not the power to authorize such a seizure? And if he might authorize a seizure by the army or navy, why not by private individuals, if they will volunteer for the purpose?—The act declaring war authorized the executive to employ the land and naval force of the United States to carry it into effect. When and where should he carry it into effect? Congress had not declared that any captures should be made on land; and if this be a substantive power, not included in a declaration of war, how could the executive make captures on the land, when Congress had not expressed their will to this effect? The power to employ the army and navy might well be exercised in preventing invasion, and the common defence, without necessarily including a right to capture, if the right of capture be not an incident of war: and upon what ground then could the executive plan and execute foreign expeditions and foreign captures? Neither the power to seize and capture enemy's property which was without the territory, at the commencement of the war, nor the power to seize that which was within the territory at the same period, were expressly given or denied (except as to private armed vessels) and how could either be assumed except as an incident of war? The act respecting alien enemies and prisoners of war may, in general be deemed mere regulations of war, limiting and directing the discretion of the executive; and it cannot be doubted that Congress had a perfect right to prescribe such regulations. To regulate the exercise of the rights of war as to enemies does not, however, imply that such rights have not an independent existence. Besides, it is clear that the act respecting alien enemies applies only to aliens resident within the country, and not to the property of aliens who are not so resident.—When the legislative authority, to whom the right to declare war is confided, declares war in its most unlimited manner, the executive authority, to whom the execution of the war is confided, is bound to carry it into effect. He has a discretion vested in him, as to the manner and extent; but he cannot lawfully transcend the rules of warfare established among civilized nations. He cannot lawfully exercise powers or authorise proceedings which the civilized world repudiate and disclaim. The sovereignty, as to declaring war and directing its effects, rests with the legislature. The sovereignty, as to its execution, rests with the President. If the legislature do not limit the nature of the war, all the regulations and rights of general war attach upon it. It was not therefore contended that the modern usage of nations constitutes a rule, acting on enemy's property so as to produce confiscation of itself, and not through the sovereign power. On the contrary, it is considered, that enemy's property is in no case confiscated by the mere declaration of war; it is only liable to be confiscated, at the discretion of the sovereign power, having the conduct and execution of the war. The modern usage of nations was resorted to merely as a limitation of this discretion, not as conferring the authority to exercise it. The sovereignty to execute it is supposed already to exist in the President by the very terms of the constitution: and it is again asked, if this general power to confiscate enemy's property does not exist in the executive, to be exercised in his discretion, how could he have authority to seize and confiscate any enemy's property, coming into the country after the war, or found in the enemy's territory?(e)

Thus also where salvage had been decreed upon property which was the property of a friend at the time of its being rescued, but war being subsequently declared, and existing at the time of adjudication, prevented the owner, who was entitled to the residue after paying the amount of salvage, from interposing a claim in the courts of the belligerent state. But as this property was found within the territory of that state at the declaration of war, it was decided that it must stand on the same footing with other enemy's property similarly situated. Although property of that description is liable to be disposed of by the legislative power of the

(e) Per STORY, J.

country, yet, until some act is passed on the subject, it is still under the protection of the law, and may be claimed upon the termination of war, if not previously confiscated. The court would therefore make such order respecting it, as would preserve it, subject to the will of the court, to be disposed of as future circumstances should render proper.(f)

As to the first of the above cases it should be observed that there was no affidavit in the court below shewing the timber to be partly resting on land, but that it appeared to be water borne. The decisions in both may well consist and stand with the principles hereinafter laid down as to seizures in port by non-commissioned captors; for the only real question of doubt or difficulty in the cases above referred to was one of municipal law,—Whether the state had declared its will to confiscate? Had the court deemed it within the authority of the judicial power under our municipal constitution, it might have applied the law of vindictive retaliation to these cases, it having been proved in the first, that American vessels and spars floating along side of them had been condemned in Great Britain during the then present war under like circumstances. *Vide infra*, § 13.

4. So also nations have been induced for their mutual benefit, and influenced by the increasing civilization and refinement of the age, to temper the extreme rigor of this right of seizing and confiscating enemy's property found within the territory by conventional agreements.

Thus by the treaties between the United States and France, Sweden, and Morocco, from six to nine months are allowed the merchants of those nations respectively, to withdraw themselves and their effects, in case of war. And it is stipulated in the treaty of 1794 between the United States and Great Britain, That in case of a rupture be-

(f) Per JOHNSON, J. The *Adventure*, Supreme Court of the United States, February Term, 1814. M. S. *Vide infra*, Chapter X. § 6.

tween them, the merchants and others of each of the two nations residing in the dominions of the other, shall have the privilege of remaining and continuing their trade, so long as they behave peaceably, and commit no offence against the laws; and in case their conduct should render them suspected, and the respective government should think proper to order them to remove, the period of twelve months from the publication of the order, shall be allowed them for that purpose, to remove all their families, effects, and property; but this favour shall not extend to those who act contrary to the established laws. *Art.* 26. The act of 5 Cong. c. 83, declares, That aliens, with whose nations we have any treaty, shall in case of war, be permitted to remain in the United States the full time stipulated by treaty; and where there is no such treaty, the President may ascertain and declare such reasonable time for their departure, as may be consistent with the public safety, and according to the dictates of humanity and national hospitality.

5. The war of 1756 having been commenced by Great Britain against France without a declaration or the issuing of general letters of marque and reprisal, the question was agitated in the latter country between the insured who had stipulated to pay an increase of premium *in case of war* and the insurers who were to receive it, whether hostilities of this nature were to be considered as within the words of the policy. For the insured it was contended that such hostilities could not constitute *a war*, because by the law of nations no other war is known but that which is declared in a public and solemn manner by one state against another: *Hostes sunt quibus bellum publice populus Romanus decrevit, vel ipsi populi Romano*, L. 24. *Ff. de Capt. et Post.* On the other hand it was argued, that being authorized by the British government, they were to be considered as true acts of hostility between nation and nation, and to be assimilated to a war. In fact by the memorial

sent to the court of London on the 21st December, 1755, the French king demanded the prompt and complete restitution of the vessels and effects of his subjects which had been taken, at the same time announcing that in case of refusal he should consider such denial of justice as *an actual declaration* of war on the part of the court of London. The question was finally decided against the insured, and it was determined that the premium should be increased in the same manner as if the words *hostilities and reprisal* had been used in the policy.(g)

6. As it may happen that seizures of the vessels and effects of the enemy may be made before the commencement of hostilities, and by way of reprisals; and as such seizures may be made either before or subsequent to the commencement of hostilities, by non commissioned captors it becomes an important question to determine in whom vests the proceeds of such seizures, should the injustice of the adverse power ultimately induce their confiscation. By the universal law and usage of nations the right to all captures and seizures made from an enemy vests in the sovereign or state. The municipal law of every particular nation regulates the distribution of the proceeds thereof. As to captures made after the commencement of hostilities, and in virtue of instructions given to the public armed vessels of the state, and of letters of marque issued to private armed vessels, their proceeds are distributed with certain reservations, to the individual captors. In respect to seizures made before the commencement of hostilities, and those made by non commissioned captors, they vest in the sovereign or state, except such portions of them as may have been granted to others. And by the law of most of the maritime nations of Europe, certain of those portions have been granted to, and consequently vest in, the person

(g) *Pothier, d'Assurance*, No. 84. *Valin, sur l'Ordonnance*, L. 3. tit 6. *des Assurances*, Art. 3.

sustaining the office of Admiral. Hence, in England these portions are termed *Droits of Admiralty*. But in cases of seizures by non-commissioned captors, it is usual to reward the takers with a liberal share of the property, which is determined by the proper court upon reference to it.[h]

7. And by the antient law of France, those only who had commissions from the Admiral could lawfully capture for their own use; so that if the master of a merchant vessel, who had no commission or letter of marque, was attacked at sea by an enemy's ship, and in defending himself, captured the ship of the enemy, the prize did not vest in the captor, but belonged to the Admiral, to whom the rights of the sovereign had been granted: but it was customary for the Admiral to allow the captor a liberal portion of the prize as a reward for his exertions; with a reservation, however, that this act of bounty should not be construed into a right.[i]

So also, in England, when enemy's vessels come into port from distress of weather, or want of provisions, or from ignorance of war existing, and are seized in port, they belong to the lord high admiral; or as that office is now practically constituted, to the king in his office of admiralty. This is likewise the case with enemy's ships and goods met at sea, and seized by any vessel not commissioned. All rights of prize belong originally to the crown, and the beneficial interest derived to others can proceed only from the grant of the crown. It was thought expedient to assign a certain portion of those rights, to maintain the dignity of the lord high admiral, who now exists only in contemplation of law. This grant, whatever it conveys, carries with it a total and perpetual alienation of the rights of the crown. Captors can therefore have no interest in prizes taken under such circumstances; a perpetual aliena-

(h) 1 *Robinson*, 286. The Haase. *Ib.* 303. The Amor Parentum.

(i) *Pothier, De Propriété*, No. 93. *Valin, Sur l'Ordonnance*, L. 3: tit. 9. *des Prises*, Art. 1.

tion of the crown's original right to them having been made to the lord high admiral.(k)

8. And by the law of France, enemy's vessels driven on shore from distress of weather, or other causes, are condemned to the crown. Such are the provisions of the ordinance of the 12th of May, 1696, *concerning the adjudication of vessels driven on shore by distress of weather, or otherwise.* His majesty being informed that certain disputes have arisen concerning the adjudication of stranded vessels, either in respect to those which being of foreign built are unprovided with a bill of sale, or in respect to goods unaccompanied by a bill of lading, under the pretext that the regulation of the 17th February, 1694, appears to be confined to captured vessels, and that the article of the ordinance of August, 1681, which confiscates goods unaccompanied by bills of lading is invested under the title of *prizes*; his majesty being desirous to provide a remedy herein, in order that the said goods and vessels, which are really enemy's property, but often claimed by the subjects of neutral princes, may not in any case be withdrawn from the confiscation to which they are justly liable by the laws of war, and by the antient and modern ordinances; his majesty hath ordained and doth hereby ordain that the vessels which are stranded upon the coasts, or driven thither by distress of weather, or otherwise, shall be judged according to the ordinance of August, 1681, under the title of prizes, and according to the regulation of the 17th February, 1694; so that every vessel stranded, which is of enemy built, or originally belonging to an enemy proprietor, shall not be considered as neutral, but shall be wholly confiscated to *his majesty's use*, unless the sale was made in the presence of some public magistrate before whom such transfers are usually made, and unless the bill of sale be found on board accompanied by a legal power given by the

(k) 6 *Robinson*, 282, The Maria Francaise.

former owner in case the sale is made by his agent. His majesty likewise ordains that the goods of the cargo of such stranded vessels, unaccompanied by bills of lading, shall be and remain entirely confiscated *to his use*; it not being, however, his majesty's intention to include in the present ordinance stranded vessels, whose papers may have been lost by distress of weather and the calamity of shipwreck, in case the master or commander makes a declaration thereof forthwith, and the facts justify the presumption of its truth; in which case his majesty ordains that the claimants shall have liberty to produce a certified copy of the bill of sale, and duplicates of the bills of lading.

9. And where Dutch property was seized in England before a declaration of war against Holland, it was condemned to the crown, upon the ground that the declaration had a retroactive effect, applying to all property previously detained, and rendering it liable to be considered as the property of enemies taken in time of war. The seizure was determined to be provisional and equivocal as to the effect, and liable to be varied by subsequent events. If the relations of peace had been ultimately re-established, then the seizure, though made with the character of a hostile seizure, would have proved, in the event a mere embargo, or temporary sequestration. The property would have been restored, as is usual at the conclusion of embargoes; a process often resorted to in the practice of nations, for various causes not immediately connected with any expectation of hostility. Such would have been the retroactive effect of that course of circumstances. On the contrary if the transactions end in hostility, the retroactive effect is directly the other way. It impresses the direct hostile character upon the original seizure. It is declared to be *no embargo*; it is no longer an equivocal act subject to two interpretations; there is a declaration of the *animus* by which it was done, that it was done *hostile animo*, and is

to be considered as a hostile measure *ab initio*. The property taken is liable to be treated as the property of persons trespassers *ab initio*, and guilty of injuries which they have refused to redeem by any amicable alteration of their measures. This is the necessary course, if no particular compact intervenes for the restitution of such property before a formal declaration of hostilities.(l)

10. Where the capture was made by a vessel sent out by the captain of a man of war, but not attached as a tender to the ship of war, it was condemned as a droit of admiralty, upon the ground of its being taken by a non-commissioned vessel. The only parties that can maintain an interest in prize are public ships of war and private armed vessels commissioned as letters of marque. Commanding officers of those ships may have a right to put their men, arms, and stores on board another vessel; but by so doing an officer cannot be said to put that other vessel into commission, and entitle it to the privilege of being reckoned amongst the description of vessels, to which the interest in prize is given by law. If a capture is made by a tender attached by the interposition of public authority; on every principle which a capture by a boat would entitle its ship, a capture made by a tender, specially employed in that capture by the ship of war to which she belonged, might, perhaps, entitle that ship. But not so with a tender attached by the private act of the officer hiring and manning her himself. The character of a part of the navy is not to be impressed without the intervention of some public authority.(m)

The same doctrine was held by the Lords Commissioners of Appeals in Prize Causes in England, on the claim of the Abergavenny ship of war to share in the capture of Curacoa, in virtue of the presence and co-opera-

(l) 5 *Robinson*, 233. The Boedes Lust.

(m) 5 *Robinson*, 41, The Melomasne.—*Ib.* 280. The Charlotte.

tion of a tender *so constituted*, and sent out to cruize by the captain of the ship without the intervention of any public authority; when the court decided against the claim, May 4th, 1805.(n)

11. And where private armed vessels having letters of marque against one enemy power, and a war broke out with another; the captures made from that other were condemned not to the captors, but as droits of admiralty.(o)

12. Notwithstanding the above principles relative to prizes made by non-commissioned captors appear to be well settled as a part of the law and practice of nations, yet they are apparently controverted by the learned Bynkershoek in the single case of a capture made by a merchant vessel, attacked at sea by an enemy's ship, and who in defending herself captures the ship of the enemy. In this case, he labours to shew that the master and crew of the merchant vessel are alone entitled to the prize to the exclusion of the owners and freighters.(p) But it is evident that this must depend upon the municipal regulations of the belligerent nation. For the right to prize is originally inherent in the sovereign or state. No person can have any interest in it but what he takes as the gift or grant of the sovereign or state. The right of making war and peace is exclusively in them: the acquisitions of war belong to them: and the disposal of these acquisitions may be of the utmost importance for the purposes both of war and peace. This is generally received as a necessary principle of public jurisprudence by all writers on the subject, *Bello parta cedunt Reipublicæ*. It is not to be supposed that this wise attribute of sovereignty is conferred without reason; it is given for the purpose assigned, that the power to whom it belongs to de-

(n) 5 *Robinson*, Ib. *In Notis*.

(o) 2 *Brown's* c. iv. & *Adm. Law*, 526. Appendix. 4 *Robinson*, 72. The Abigail.

(p) *Q. J. P.* L. 1. c. 20.

cide on peace or war, may use it in the most beneficial manner for the purposes of both. A general presumption arising from these considerations is, that government does not mean to divest itself of this universal attribute of sovereignty, conferred for such purposes, unless it is so clearly and unequivocally expressed.(q) Vain is it to allege that the captors, in the case stated above, act under the natural law of self defence, paramount to all civil laws whatsoever. For this right conferred by the law of nature is merged in the social compact, or at least must be exercised in subordination to the regulations of civil society. Unless therefore the municipal law of the belligerent state has otherwise ordained it, the right to prizes captured under these circumstances must vest in the sovereign or state. In Great Britain, a statute provision divides the proceeds of the prize thus captured between the master and crew, and the owners of the merchant vessel, in the same manner as is practised in the case of private armed vessels, Stat. 22 & 23 Charles II. c. 2. And in case of recaptures by non-commissioned vessels, the property retaken becomes a droit of admiralty; but it is always referred to the court of admiralty to fix the proportion of reward due to the salvors.(r)

13. As the United States have not alienated their original right to prizes, except as to those made by public and private armed and commissioned vessels, it follows, that, in this country, the right to prizes made before a declaration of war, or by non-commissioned captors, vests in the United States. If, therefore, property which has been subjected to an embargo or temporary sequestration, or which has been seized by non-commissioned captors, is finally condemned as enemy's property, it must be condemned to the United States, the captors having no legal interest in prizes made under such circumstances. And non-commis-

(q) 5 *Robinson*, 173, The Elsebe.

(r) 1 *Robinson*, 178, The San Bernado. *Ib.* 286, The Haase.

sioned captors are rewarded in this country not by the executive authority, but by the legislature. *Vide* the several acts of Congress passed during the late war granting to individuals vessels, and other property captured by them without a letter of marque.

It is evident that none of the preceding principles can be applicable to vessels and goods *wrongfully* taken and detained before a declaration of war. Such property cannot be confiscated after the declaration, but ought to be restored to the enemy owners; because had it not been for the wrong first done it would not have been in the possession of the belligerent state. *Vide* the famous Report of Sir George Lee, &c. on the Memorial of the Prussian Minister to Great Britain, of the 18th of January, 1753, by which it appears that French ships and effects, wrongfully taken before France became a party to the war which was terminated by the treaty of Aix La Chapelle, were restored to the French owners by decree of the English courts of prize, *flagrante bello*. Nothing can justify a departure from this course, unless indeed it be the conduct of the enemy; for we are told by authority equally high with that of the authors of this Report, that it is the constant practice of Great Britain to condemn property seized before the war, if the enemy condemns, and to restore if the enemy restores.(*)

(*) Per Sir W. Scott, in the Santa Cruz, 1 Rob. 64.

CHAPTER II.

Of the authority to make captures, and what things are exempt from capture.

1. THE sovereign power of the state has, alone, authority to make war. But as the different rights which constitute this power, originally resident in the body of the nation, may be separated or limited according to the national will, it is in the municipal constitution of each particular state that we are to seek the power of making war.[a] Thus in the United States the Congress are invested with this power. *Constitution*, art. 1. § 8. 10.

2. Whatever belongs to the enemy state or sovereign, or to their citizens or subjects, may be termed things belonging to the enemy, *res hostiles*.[b]

A state taking up arms in a just cause has a double right against its enemy. 1st, A right of putting itself in possession of what belongs to it, and which the enemy witholds; and to this must be added the expenses incurred to this end, the charges of the war, and the reparation of damages. For were the belligerent state obliged to bear these expenses and losses, it would not fully obtain what is its due, or what belongs to it. 2d, It has a right of weakening the enemy for the purpose of disabling him from supporting an unjust violence; the right to take from him all means of resistance. Hence arise all the rights of war with regard to things belonging to the enemy.[c]

(a) *Vattel*, L. 3. c. 1. § 4. *Martens*, L. 8. c. 2. § 1.

(b) *Vattel*, L. 3. c. 5. § 73.

(c) *Ib.* L. 3. c. 9. § 1. *Martens*, L. 8. c. 3. § 9.

3. All things belonging to the enemy are therefore subject to capture.(d) This, however, must be understood with certain exceptions, which will be hereafter explained.

4. All moveable things taken from the enemy belong to the sovereign or state making war. They may reserve the property to themselves, or grant it to the captors. The title to it is vested in them, and thence derived to the individual captors according to the municipal regulations of each particular state.(e)

5. Captures made by public armed vessels are made in pursuance of the instructions given them by the sovereign or state. Those made by private armed vessels or merchantmen are in virtue of commissions or letters of marque granted to them.

Subjects are not obliged to weigh scrupulously the justice of the war; but in case of doubt are to rely upon the judgment of the supreme power of the state. Nor can there be any doubt that they may with a safe conscience serve their country by fitting out private armed vessels to cruise against the commerce of the enemy, unless the war be evidently unjust. These adventurers have been sometimes denominated *free-booters* or *pirates*: but this is manifestly absurd, for what they do is done under the sanction of public authority.(f)

By the law of France private armed vessels can only be fitted out by a commission from the government, which cannot be obtained without giving security for their responsibility on account of unlawful conduct. The amount of this security was fixed at seventy four thousand francs by a decree of the 2d Prairial, 11th year, 22d May, 1813.

(d) *Bynkershoek*, Q. J Pub. L. 1 c. 1.

(e) *Vattel*, L. 3. c. 9. § 164. *Azuni*, Part 2. c. 4. art 2. § 1. *Quam princeps sit, cujus auspiciis bellum geritur, idemque et sumptus et onera ferat, præda ipsi cedit.—Heinnecius*, De nav ob vet. mer. vec. com. § 13.

(f) *Vattel*, L. 3. c. 15. § 229. *Bynkershoek*, Q. J. Pub. L. 1. c. 18. *Azuni*, Part 2. c. 5. art. 3. § 1. 2.

This amount is reduced to one half, if the vessel is manned by less than one hundred and fifty men. The owners, the commander, and two sureties are required to join in the stipulation for this purpose.

In Great Britain letters of marque cannot issue to any private armed vessel until a stipulation in the nature of bail is given before the judge of the high court of admiralty or his surrogate, in the sum of three thousand pounds sterling, if the ship carries above one hundred and fifty men; and if a less number, in the sum of fifteen hundred pounds sterling, with condition to render full satisfaction for any damage or injury done to British subjects or the subjects of foreign states, in amity with Great Britain.(g)

By the act of congress of 1812, concerning letters of marque, prizes, and prize goods, it is provided that before any commission of letters of marque and reprisal shall be issued, the owner or owners of the ship or vessel for which the same shall be requested, and the commander thereof for the time being, shall give bond to the United States, with at least two responsible sureties, not interested in such vessel, in the penal sum of five thousand dollars: or if such vessel be provided with more than one hundred and fifty men, then in the penal sum of ten thousand dollars; with condition that the owners, officers, and crew, who shall be employed on board such commissioned vessels, shall and will observe the treaties and laws of the United States, and the instructions which shall be given them according to law for the regulation of their conduct; and will satisfy all damages and injuries which shall be done or committed contrary to the tenor thereof by such vessel, and to deliver up the same when revoked by the President of the United States.

So also by the act of congress of 1815, for the protection of the commerce of the United States, against the Alge-

(g) 2 *Robinson*, Appendix, No. 8. P. 13.

rine cruizers, Sec. 3. it is provided, That on the application of the owners of private armed vessels of the United States, the President of the United States may grant them special commissions in the form which he shall direct, under the seal of the United States; and such private armed vessels, when so commissioned, shall have the like authority for subduing, seizing, taking and bringing into port any Algerine vessel, goods or effects, as the beforementioned public armed vessels may by law have; and shall therein be subject to the instructions which may be given by the President of the United States for the regulation of their conduct; and their commissions shall be revocable at his pleasure. *Provided*, That before any commission shall be granted as aforesaid, the owner or owners of the vessel for which the same may be requested, and the commander thereof for the time being shall give bond to the United States, with at least two responsible sureties, not interested in such vessels, in the penal sum of seven thousand dollars, or if such vessel be provided with more than one hundred and fifty men, in the penal sum of fourteen thousand dollars, with condition for observing the treaties and laws of the United States, and the instructions which may be given as aforesaid, and also for satisfying all damages and injuries which shall be done contrary to the tenor thereof, by such commissioned vessel, and for delivering up the commission when revoked by the President of the United States.

6. A question here arises whether the owners and officers of a private armed vessel are liable for illegal acts committed during the cruize beyond the amount of the security thus given, and if so, whether they are thus liable to a greater extent than the value of the vessel, her tackle, apparel and arms. No doubt can be entertained as to the commander that he ought to be held liable for the immediate consequences of his own acts. And as to the owners, it seems equally clear that their liability is not limited

by the amount of the penalty of the bond or stipulation they are compelled to give; but the only doubt that can arise is, whether this liability ought not to be restricted to the value of the vessel, her tackle, apparel, and arms. Pothier decides that the owner may entirely discharge himself from his responsibility beyond the amount of the penalty by abandoning the vessel to the injured party.[h] But there is some reason to believe that this decision is founded upon a deduction from the provision of the civil law in respect to the actions *de pauperie* and *noxalis*; the first of which was given against the owner of a quadruped who had done an injury to some person by kicking, biting, &c. which was called *pauperiem facere*. Inst. L. 4. tit. 9. Dig. L. 9. tit. 1. The second lay against the master of a slave for any injury done by him, Dig. L. 9. tit. 4. and in both these the owner or master was discharged by delivering up the *quadruped* or *slave*. But no correspondent provision is to be found in our municipal law, the responsibility of the owners of merchant vessels not being limited to the value of the vessels and freight, as in Great Britain[i] and France.[k] The modern law of France goes even beyond this decision of Pothier, and provides that the owners of private armed vessels shall in no case be responsible for torts and depredations committed by their officers and crews upon the high seas beyond the amount of the security given by them, unless they were accessory to the committing of the same. *Code de Commerce*, Art. 217. But it is evident that this limitation of the liability of the parties must depend upon the positive provisions of municipal law; and that unless it be thereby expressly confined to the value of the vessel and her appurtenances, it must be indefinite in its extent. If they are not personally bound

(h) *Pothier*. de Propriètè, No. 92.

(i) Stat. 7 Geo. II. c. 15.

(k) *Code de Commerce*, Art. 216.

to a further extent than the value of the vessel and her appurtenances, why is a specific sum required which may, in many instances, greatly exceed that value? If the law contemplated that this value should fix the extent of their liability, it would direct the ship to be valued, and order securit to be taken in the precise amount of the valuation. The commander who captures, in consequence of an authority which he has received, is appointed for that special purpose, and those who appoint him are responsible for the execution of the trust. Thus the civil law gives the action *exercitoria*, Dig. L. 14. tit. 1, against the owner of a vessel for the act of the master, when the latter is acting in the course of his employment as such. If the owner be thus liable, it clearly follows, that he is so to the amount of his whole property, and that he is not discharged by delivering up the vessel. Therein our own municipal law agrees with the civil.

The prize acts of 1812, provides, Sec. 6. That if the capture be made without probable cause, or otherwise unreasonably, the courts may order and decree damages and costs to the party injured, and for *which the owners and commanders of the vessels making such captures, and also the vessels, shall be liable*; and our own courts of prize have adjudged that the owners of a privateer are responsible for the conduct of their agents, the officers and crew, to all the world; and that the measure of such responsibility is the full value of the property injured or destroyed.(l) And all the owners are responsible *in solidum*; nor can a part owner exempt himself from his general responsibility by compensation *pro tanto*, and a release from the claimant as to him.(m)

7. By the laws of the United States it is enacted that, If any citizen shall, within the territory or jurisdiction of

(l) 3 *Dallas*, 333. Del Col. vs. Arnold.

(m) 5 *Robinson*, The Karasan.

the United States, except and exercise a commission to serve a foreign prince or state in war, by land or sea, the person so offending shall be deemed guilty of a high misdemeanor, and shall be fined not more than two thousand dollars, and shall be imprisoned not exceeding three years. And it is likewise provided, That if any person shall, within any of the ports, harbours, bays, rivers, or other waters of the United States, fit out and arm, or attempt to fit out and arm, or procure to be fitted out and armed, or shall knowingly be concerned in the furnishing, fitting out, or arming of any ship or vessel, with intent that such ship or vessel shall be employed in the service of any foreign prince or state, to cruize or commit hostilities upon the subjects, citizens, or property of another foreign prince or state, with whom the United States are at peace, or shall issue or deliver a commission within the territory or jurisdiction of the United States, for any ship or vessel, to the intent that she may be employed as aforesaid, every such person, so offending, shall, upon conviction, be adjudged guilty of a high misdemeanor, and shall be fined and imprisoned at the discretion of the court in which the conviction shall be had, so as the fine to be imposed shall in no case be more than five thousand dollars, and the term of imprisonment shall not exceed three years, and every such ship or vessel, with her tackle, apparel, and furniture, together with all the materials, arms, ammunition, and stores, which may have been procured for the building and equipment thereof, shall be forfeited, one half to the use of any person who shall give information of the offence, and the other half to the use of the United States.[n] And by a subsequent act it is also provided, That if any citizen of the United States shall, without the limits of the same, fit out or procure to be fitted out, or knowingly be concerned in the fitting out of a privateer for the purpose of cruizing

[n] 3 Laws U. S. 89.

against the subjects of a nation in amity with the United States, or shall take the command, or serve on board of such privateer, or purchase any interest in the same, he shall be adjudged guilty of a high misdemeanor, and be punished by a fine not exceeding ten thousand dollars, and imprisonment not exceeding ten years.(o)

And by the law of France, its subjects were forbidden to take commissions from any foreign kings, princes, or states, for the purpose of arming ships of war, and cruising therewith on the high seas under the foreign flag, unless by permission of the government, under the penalty of being considered as pirates.(p)

Similar prohibitions are contained in the municipal laws of most countries; and it may be doubted whether cruising under commissions from two or more different powers be permitted by the law of nations. An opinion is expressed by D'Habreu, *Tratado de las Presas*, Part 2. c. 1. § 7. that the taking commissions from two or more different princes *allied in the same war* may be justifiable. But this distinction is rejected by Valin, who urges against it the conclusive objection that though the two princes or states may be allies, one or the other of them may be in amity with a power with whom the other is at war; and that consequently to indulge such a deviation from the general rule might compromit the rights of the sovereign and the peace of the country. And Sir Leoline Jenkins considers those who commit depredations under commissions from two or more sovereigns or states, as pirates in the same degree with those who cruize without any commission.(q)

8. The conduct of public vessels of war, or of private armed vessels commissioned as letters of marque, is regu-

(o) 4 Laws U. S. 3—Vide 3 *Dallas*, 133. Talbot vs. Janson. 2 *Dallas*, 321, The United States vs. Guinet.

(p) *Ordonnance de la Marine*, L. 3. tit. 9. *des Prises*, art. 3.

(q) *Sir L. Jenkin's Works*, 714.

lated by instructions from the sovereign, or supreme executive power of the state.

Thus by the prize act of 1812, the President of the United States is authorized to establish and order suitable instructions for the better governing and directing the conduct of vessels commissioned according to the act, their officers and crews, copies of which shall be delivered, by the collector of the customs, to the commanders of the same when they shall give bond as required by the act.

Under this authority the President issued on the 28th August, 1812, an instruction, commanding private armed vessels not to interrupt any vessels belonging to citizens of the United States, coming from British ports to the United States, laden with British merchandize, in consequence of the alleged repeal of the British orders in council. It was adjudged to be necessary that the instruction should either have been actually delivered to the privateer, or that she should have been in port after it was issued, in order to invalidate a capture made contrary to its letter and spirit.[r]

So also where a capture was made by a private armed vessel having the instruction on board, a question was made whether the capture was lawful, and that depended upon the authority of the President to issue this instruction, and upon its true import, if rightly issued. The language of the provision in the prize act is very general, and it is entitled to a liberal construction both upon the manifest intent of the legislature, and the ground of public policy.

It had been argued, that privateers acquire, by their commissions, a general right of capture under the prize act, which it is not in the President's power to narrow or restrain, while the commission is in force; that therefore his

[r] The Frances and the Mary, Supreme Court of the U. S. February Term, 1814. M. S.

right to issue instructions must be construed as subordinate to the general authority derived from the commission; and that, in this view, his instruction should extend only to the internal organization, discipline, and conduct of privateers. But it is very clear that the President had, under the prize act, power to grant, annul, and revoke at his pleasure the commissions of privateers; and by the act declaring war, he was authorized to issue the commissions in such form as he should deem fit. The right of capture is entirely derived from the law: It is not an absolute vested right which cannot be taken away or modified by law: It is a limited right, which is subject to all the restraints that the legislature imposes, and is to be exercised in the manner its wisdom prescribes. The commission, therefore, is to be taken in its general terms, with reference to the laws under which it emanates, and as containing within itself all the qualifications and restrictions which the acts, giving it existence, prescribe. In this view, the commission is qualified and restrained by the power of the President to issue instructions. The privateer takes it subject to such power and contracts to act in obedience to all the instructions which the President may lawfully promulgate.

Public policy, also, would confirm this construction. It has been the great object of every maritime nation to restrain and regulate the conduct of its privateers: they are watched with great anxiety and vigilance, because they may often involve the nation, by irregularities of conduct, in serious controversies, not only with public enemies, but also with neutrals and allies. If a power did not exist to restrain their operations in war, the public faith might be violated, cartels and flags of truce might be disregarded, and endless embarrassments arise in the negotiations with foreign powers. Considerations of this weight and importance are not lightly to be disregarded, and when the language of the act is so broad and comprehensive, the court stated they should not feel at liberty to narrow or weaken its force by a construction not presented by the letter, or spirit, or policy of the clause; and were therefore of the opinion that the instruction in question was within the authority delegated to the President by the prize act.[a]

9. And though such instructions may bind the judges of the prize courts of the nation under whose authority they are issued, where those instructions relax the law of nations in favour of neutrals, yet if they attempt to extend that law to the prejudice of neutrals, they are not conclusive upon the judges, whose decisions must in that case be regulated by the paramount authority of the law of nations.

It was upon these principles that Sir James Mackintosh determined in the case of the American ship Minerva in the Prize Court at Bombay, which ship had been captured on a voyage supposed to be interdicted under the British doctrine which subjects to capture a neutral trade not open in time of peace. The ship left Providence, Rhode Island, in August, 1805; had touched at the Isle of France, from which place she sailed to Batavia, thence she went to Tegall and Manilla, and on her voyage from this last place back again to Batavia she was detained. Her cargo consisted chiefly of indigo and dollars. It appeared that she was under the direction of a supercargo on board, as to her employment in trade, both in respect of the cargoes and the intermediate ports to which she was to trade, previously to her return to Providence, or some other port in America, where her voyage was to end. For the captors, it was contended that she was trading between enemies colonies, and therefore acting in direct violation of the letter and spirit of his majesty's instructions of June, 1803, which command the commanders of ships of war and privateers not to seize any neutral vessel which should be carrying on trade directly between the colonies of the enemy and the

(a) Per STORY, J. The Thomas Gibbons, Supreme Court of the U. S. February Term, 1814. M. S.

neutral country to which the vessel belonged. For the claimants it was insisted, that neither Manilla, nor Batavia, nor the Isle of France were enemies colonies of such a nature, as to render the trading thereto by a neutral in time of war illegal; inasmuch as the trade to those places was open in time of peace. The court had directed commissions to be sent to Bengal and Madras, to ascertain whether the ports of Batavia and Manilla were, during the last peace, open to any foreigners from the ports of India, Europe, or America; and if open, whether under any and what restrictions; and also to enquire into the state of those ports in these respects before the war which broke out between Great Britain and Spain in 1796. These commissions being in part returned, and it appearing that these ports were open to all foreigners during the last peace, without any restrictions except as to opium, and specie at the port of Batavia, Sir James Mackintosh pronounced judgment of restitution. The captors, he said, were fully justified in detaining this vessel, because in so doing they were acting in obedience to the letter of the instructions of June, 1803. Batavia and Manilla were certainly colonies of the enemy, and this vessel was certainly not trading directly between America and such colonies. But though the officers in his majesty's service were bound to obey these instructions, he did not conceive himself, sitting as a judge of prize, in a court whose decisions were to be regulated by the law of nations, as bound and concluded by them. He believed indeed that he was the first and only judge who had ventured to pronounce such a doctrine. In every court, in every country, by all writers on the subject, and all administrations of the law, the instructions of the sovereign were regarded as a law to the judge. But he considered the law of nations as paramount to such instructions; and the king as having indeed a right to dispense with such law, but not a right to extend it. As far therefore as any of his majesty's instructions were a relaxation of the law of nations in favour of neutrals, he should consider himself bound by them; but if he saw in such instructions any attempt to extend the law to the prejudice of neutrals, he should not obey them, but regulate his decisions according to the known and recognized law of nations. In the present case, after great deliberation, he felt himself bound to say, that neither Batavia nor Manilla were such colonies as to render any trading by neutral nations, in time of war, illegal. It is not their being called colonies that will render such a trading unlawful, notwithstanding the letter of the instructions of 1803; something further is necessary, and that is, that the trade to and with these colonies was prohibited to such neutrals in time of peace.

10. A maritime capture is the seizure of a vessel or goods on board the same, or both, belonging to a real or supposed enemy, or from some other cause justifiable by the laws of nations, under authority from the belligerent state; with the intent to divest the actual owner of the property, and to carry it into port for adjudication before some competent court.

11. The time of capture is to be dated not from the actual taking possession, but from the striking of the colours, which last is to be deemed the real *deditio*: Unless indeed the enemy succeed in defeating that surrender, and this act of formal submission is thus discontinued.(t)

12. And a seizure under an agreement with the neutral master to bring in his vessel was held to be a legal capture.(u)

So also where it was objected to the legality of a capture that it was defeated by subsequent abandonment on the part of the captors, because one man only was put on board from the armed vessel with the consent of the captured,

(t) 1 *Robinson*, 233. The Rebeckah.

(u) 6 *Robinson*, 13. The Resolution.

and the prize was thus permitted to proceed to the port of her original destination; it was determined that the inability of the prize master to secure the captured vessel, his inability to bring in the vessel without the aid of the crew belonging to her, were, in reason, no proof of abandonment. If the circumstances of the captured vessel be such as to do away all apprehension of rescue, and inspire confidence that the crew will bring her into port, no reason is perceived why the property of the captor may not be retained as well by a prize master alone, as by a considerable detachment from the crew of the capturing vessel.(v)

So also where a merchantman, which had separated from her convoy during a storm, and had been brought to by an enemy's vessel of war, which came up and told the master to stay by her till the storm moderated, when she would send a boat on board, it was held to be a legal capture. The sending of a prize master on board is a very natural act of possession, but by no means essential to constitute a capture. If the merchantman, as in this case, is obliged to lie to and obey the direction of the enemy's vessel, and await her further orders, there being no ability to resist and no prospect of escape, the capture must be considered as consummated.(w)

But the master or crew of a neutral vessel captured is not bound to assist in carrying the vessel into port for adjudication, unless a compromise or agreement to that effect is made by them with the commander of the armed vessel making the capture. They owe no service to the captors, and are still to be considered answerable to the owners for their conduct, so that they make no actual resistance. It is the duty as well as the interest of the captors to make the capture sure; and if they neglect it from any anxiety

(v) Per Marshall, C. J. The Alexander, Supreme Court of the U. S. February Term, 1814. M. S

(w) 3 *Robinson*, 305. The Edward and Mary.

to make other captures, or thinking the force already furnished sufficient, it is exclusively as their own peril.(x)

13. It results from the above definition of legal capture that a taking by pirates has none of the effects of such a capture. It does not divest the actual owner of the property, and cannot be followed by a sentence of condemnation in a competent court.(y) *A piratis et latronibus capta dominium non mutant*, is the maxim of the civilians, which has been adopted by modern writers on public law. But a taking by pirates must not be confounded with a capture by non commissioned captors. For, as we have before seen, a seizure of enemy's vessels in port, before a declaration of war or the issuing of letters of marque and reprisal; and of enemy vessels coming into port from distress of weather, want of provisions, or ignorance of war; captures made by private armed vessels having letters of marque against one enemy power of the property of another with whom war had broken out; and a capture made by a merchant vessel, attacked at sea by an enemy's ship, who in defending herself takes the ship of the enemy,—are all lawful captures, although the prizes are condemned not to the actual captors, but to the sovereign or state, unless otherwise provided by the municipal law of the belligerent power.

Though all things belonging to the enemy are, generally speaking, subject to capture; yet there are certain exceptions to this general rule.

14. Thus the rights of war can only be exercised in the territories of the belligerents, upon the high seas, or in a territory belonging to no one. Hence it follows that hostilities cannot be exercised within the territorial jurisdiction

(x) *Acton*, 37. The Pennsylvania.

(y) *Albericus Gentilis* De Jure Belli, L. 1. c. 4. *Grotius*, De J. B. ac P. L. 3. c 9. § 16 Loccenius, De J. M. L. 1 c. 3. No. 4. *Bynkershoek*, 2. J. P. L. 1. c. 17. *Azuni*, Part. 2, c. 5, art. 3. § 12.

of a neutral power who is the common friend of the belligerents.[y]

This jurisdiction extends to the ports, harbours, bays, and chambers formed by head lands of the neutral power. The usual addition allowed to this is a distance of three English miles, or a marine league, or as far as a [z] cannon shot will carry from the coasts or shore. And by the laws of the United States it is provided, that the district courts shall take cognizance of complaints, by whomsoever instituted, in cases of captures made within the waters of the United States, or within a marine league of the coasts or shores thereof.

Captures made by armed vessels stationed in a river of a neutral power, or in the mouth of a river, or in his harbours, for the purpose of exercising the rights of war from that river or harbour, are likewise invalid.[a] So also where a belligerent ship, lying within neutral territory, made a capture, with her boats, out of the neutral territory, the capture was held to be invalid. For though the hostile force employed was applied to the captured vessel *lying out* of the territory; yet no such use of a neutral territory for the purposes of war is to be permitted. This prohibition is not to be extended to *remote* uses, such as procuring provisions and refreshments, and acts of that nature, which the law of nations universally tolerates; but no *proximate* acts of war are in any manner to be allowed to originate on neutral grounds. That a ship should sta-

(y) *Grotius*, De J. B. ac P. L 3. c 4 § . *Bynkershoek*, Q. J. P. L. 1. c 8. *Vattel*, L. 3. c. 7. § 132. *Martens*, L. 8. c. 6. § 6. *D'Habreu*, Tratado sobre las Presas, Part 1, c. 5. § 14. *Azuni*, Part 2, c. 5. art. 1. § 16. *Ib.* Part 2, c. 1. art. 6. § 4.

(z) 5 *Robinson*, 15. The Vrow Anna Catharina. *Ib.* 373. The Anna. *Vattel*, L. 1 c. 22. § 289. *Bynkershoek*, Q. J. P. L. 1. c. 8. *Id.* De Domni. Maris, c. 2. § 5. *Martens*, L. 4. c. 4. § 4. *Azuri*, Part 1. c. 2. art, 2. § 15. *Vide Bee's Adm. Reports*, 204. Soult v. L'Africaine.

(a) 5 *Robinson*, 373. The Anna.

tion herself on neutral territory, and send out her boats on hostile enterprizes, is an act of hostility much too immediate to be permitted: for supposing that even a *direct hostile use* should be required to bring it within the prohibition of the law of nations, nobody will say, that the very act of sending out boats to effect a capture, is not itself an act directly hostile,—not complete indeed, but inchoate, and clothed with all the characters of hostility. If this could be defended, it might as well be said, that a ship lying in a neutral station, might fire shot on a vessel lying out of the neutral territory; the injury in that case would not be consummated nor received on neutral ground; but no one would say that such an act would not be a hostile act, immediately commenced within the neutral territory: And what does it signify to the nature of the act considered for the present purpose, whether I send out a cannon shot which shall compel the submission of a vessel lying at two miles distance, or whether I send out a boat armed and manned to effect the very same thing at the same distance? It is in both instances the direct act of the vessel lying in neutral ground; the act of hostility actually begins in the latter case with the launching and manning and arming the boat that is sent out on such an errand of force. But direct hostility appears not to be necessary; for whatever has an immediate connexion with it is forbidden: you cannot, without leave, carry prisoners or booty into a neutral territory, there to be detained, because such an act is an immediate continuation of hostility. In the same manner an act of hostility is not to take its commencement on neutral ground: It is not sufficient to say it is not completed there—you are not to take any measure there that shall lead to immediate violence; you are not to avail yourself of a station on neutral territory, making as it were a vantage ground of the neutral country, a country which is to carry itself with perfect equality between both belligerents, giving neither the one nor the other any advantage.([b])

Although the immunity of neutral territory from the exercise of any belligerent act is generally admitted; yet an exception to it has been attempted to be raised in the case of an enemy vessel met on the high seas, and pursued; which it is said may, in the pursuit, be chased into the limits of a neutral jurisdiction. The only writer of eminent authority who has maintained this anomalous principle is Bynkershoek. He himself admits that he had never seen it mentioned in the writings of the publicists or among any of the European nations, the Dutch only excepted; thereby leaving the inference open, that even if reasonable in itself, it neither rested upon authority, nor was sanctioned by general usage. There is besides some reason to believe that he meant to confine the doctrine within narrower limits than have been since sought to be given to it. Be this as it may, it is sufficient to observe that the extreme caution with which he guards this license to belligerents is wholly inconsistent with the exercise of it. For how is an enemy to be pursued in a hostile manner within the jurisdiction of a friendly power without imminent danger of injuring the subjects and property of the latter? *Dum fervet opus*—in the heat and animation excited against a flying foe, there is too much reason to presume little regard will be paid to the consequences that may ensue to the neutral.

When the fact of a capture within a neutral jurisdiction is established, the capture is done away, and the property must be restored notwithstanding that it may actually belong to an enemy. But it has been held that a suggestion of neutral territory cannot be set up by an individual claimant, but that it must proceed from the government, whose territory is asserted to have been violated.([c])

([b]) 3 *Robinson*, 162. The Twee Gebroeders.

([c]) 5 *Robinson*, 15. The Vrow Anna Catharina. 3 *Robinson*, 162, *In*

15. The practice of exchanging prisoners taken in war has been gradually introduced in the place of the older practice of ransoming, which succeeded to the still more antient practice of making slaves of them, which again was substituted for that of putting them to death. It is a practice of a nature highly deserving every degree of favourable consideration, upon the same principles as are all other *commercia belli*, by which the violence of war may be allayed, as far as is consistent with its purposes; and by which, something of a pacific intercourse may be kept up, which, in time, may lead to an adjustment of differences, and end ultimately in peace. The cartel-ships employed in this service are therefore exempt from capture; and are protected in this office both in carrying prisoners, and returning from that service.[d] But this service is so highly important to the interests of humanity, that it is peculiarly incumbent on all parties to take care, that it should be conducted in such a manner as not to become a subject of distrust and jealousy between the two belligerent nations. It is not a question of gain, but one on which depends the recovery of the liberty of individuals who may happen to have become prisoners of war; it is, therefore, a species of navigation which on every consideration of humanity and policy must be conducted with the most exact attention to the original purpose, and to the rules which have been built upon it, since, if such a mode of intercourse is broken off, it cannot but be followed by consequences extremely calamitous to individuals of both countries. It is a species of navigation, therefore, which more than any other requires to be narrowly watched. There is no way by which this

Notis. And it will be found in all the cases reported by Sir C. Robinson, that the claim of territory was interposed by direction of the neutral government whose territory was alleged to have been violated.

(d) 3 *Robinson*, 139. The Daifje. See also the case of La Gloire, 5 *Robinson*, 192, and the Mary. Ib. 200.

purity of conduct can be maintained, but by considering the owner as answerable for the due execution of the service on which his vessel is employed: It is the very last description of cases in which the responsibility of the owner ought to be relaxed. Cartel-ships are subject to a double obligation to both countries, not to trade. To engage in trade may be disadvantageous to the enemy, or to their own country; both countries are mutually engaged to permit no trade to be carried on under a fraudulent use of this intercourse; all trade must, therefore, be held to be prohibited, and it is not without the consent of both governments that vessels engaged on that service can be permitted to take in any goods whatever. The penalty of confiscation is affixed to the abuse of the privileges of a cartel ship, and whether the vessel belong to the belligerent state or to the enemy it is liable to capture and condemnation.[e]

16. A vessel with the cargo laden on board sailing under a passport, safe-conduct, or license from the belligerent state, whether the property belong to the citizen or subjects of the belligerent state, or to the enemy, is exempt from capture by the armed vessels of the belligerent state.

A passport or safe-conduct is granted to protect the persons and property of an enemy from hostilities within the places and times limited therein. They may be granted for various purposes; and it is the sovereign power of the state which is to judge of the expediency of granting them.

But this authority may be delegated to, and exercised by its officers. Thus it is incidental to the commission with which an admiral or a general is invested that they should have the authority to issue these documents of protection.[f]

(e) 4 *Robinson*, 355. The Venus. 6 *Robinson*, 336. The Carolina.

(f) *Vattel*, L. 3. c. 17. § 265. 1 *Blackstone's Commentaries*, 259.

And it is provided by the laws of the United States, that if any person shall violate any safe-conduct, or passport, duly obtained and issued under the authority of the United States, the person so offending, on conviction, shall be imprisoned not exceeding three years, and fined at the discretion of the court.

17. Of the same nature are licenses granted by the belligerent state to trade with its enemy. All commercial intercourse being suspended by war, such trade can only be legalized by license granted by the sovereign power of the state, which is alone competent to decide on all the considerations of commercial and political expediency, by which such an exception from the ordinary consequences of war must be controlled.(g) And these licenses are by no means, as has been commonly supposed, an invention of the present times. For Valin, speaking of the frauds by which the commerce and property of the enemy were screened from capture, not only on the high seas, but even in the ports of France—observes that before the Ordinance on which he was commenting, no other means of counteracting these frauds had been discovered than that of delivering passports to the vessels of the enemy permitting them to trade with the ports of the kingdom upon the payment of a duty of a crown per ton. This was done by an ordinance of 1673, upon the ground that as the enemies of the king availed themselves of neutral vessels in order to carry on their trade with France, good policy required that by means of this tonnage duty the profit heretofore acquired by neutrals should be appropriated to the kingdom.

18. And, finally, it has been usual in maritime wars to exempt from capture fishing boats and their cargoes, both from views of mutual accommodation between neighbouring countries, and from tenderness to a poor and industrious order of people. This custom, so honourable to the

(g) 4 *Robinson*. Vide M. S. The *Cosmopolite*.

humanity of civilized nations, has fallen into disuse; and it is remarkable that both France and England mutually reproach each other with that breach of good faith which has finally abolished it.[h]

[h] 1 *Robinson*, 20. The Young Jacob and Johanna. *Valin*, Sur l'Ordonnance, L. 5 tit. x. *Bynkershoek*, Q. J. P. L. 1. c. 3.

CHAPTER III.

Of enemy's property considered as an object of capture.

1. SUBJECT to the exceptions mentioned in the foregoing chapter, all things belonging to the enemy are liable to capture. And such captures may be made of enemy's vessels and his goods laden therein; or of enemy's goods laden in neutral vessels.

2. By the general usage of maritime nations, transfers of ships and other vessels are made in writing. If therefore the vessel captured has been transferred from the original proprietor, it seems reasonable to require the production of the bill of sale in order to determine the validity of the capture.[a] Where it appears that the transfer was made from an enemy to a neutral during the war, various rules have been adopted by the particular Ordinances of belligerent nations as to the effect of such transfers, and to determine under what circumstances they shall be deemed valid, or otherwise.

3. Thus by the British order in council of the 11th November, 1807, it was provided, That the sale to a neutral of any vessel belonging to his majesty's enemies, shall not be deemed to be legal, nor in any manner to transfer the property, nor to alter the character of such vessel: and all such vessels now belonging, or which shall hereafter belong to any enemy of his majesty, notwithstanding any sale, or pretended sale to a neutral, after a reasonable time shall have elapsed for receiving information of this his majesty's

(a) 1 *Robinson*, 122. The Welvaart.

order at the place where such sale was effected, shall be captured and brought in, and shall be adjudged as lawful prize to the captors.

And by the French Regulations of the 23d July, 1704, the 10th October, 1744, and the 26th July, 1778, it is provided that no such transfer to a neutral shall be valid unless made before the declaration of war.

4. But as these Ordinances make no part of the law of nations, so neither are they founded on the principles of justice. For as ships are an article of commerce, to prohibit their sale to neutrals, is to pronounce an absolute interdiction of a branch of trade, which is perfectly innocent if carried on with good faith, and which ought not to be prohibited by a sweeping rule founded upon an undistinguishing presumption of fraud, that may as well be applied to any other commercial transaction as to this. It is vain to allege, in vindication of such innovations upon the law of nations, the example of a similar regulation and practice on the part of the enemy, as is done in the above British order in council. For retaliation, in order to be just, must strike only the offending power: and *the true mode of correcting the irregular practice of a nation is, by protesting against it, and by inducing that country to reform it: it is monstrous to suppose, that because one country has been guilty of an irregularity, every other country is let loose from the law of nations; and is at liberty to assume as much as it thinks fit.*(b) Nor have these Ordinances any binding force even upon the prize courts of the nation under whose authority they are issued; for all captures must be judged by those tribunals according to the law of nations and treaties, and not according to the municipal law of the belligerent state.(c)

(b) 1 *Robinson*, 142. The Flad Oyer.

(c) *Report of Sir George Lee, &c.* of the 18th January, 1753. FOURTH PROPOSITION. Chap. 11. Note f.

5. The rules which have been laid down by the Ordinances of belligerent nations requiring the production of certain prescribed proofs to ascertain the *bona fide* nature of such transfers, and inferring the existence of enemy interests from the absence of such proofs, are more just and conformable to the law of nations. Thus by the French regulations of the 17th February, 1694, the 12th May, 1696, and the 26th July, 1778, revived by decree of the Consuls of the 29th Frimaire, 8th year of the Republic, it is provided, That no vessel of enemy built, or originally belonging to an enemy proprietor, shall be considered as neutral, unless the sale was made in the presence of some public officer, before whom such transfers are usually made, and unless the bill of sale is found on board, accompanied by a legal power given by the former owner, in case the sale is not made by himself.

6. So also it has been held that such transfers made by an enemy to a neutral in time of war, must be an absolute and unconditional sale. This rule is applied to guard against the frauds which might otherwise be practised, and by means of which enemy interests might still be preserved and protected from capture.(d) And if the vessel, ostensibly transferred, still continues under the control and management of her former owner, and in the same trade and navigation in which she was previously employed, these circumstances are deemed sufficient to make void the transfer, and to indicate the continued existence of enemy interests rendering the property liable to capture.(e) This last rule seems nothing more than a just application of the principle of municipal law, by which a sale or other transfer is only valid where the actual delivery of the thing ac-

(d) 2 *Robinson*, 137. The Noydt Gedacht. 4 *Robinson*. 100. The Sechs Geschwistern.

(e) 1 *Robinson*, 1. The Vigilantia. 4 *Robinson*, 31. The Jemmy. 3 *Robinson*, 41. The Jonge Amelia *in the Portland*.

companies the transfer; whilst if it still continues in the possession of the original proprietor, it is subject to attachment for his debts, and if sold cannot be reclaimed by the first vendee.(f) Thus it is a maxim of the civil law, *Traditionibus, non nudis conventionibus, dominia transferuntur*, which seems to be peculiarly applicable to transfers of enemy's property, which, if such transfers were permitted without an actual delivery, might easily be veiled with the neutral character and effectually guarded from capture.

7. If on the other hand no transfer has been made, as the laws of most maritime countries require ships and vessels to be registered in a public registry, the certificate of registry is the proof naturally to be looked for. And as the same laws require that the master and a certain proportion of the crew of the vessel should be of the nation whose flag she bears, the national character of the vessel must be determined by those laws.

Besides these, the following proofs of property in the vessel and cargo are usually required.

1st. The Passport or Sea Letter. This is a permission from the neutral state to the master of the vessel to proceed on the intended voyage, and usually contains his name and residence, the name, description, and destination of the vessel, with such other matters as the local law and practice require. According to those treaties which determine the character of the goods by that of the vessel on board of which they are laden, and consequently that free ships shall make free goods, this is the only document or proof of property required. So also by the treaties between different maritime nations, and Turkey and the Barbary powers, it is stipulated that the production of a pass from the government whose flag the vessel bears shall

(f) *Pothier, De Propriété*, No. 245. 247. 3 *Coke*, R. 80. b. Twine's Case.

be conclusive evidence of the property, and shall exempt the vessel and cargo from further search and detention.

2d. The Muster Roll, or *Role d'Equipage*, contains the names, ages, quality, and national character of every person of the ship's company.

3d. The charter party; if the vessel has been let to hire.

4th. The bills of lading, by which the master acknowledges the receipt of the goods specified therein, and promises to deliver them to the consignee or his order. Of these there are usually several duplicates; of which, one is delivered to the master, one retained by the shipper of the goods, and one sent to the consignees.

5th. The invoices, which contain the particulars and prices of each parcel of the goods, with a statement of the charges thereon, which are usually transmitted from the shippers to the consignees.

6th. The log-book, or ship's journal, which contains an accurate account of the vessel's course, with a short history of the occurrences during the voyage.

8. As the whole of these papers may be fabricated, their presence does not necessarily imply a fair case; neither does the absence of any of them furnish a conclusive ground of condemnation, as has been most unjustly provided by the Ordinances of certain belligerent powers. As they furnish presumptive evidence only of the property in the vessel and cargo belonging to those to whom it purports to belong; so on the other hand their absence affords only presumptive evidence of the existence of enemy interests, which may be rebutted by other proof of a positive nature accounting for the want of them and supplying their place according to the circumstances of each particular case. Equally unjust and erroneous are the provisions of those Ordinances which prescribe what proportion of the vessel's crew shall be of the nation whose flag she bears in order to entitle her to the privileges of the national character;

since it is evident that this must be determined by the municipal law of her own country.

It was upon these principles that the Council of Prizes at Paris determined in the case of the American ship Pigou, which had been condemned by the inferior prize court upon the ground of the *role d'Equipage* not being found on board as required by several French ordinances. The commissary of the government, M. Portalis, in his *Conclusions*, premised, That all questions of neutrality are what are termed in law questions regarding *bona fides.* He then proceeded to state that neutrality is to be proved; and hence the several regulations in the ordinances and decrees of France which required the neutral character of vessels and their cargoes to be proved by certain enumerated documents, among which is mentioned a *role d'Equipage* in due form; but that it would be a gross error to infer from thence that the want of, or a trifling irregularity in one of these papers, would in every case have the effect of condemning the property. Sometimes regular papers cover enemy's property, which other circumstances unmask. In other cases the stamps of neutrality break through omissions and irregularities in the forms, originating in mere negligence, or grounded on motives free from fraud. We must therefore decide not merely by strict forms, but by the principles of good faith; we must say with the law that mere omissions and irregularities in the forms cannot prejudice the truth, if it can be made otherwise to appear, and *si aliquid ex solemnibus deficiat, cum equitas poscit, subveniendum est.* In conformity with these reasonings the Council reversed the sentence of the inferior court and decreed restitution of the ship and cargo to the American claimant.

9. It is evident that goods the property of the enemy laden in enemy's vessels are subject to capture. But that the goods of a neutral laden on board the vessels of an enemy should be subject to capture and condemnation is

manifestly contrary to reason and justice. But unreasonable and unjust as this rule may be, it has been incorporated into the prize laws of certain nations, and by them enforced at different periods.

Thus by the French Ordinances of 1543 and 1584, the goods of a friend laden on board enemy's vessels are declared good prize. The contrary was provided by the Declaration of February, 1650; but by the Ordinance of August, 1681, L. 3. tit. 9. *des Prises*, art. 7. the former rule was again established. Valin and Pothier are able to find no better arguments in support of this rule than that those who lade their goods on board enemy's vessels thereby favour the commerce and navigation of the enemy, and by this act are considered in law as submitting themselves to abide the fate of the vessel; and Valin triumphantly asks, How can it be that the goods of friends and allies, found in an enemy's ship, should not be liable to confiscation, whilst those even of *subjects* are liable to it? To which Pothier himself furnishes the proper answer, That in respect to goods the property of the king's subjects, in lading them on board enemy's vessels, they contravene the law, which interdicts to them all commercial intercourse with the enemy, and they deserve to lose their goods for the violation of the law.(g) And the fallacy of the arguments by which this rule is attempted to be supported consists in assuming what requires to be proved, that by the act of lading his goods on board an enemy's vessel the neutral submits himself to abide the fate of the vessel. For it cannot be pretended that the goods are subject to capture and confiscation *ex re*, since their character of neutral property exempts them from this liability. Nor can it be shewn that they are thus liable *ex delicto*, unless it be shewn that the act of thus lading them on board is an

(g) *Valin*, Sur l'Ordonnance, L. 3. tit. 9. *des Prises*, art. 7. *Pothier*, De Propriété, No. 96.

offence against the law of nations. It is therefore with reason that Bynkershoek concludes that this rule, established by the ordinances of certain belligerent powers and incorporated in some treaties, cannot be defended upon sound principles: for why, he asks, should I not be allowed to make use of my friend's ship to carry my property, notwithstanding his being at war with you? If treaties do not prohibit, I am at liberty to trade with your enemy; and if so, I may likewise enter into any kind of contract with him, buy, sell, let, hire, &c. Therefore, if I have engaged his vessel and his labour, to carry my goods across the seas, I have done that which was lawful on every principle. You, as his enemy, may take and confiscate his ship, but by what law will you also take and confiscate the goods that belong to me, who am your friend? All that I am bound to do, is, to prove that they are really mine. But what shall we say, continues he, if the owners of the goods knew and consented that they should be shipped on board the vessel of their friend, indeed, but of your enemy? I should think that this knowledge and consent do not authorize a confiscation. The matter depends upon this question only, whether the owners of the goods, in shipping them on board of an enemy's vessel have acted lawfully or unlawfully? I have contended for the former position, because, as I may lawfully carry on any kind of trade with your enemy, I think that I may therefore enter into any kind of contract with him, and make use, for a valuable consideration, of his ship for my own utility. Take if you can, every thing which belongs to your enemy, but restore to me what is my own, because I am your friend, and in shipping my goods, I have not intended to do you any injury.[h]

And in conformity with these principles is the doctrine of the law of nations as laid down by the most eminent

[h] *Du Ponceau's Bynkershoek*, c. 13. p. 104.

authorities, from that venerable code of public and maritime law the *Consolato del Mare*, to the most modern writers.(i)

10. A question arises whether the captor of an enemy's ship be entitled to freight upon the goods of a neutral thus captured and restored according to the foregoing principle. And the *Consolato del Mare*, c. 273, has determined that the freight is to be paid to the captor by the neutral in the same manner as if the voyage had been terminated. But this determination is justly contested by Bynkershoek, upon the ground that the freight was not due to the ship unless the goods had been carried to their destined port, or the captor is ready to carry them thither.(k) This doctrine is adhered to in practice; freight being paid to captors only where the ship and cargo are carried to the port of their original destination for adjudication, and the former condemned, whilst the latter is restored:(l) and to captors carrying the goods *not to* the actual port of destination, but to the claimants' own *country*, and to the ports to which they would have consigned them if not prevented by the regulations of the country to which they had *actually* consigned them.(m) But where freight was demanded by the captors, upon the ground that the goods were *sold advantageously* for the neutral claimants in the country of the captors, and at the particular request of the claimants, it was refused; because this ground of distinction was held not to be sufficient to take the case out of the general rule. In all cases, except those

(i) *Consolato del Mare*, c. 273. *Grotius*, de J. B. ac P. L. 3. c. 6. § 26 *Heinnecius*. De nav. ob vect. mero. com. c. 9. § 9. *Vattel*, L. 3 c. 7. § 116. *Burlemaqui*, Tome 3. Part 4. c. 4. § 1. *Loccenius*, De J. M. L. 3. c. 4.—*Voet*, In Pandect. L. 49. tit. 15. § 5. *Hubner*, Tome 1, c. 9. § 1. *Martens*, L. 8. c. 6. § 10.

(k) *Bynkershoek*, Q. J. P. L. 1. c. 13.

(l) 4 *Robinson*, 278. The Fortuna.

(m) 5 *Robinson*, 67. The Diana.

before mentioned, freight is held not to be due, although the ship may have performed a very large part of her intended voyage, and so large a portion, as to raise at first sight an appearance of hardship and injustice in the refusal of freight, and to suggest a doubt whether it might not be a better rule to allow a proportion of freight *pro rata iteneris peracti*. But such a rule would be found to be productive of much practical injustice, and would lead to endless litigation and uncertainty, in the discussion of the particular circumstances that would be relied on in every case. The possible *advantage* or *disadvantage* of an interruption of the original voyage by capture, is but an accidental circumstance to which a court of prize will but slightly attend. It would introduce a labyrinth of minute considerations through which the court could not find its way.(n)

11. The regulations and practice of certain nations, at different periods, have not only considered enemy's goods laden in neutral vessels as subject to capture, but have also confiscated the neutral vessels, on board of which they were laden. Thus by the French Ordinance of August, 1681, *des Prises*, art. 7. all vessels taken with enemy's goods laden on board are declared good prize. The contrary rule had been adopted by preceding Ordinances, and was revived by the Regulation of the 21st October, 1744, by which it was declared, That in case there should be found on board of neutral vessels, of whatever nation, goods or effects belonging to his majesty's enemies, the goods or effects shall be good prize, and the vessels shall be restored. Valin admits that this jurisprudence, which continued to prevail in the French courts of prize from 1681 to 1744, was peculiar to them and to the Spanish; but that the usage of other nations was only to confiscate the goods of

(n) 6 *Robinson*, 269. The Vrow Anna Catharina. 1 *Edwards*, 56. The Fortuna.

the enemy.(o) The Regulation of the 21st October, 1744, continued to be observed in the prize courts of France from its date until the French revolution; when by a law of the 29th Nivose, 6th year of the Republic, it was provided that, The neutral or enemy character of vessels shall be determined by that of the cargo; consequently every vessel found at sea, laden in whole or in part with merchandize the product of England or her possessions, shall be pronounced good prize, to whomsoever the said merchandize may belong. This law was again repealed by that of the 23d Frimaire, 8th year of the Republic, and by the decree of the Consuls of the 29th of the same month. The following treaties and edicts of belligerent powers likewise involve the confiscation of neutral vessels together with their cargoes, whether the latter are the property of enemies or not. By the Treaty of the 22d August, 1689, between Great Britain and Holland, it was declared, That the contracting powers, having declared war against the Most Christian King, it behoves them to do as much damage as possible to the common enemy, in order to bring him to agree to such conditions as may restore the repose of Christendom: and that, for this end, it was necessary to interrupt all trade and commerce with the subjects of the said king; and that, to effect this they had ordered their fleets to block up all the ports and havens of France. And in the 2d and 3d article, it is agreed, That they would take any vessel, whatever king or state it may belong to, that shall be found sailing into or out of the ports of France, and condemn both vessel and merchandize as lawful prize; and that this resolution should be notified to all neutral states. By the British Order in Council of the 11th November, 1807, it is declared, That all the ports and places of France and her allies, or of any other country at war with his majesty, and all other ports

(o) *Valin*, Sur l'Ordonnance, L. 3. tit. 9. des Prises, art. 7.

and places in Europe, from which, although not at war with his majesty, the British flag is excluded, and all ports or places in the colonies belonging to his majesty's enemies, shall, from henceforth, be subject to the same restrictions in point of trade and navigation, as if the same were actually blockaded by his majesty's naval forces, in the most strict and rigorous manner. And that all trade in articles which are of the produce and manufacture of the said countries or colonies, shall be deemed and considered to be unlawful; and that every vessel trading from or to the said countries or colonies, shall be captured and condemned as prize to the captors. And by the French decree issued at Milan on the 17th December, 1807, it is provided, That every vessel submitting to be searched by English cruizers, or paying duties to the English government, or sailing from the ports of England, and those of the English colonies, or countries occupied by English troops, shall be considered as good and lawful prize, and may be captured by our ships of war or privateers, and adjudged to the captors. It is evident that these edicts, however they may be attempted to be justified, are of a temporary nature only; must cease with the extraordinary circumstances that gave birth to them; and could make no permanent alteration in the law of prize.

The above rule, by which neutral vessels are involved in the confiscation of enemy's goods laden on board, seems to have been derived from a misapplication of that provision of the civil law which ordains the confiscation of the ship as a penalty for an unlawful lading put on board. *Dominus navis, si illicitè aliquid in nave, vel ipse, vel vectores imposuerint, navis quoque fisco vindicatur.* Ff. De Public. & Vectig. L. 11. § 2. It is evident that this is a mere fiscal regulation which cannot be applied to an act, such as that of carrying enemy's goods, which is perfectly lawful in the neutral, and therefore cannot induce the confiscation of the vehicle, which is his property.

12. Another, and a more difficult question presents itself, regarding enemy's goods laden in neutral vessels; and this is, whether the goods themselves are lawfully subject to capture and condemnation?

The conventional law of maritime nations on this question has fluctuated; but has most commonly decided that *free ships should make free goods*. The customary law and practise of those nations has varied less, and has generally determined that enemy's property on board the ships of a friend should be liable to capture and condemnation.

Without going back beyond the middle of the seventeenth century, the times preceding which partake too little of the spirit of civilization and humanity to furnish precedents of conventional law for the present age, we may enumerate the treaties mentioned in the margin which sanction the principle that *free ships make free goods*.(p)

(p) The treaty of 1646 between France and Holland. Of 1655 between France and the Hanse Towns. Of the same year between France and England. Of 1656 between England and Sweden. Of 1659 between France and Spain. Of 1661 between Portugal and Holland. Of 1662, of 1678, and of 1697 between France and Holland. Of 1662 and of 1742 between France and Denmark. Of 1672 between France and Sweden. Of 1677 between France and England. Of 1667 and 1670 between England and Spain. Of 1667, of 1675, and of 1679 between Sweden and Holland. Of 1668 and of 1674 between Holland and England. Of 1725 between the Empereror of Germany and Spain. Of 1742 between Spain and Denmark. Of 1748 between Denmark and Naples. Of 1756 between Denmark and Genoa. Of 1752 between Naples and Holland. The treaties of navigation, and commerce of Utrecht, 1713. The treaty of 1720 between Great Britain and Sweden. The treaties of 1721 and 1739 between Great Britain and Spain, confirming the treaties of Utrecht. The treaty of Aix la Chapelle, 1748, of Paris, 1763, of Versailles, 1783, and of commerce between Great Britain and France, 1786, all confirming the treaties of Utrecht. In the negotiations at Lisle in 1797, between Great Britain and France, it was proposed by the British plenipotentiary to renew these treaties confirmatory of those of Utrecht; which proposition was objected to by the French plenipotentiaries for several reasons foreign to the present subject: to which the British plenipotentiary, Lord Malmesbury, replied, that these treaties were become the law of nations,

The only treaties now existing, and observed by the parties to them, which adopt the principle that the character of the vessel shall determine that of the cargo, and that,

and that infinite confusion would result from their not being renewed. They were not, however, renewed by the treaty of Amiens of 1802, nor by that of Paris of 1814. The principle that free ships make free goods was also recognized by the treaty of 1778, between the United States and France; of 1782 between the United States and Holland; and of 1783, between the United States and Sweden. The same stipulation was contained in the treaty of 1785 between the United States and Prussia; but this treaty having expired, and a new one having been concluded in 1799, the article embracing this stipulation was not renewed: but the following was substituted in its place. Article XII. Experience having proved that the principle adopted in the twelfth article of the treaty of 1785, according to which, *free ships make free goods*, has not been sufficiently respected during the two last wars, and especially in that which still continues, the two contracting parties propose, after the return of a general peace, to agree either separately between themselves, or jointly with other powers alike interested, to concert with the great maritime powers of Europe, such arrangements and such permanent principles, as may serve to consolidate the liberty and safety of neutral navigation and commerce in future wars. And if in the interval either of the contracting parties should be engaged in a war, to which the other should remain neutral, the ships of war and privateers of the belligerent power shall conduct themselves towards the vessels of the neutral power, as favourably as the course of the war then existing may permit, observing the principles and rules of the law of nations generally acknowledged. In 1780, Russia published a declaration of what are called the principles of the *armed neutrality*, which were adopted by the treaties of the same year between Russia and Sweden and Denmark. To this declaration Holland acceded in 1780; Prussia, and the Emperor of Germany in 1781; Portugal in 1782; and Naples in 1783. Among the belligerent powers, France, Spain, and the United States acknowledged its principles; and Holland having become subsequently involved in the war, the British government offered to make peace with her on the basis of the treaty of 1674 between Great Britain and the Republic: a treaty, by which the principles of the armed neutrality are established in their widest extent. *Mr. Secretary Fox's letter to Mr Semolin, the Russian minister in London, 4th May*, 1782. These principles were again recognized by the convention of 1800 between the United States and France, and were renewed by the second armed neutrality of 1801; which was dissolved by the naval power of Great Britain, and the particular principle in question relinquished by consequently, *free ships shall make free goods*, are the following.

By the 15th article of the treaty of the 27th October, 1795, between the United States and Spain, it is stipulated that free ships shall give freedom to goods, and that every thing shall be deemed free and exempt which shall be found on board the ships belonging to the subjects of either of the contracting parties, although the whole lading, or any part thereof, should appertain to the enemies of either: Contraband goods being always excepted.

By the 23d article of the treaty of the 10th July, 1654, between the Republic of England and the king of Portugal, it is provided, That all goods and merchandize of the said Republic or King, or of their people or subjects, found on board the ships of the enemies of either, shall be made prize, together with the ships, and confiscated. But all the goods and merchandize of the enemies of either, on board the ships of either, or of their people or subjects, shall remain free and untouched.

It has been decided in the English courts of prize that the former provision of this article which subjects to condemnation the goods of either of the high contracting parties found on board the ships of the enemy of either, could not be fairly applied to the case of property *shipped* before the contemplation of war, and before the vessel herself had acquired a hostile character. In this adjudication it was observed, that it did not follow, that, because Spanish property put on board a Portuguese ship, would be protected in the event of the occurrence of war between England and

Russia: enemy's property on board neutral vessels being liable to capture and confiscation by the convention of the 5th June, 1801, between Great Britain and Russia. In 1807, in consequence of the treaty of Tilsit with France, a declaration was issued, by which the principles of the armed neutrality were proclaimed anew, and the convention of 1801, annulled. In 1812 a treaty of alliance was signed between Great Britain and Russia; but no treaty of commerce and navigation has been concluded between the two powers since that of 1801.

Spain, therefore Portuguese property on board a Spanish ship should become instantly confiscable on the breaking out of hostilities with Spain: that in one case the conduct of the parties would not have been different if the event of hostilities had been known. The cargo was entitled to the protection of the ship generally by the stipulation of the treaty even if shipped in open war; and *a fortiori*, if shipped under circumstances still more favourable to the neutrality of the transaction. In the other case there might be reason to suppose that the treaty referred only to goods shipped on board an enemy's vessel, in an avowed hostile character; and that the neutral merchant would have acted differently, if he had been apprized of the character of the vessel at the time when the goods were put on board.(q)

(q) 6 *Robinson*, 29. The Marianna. The treaty of 1783 between the United States and Sweden (which has expired) excepts from the terms of the article, importing confiscation of *neutral property found on board enemy's vessels*, such goods and merchandizes as were put on board before the declaration of war, or even six months after the declaration. Article XVI. It is obvious that this privilege of the neutral flag of protecting enemy's property, whether conferred by treaty or by the ordinances of belligerent powers, cannot extend to a fraudulent use of the flag to cover enemy's property in the ship as well as cargo. 6 *Robinson*, 358. The Citade de Lisbon. And when during the war of the American revolution, the United States recognizing the principles of the armed neutrality, exempted by an ordinance of Congress all neutral vessels from capture, except such as were employed in carrying contraband goods, or soldiers, to the enemy; it was held that this exemption did not extend to a vessel which had forfeited her privilege by grossly unneutral conduct in taking a decided part with the enemy by combining with his subjects to wrest out of the hands of the United States and of France the advantages they had acquired over Great Britain by the rights of war in the conquest of Dominica. By the capitulation of that island, all commercial intercourse was interdicted with Great Britain. In the case in question the vessel was purchased by neutrals in London, who supplied her with false and colourable papers, and assumed on themselves the ownership of the cargo for a voyage from London to Dominica. Had she been employed in a fair commerce, such as was consistent with the rights of neutrality, her cargo, though the property of an enemy

A celebrated controversial writer has criticised the above expression *conventional law of nations*, as used by those modern champions of neutral rights, Hubner and Schlegel; but it is evident that this criticism can only apply with force to its use in an unlimited extent. For, as between the nations stipulating, a treaty must be the law, 1st, So long as it subsists, 2d, So long as its provisions are to subsist by its terms. Such treaty must also be the law as between the contracting parties, and all others to whom its provisions, relaxing the primitive rigour of the customary law of nations, are to be extended; and it must be the law as between themselves, and to be observed by them towards all the rest of the world, if the provisions of the treaty be declaratory of the original and pre-existing law of nations. This last characteristic applies to the convention of 1801, between Great Britain and Russia, which Lord Grenville in his speech delivered in the British House of Lords on the 13th November, 1801, *states*, and conclusively *proves*, to be a recognition of universal and pre-existing rights, which, as such, could not justly be refused by the contracting powers to any other independent state.

13. Considering the question in regard to the customary law and practice of maritime nations, we shall find that enemy's goods in neutral vessels were declared to be liable to capture by the *Consolato del Mare;* in the 273d chapter[r] of which it is laid down, that, If the ship or vessel

could not be prize; because Congress had said by their ordinance, that the rights of neutrality should extend protection to such effects and goods of an enemy. But, if the neutrality were violated, Congress had not said, that such a violated neutrality shall give such protection: Nor could they have said so, without confounding all the distinctions of right and wrong; and Congress did not mean, by their ordinance to ascertain in what cases the rights of neutrality should be forfeited, in exclusion of all other cases; for the instances not mentioned are as flagrant as the cases particularized. 2 *Dallas*, 34. Darby *et* al v. The Erstern.

(r) Chap. 276, § 1004, of M. Boucher's French translation.

which shall be taken, belong to a friend, and the merchandize which she carries belong to an enemy, the commander of the armed ship or vessel may force and constrain the master of the ship or vessel, which he has taken, to carry into some port the effects of his enemy which are on board. And in conformity with this rule are the authorities cited in the margin.(s)

14. Bynkershoek is of the opinion that freight is not payable to the neutral carrier of enemy's property by the captor, because freight is not due, unless the goods have been carried to their port of destination.(t) But a different rule is laid down in the *Consolato del Mare*, which is more reasonable in itself, and is supported by the whole current of authorities. A capture is considered as *delivery*; and enemy's goods are condemned *ex re* only, the carrier of them not being guilty of any offence against the law of nations.

This rule is adopted by the English prize courts, but with so many exceptions and limitations that its practical

(s) *Grotius*, De J. B. ac P. L. 3. c. 6, § 6. *Heinecius*, De nav. ob vect. vet. merc. com. c. 2. § 9. *Voet*, De Jure Militari, c. 5. *Loccenius*, De Jure Maritimo, L. 2. c. 4. *Bynkershoek*, Q. J. P. L. 1. c. 14. *Vattel*, L. 3. c. 7. § 115. *Azuni*, Part 2, c. 3. art. 2. *D'Habreu*, Tratado sobre las Presas, c. 9. No. 3.

Se alcuna nave, o navilio, o altra fusta che entrerà in corso, o ne uscirà, o ci sarà, si riscontrerà con alcuna nave, o navilio di mercanzia, fusse d'amici, e le mercanzie che lui porterà sarrano d'inimici, lo Ammiraglio della nave, e navilio armato può constringere quel padrone della nave, o navilio che lui pigliato averà, che lui con quella sua nave gli debba portare quello che de suoi inimici sarà, in loco che non abbia paura, che i nimici non ne li possono torre. Consolato del Mare. Italian Edit. *Empero si la nav ho lo leyn que pres sera es de enemichs; e la mercaderia que ell aportara sera tambe de enemichs, lo Almirall dela nav ho del leyn armat pot forçar y destrenyer aquell aytal senyor de equella nav ho de aquell dit leyn que ell pres havra que ell ab aquella sua nav li deja a portar ço que de los enemichs sera: y encara que ell so te en sa nav ho en son leyn, tro que sia en loch de recabre. Ib.* Catalonian Edit. Barcelona, 1540.

(t) Q. J. P. L. 1. c. 14.

effect is almost destroyed.(u) And, 1st, It is refused to a neutral ship taken whilst engaged in the coasting trade of the enemy.(v) 2d, To a neutral ship engaged in the colonial trade of the enemy.(w) 3d, Where there has been a spoliation of papers by the master.(x) 4th, Upon the carriage of contraband.(y) As the two first of these exceptions are grounded upon a doctrine peculiar to the British courts of prize which subjects to capture a neutral trade not open in time of peace, and as this doctrine makes no part of the law of nations, and is not recognized in the practice of any other nation, it is evident that these exceptions have no legal foundation.

15. If the property in the ship or her cargo appear by the papers found on board to be in the enemy, no liens in a neutral claimant, or in a subject or citizen of the belligerent state, upon the same, by way of pledge for the payment of the purchase money or hypothecation, are sufficient to found a claim in a prize court, and to defeat the rights of the captors.

Thus where the ship appeared to have been originally a neutral vessel sold to a Spanish merchant at Buenos Ayres, and seized on a voyage to England, documented as belonging to a Spanish merchant, and sailing under the flag and pass of Spain; a claim was given on behalf of the former neutral proprietor, in virtue of a lien which he was said to have retained on the property for the purchase money; but such an interest was deemed not sufficient to support a claim in a court of prize. Captors are supposed to lay their hands on the gross tangible property, on which there may be many just claims outstanding, between other parties, which can

(u) 3 *Robinson*, 304. The Atlas. In Notis.

(v) 1 *Robinson*, 296. The Emanuel.

(w) 2 *Robinson*, 186. The Immanuel.

(x) *Ib.* 104. The Rising Sun.

(y) 1 *Robinson*, 288. The Mercurius.

have no operation as to them. If such a rule did not exist, it would be quite impossible for captors to know upon what grounds they were proceeding to make any seizure. The fairest and most credible documents, declaring the property to belong to the enemy, would only serve to mislead them, if such documents were liable to be overruled by liens which could not in any manner come to their knowledge. It would be equally impossible for the court which has to decide upon the question of property to admit such considerations. The doctrine of liens depends very much upon the particular rules of jurisprudence, which prevail in different countries. To decide judicially on such claims, would require of the court a perfect knowledge of the law of covenant, and the application of that law in all countries, under all the diversities in which that law exists. From necessity, therefore, the court would be obliged to shut the door against such discussions, and to decide on the simple title of property with scarcely any exceptions. Then what is the proprietary character of this ship? She is described as the property of a Spanish merchant. She is sailing under the Spanish flag, and is fully invested with the Spanish character not ostensibly only, but actually, and in the real intention and understanding of the parties. The objection that a part of the purchase money had not been paid can have but little weight, since it is a matter solely for the consideration of the person who sells, to judge what mode of payment he will accept. He may consent to take a bill of exchange, or he may rely on the promisory note of the purchaser, which may not come in payment for a considerable time, or may never be paid. The court will not look to such contingencies. It will be sufficient that a legal transfer has been made, and that the mode of payment whatever it is has been accepted. As to the title of property in the goods, which were going as the funds out of which the payment for the ship was to have been made. That they were going for the payment of a debt, will not alter the property; there must be something more. Even if bills of lading are delivered, that circumstance will not be sufficient, unless accompanied with an understanding, that he who holds the bill of lading is to bear the risk of the goods, as to the voyage, and as to the market to which they are consigned; otherwise, though the security may avail *pro tanto*, it cannot be held to work any change in the property.(z)

And also where a claim was interposed on behalf of a subject of the belligerent state for the amount of a bottomry bond executed to him by the master of the ship, being an enemy's vessel, previous to hostilities, the claim was rejected. For the person advancing money on bonds of this nature, acquires by that act no property in the vessel; he acquires the *jus in rem*, but not the *jus in re*, until it has been converted and appropriated by the final process of a court of justice. The property of the vessel continues in the former proprietor, who has given a right of action against it, but nothing more. If there is no change of property, there can be no change of national character. Those lending money on such security, take this security subject to all the chances incident to it, and amongst the rest, the chances of war. But it is said, that the captor takes *cum onere*; and therefore that this obligation would devolve upon him. That he is held to take *cum onere* is undoubtedly true as a rule which is to be understood to apply, where the *onus* is immediately and visibly incumbent upon it. A captor who takes the cargo of an enemy on board the ship of a friend, takes it liable to the freight due to the owner of the ship; because the owner of the ship has the cargo in his possession, subject to that demand by the general law, independent of all contract. By that law he is not bound to part with it but on payment of freight, he being in possession can detain it by his own authority, and wants not the aid of any court for that purpose. These are

(z) 6 Robinson, 25, The Marianna.

all characters of the *jus in re*—of an interest directly and visibly residing in the substance of the thing itself. But it is a proposition of a much wider extent, which affirms that a mere right of action is entitled to the same favourable consideration, in its transfer from the neutral to a captor. It is very obvious that claims of such a nature may be so framed, as that no powers belonging to the prize court can enable it to examine them with effect. They are private contracts passing between parties who may have an interest in colluding; the captor has no access whatever to the original private understanding of the parties in forming such contracts; and it is therefore unfit that he should be affected by them. His rights of capture act upon the property, without regard to secret liens possessed by third parties. In like manner his rights operate on such liens, where the property itself is protected from capture. Indeed, it would be almost impossible for the captor to discover such liens in the possession of the enemy, upon property belonging to a neutral; the consequence, therefore, of allowing, generally, the privilege here claimed would be, that the captor would be subject to the disadvantage of having neutral liens set up to defeat his claims upon hostile property, whilst he could never entitle himself to any advantage, from hostile liens upon neutral property.[a]

So where the claimant grounded his pretensions on a lien created on the goods, in consequence of an advance made to the shippers, in consideration of the consignment by the claimant's agent in the enemy's country; and on other goods, in virtue of a general balance of account due to the claimant as the factor of the shippers. To establish this fact, an order for further proof was asked for, and the question was, whether, if proved, the claim could, in point of law, be sustained? The doctrine of liens seems to depend chiefly upon the rules of jurisprudence established in dif-

(a) 5 *Robinson*, 218. The Tobago.

ferent countries. There is no doubt that, agreeably to the common law, a factor has a lien upon the goods of his principal in his possession, for the balance of accounts due to him; and so has a consignee for advances made by him to the consignor. The consignor or owner cannot maintain an action against his factor, to recover the property so placed in his possession, without first paying or tendering what is thus due to the factor. But this doctrine is unknown in prize courts, unless in very particular cases, where the lien is imposed by a general law of the mercantile world, independent of any contract between the parties. Such is the case of freight upon enemies' goods seized in the vessel of a friend, which is always decreed to the owner of the vessel. The possession of the property is actually in the owner of the ship, of which, by the general mercantile law of all nations, he cannot be deprived until the freight due for the carriage of it is paid. He has, in fact, a kind of property in the goods by force of this general law, which a prize court ought to respect and does respect. On the one hand, the captor by stepping into the shoes of the enemy owner of the goods, is personally benefitted by the labour of a friend, and ought, in justice, to make him the proper compensation:—and on the other, the ship owner, by not having carried the goods to the place of their destination, and this in consequence of an act of the captor, would be totally without remedy to recover his freight against the owner of the goods. But in cases of liens created by the mere private contract of individuals, depending upon the different laws of different countries, the difficulties which an examination of such claims would impose upon the captors, and even upon the prize courts, in deciding upon them, and the door which such a doctrine would open to collusion between the enemy owners of the property and neutral claimants, have excluded such cases from the consideration of these courts. The principal strength of the argument in favour of the claimant in this case seemed to be rested upon the position, that the consignor could not have countermanded the consignment after delivery of the goods to the master of the vessel; and hence it was inferred that the captor had no right to intercept the passage of the property to the consignee. This doctrine would be well founded, if the goods had been sent to the claimant upon his account and risk, except in the case of insolvency. But where goods are sent upon the account and risk of the shipper, the delivery to the master is a delivery to him as agent of the shipper, not of the consignee; and it is competent to the consignor, at any time before actual delivery to the consignee, to countermand it, and thus to prevent his lien from attaching.[b]

16. The property in ships and their cargoes which was enemy's property at the commencement of the voyage cannot be transferred to a neutral *in transitu* so as to protect it from capture and condemnation. In the ordinary course of things in time of peace such a transfer might be made. When war intervenes, another rule is set up by courts of prize, which interferes with the ordinary practice. In a state of war, existing or imminent, it is held that the property shall be deemed to continue as it was at the time of shipment until the actual delivery; this arises out of a state of war, which gives a belligerent a right to stop the goods of his enemy. If such a rule did not exist, all goods shipped in the enemy's country would be protected by transfers which it would be impossible to detect. A transfer may take place *in transitu,* where there is no actual war, nor any prospect of war, mixing itself with the transaction of the parties: But in time of war this is prohibited as a vicious contract; being a fraud on belligerent rights, not on-

(b) Per Washington, J. The Frances, Supreme Court of the U. S. February Term, 1814. M. S. For a further illustration of the doctrine that the rights of war operate only on the *res ipsa,* and the *onera* attaching thereon in right of possession, see the case of the Hoffnung, 6 *Robinson,* 383.

ly in the particular transaction, but in the great facility which it would necessarily introduce, of evading those rights beyond the possibility of detection. It is a road that, in time of war, must be shut up ; for although honest men might be induced to travel it with very innocent intentions, the far greater proportion of those who passed, would use it only for sinister purposes, and with views of fraud on the rights of the belligerent. But would the *contemplation of war* have the same effect in vitiating these contracts as actual war? It cannot be said that all engagements in the proximity of war, into which the speculation of war might enter, as for instance, with regard to the price, would therefore be invalid. The contemplation of war is undoubtedly to be taken in a more restricted sense. But if the contemplation of war leads immediately to the transfer, and becomes the foundation of a contract, that would not otherwise be entered into on the part of the seller; and this is known to be so done in the understanding of the purchaser, though on his part there may be other concurrent motives, such a contract cannot be held good, on the same principle that applies to invalidate a transfer *in transitu* in time of actual war. The motive may indeed be difficult to be proved—but that will be the difficulty of particular cases: supposing the fact to be established, that is a sale under an admitted necessity, arising from a certain expectation of war; that is a sale of goods not in the possession of the seller, and in a state where they could not, during war, be legally transferred, on account of the frauds on belligerent rights ;—the same fraud is committed against the belligerent, not indeed as an actual belligerent, but as one who was, in the clear expectation of both the contracting parties, likely to become a belligerent, before the arrival of the property which is made the subject of their agreement. The nature of both contracts is identically the same, being equally to protect the property from capture of war—not indeed in either case from capture at the present moment when the contract is made, but from the danger of captures when it was likely to occur. The object is the same in both instances, to afford a guarantee against the same crisis: In other words, both are done for the purpose of eluding a belligerent right either present or expected. Both contracts are framed with the same *animo fraudandi*, and are justly subject to the same rule.(c)

Where goods were shipped to be sold on joint account of the shipper and consignees, or on account of the shipper only at the option of the consignee, and the goods were claimed by the consignee, the whole question as to the exclusive property of the shipper in the goods was rested by the captors upon the option given to the consignee to be jointly concerned or not in the shipment. The court stated that the question of law was, in whom the right of property was vested at the time of capture? To effect a change of property as between seller and buyer, it is essential that there should be a contract of sale agreed to by both parties; and if the thing agreed to be sold is to be sent by the vendor to the vendee, it is necessary to the perfection of the contract, that it should be delivered to the purchaser or to his agent, which the master, to many purposes, is considered to be. The only evidence of a contract, such as that set up by the claimant, appeared in his affidavit, stating, that before the declaration of war, he was in the enemy's country, and agreed with the shipper that the latter should ship goods on joint account, when the commercial intercourse between the two countries should be opened; and that, in consequence of this agreement the shipment was made. Yet the delivery of the goods to the master of the vessel, was not for the use of the consignee, any more than it was for the use of the shipper solely; and, consequently it amounted to nothing, so as to divest the property out of

(c) 1 *Robinson*, 107. The Danckebaar Africaan, 4 *Robinson*, 207. The Carl Walter. 5 Robinson, 128, The Jan Frederick.

the shipper, until the consignee should elect to take the goods on joint account, or to act as the agent of the shipper. Until this election was made, the goods were at the risk of the shipper, which was conclusive as to the right of property.(d)

But as this is merely a rule of evidence intended for the detection of fraud, it is not applied to the case of goods transferred *in transitu* before the breaking out of hostilities, and not in contemplation of war being commenced. The rule arises out of a state of war, and cannot be applied to transactions originating in time of profound peace, which must be judged according to the ordinary rules of commerce.(e) Nor is it applied to a consignment on credit made by an enemy shipper to a neutral consignee, where the consignor learning after the shipment, that the consignee has become a bankrupt or failed, stops the goods *in transitu* on their passage to the consignee. For by the municipal law the consignor having a right in this case thus to change the consignment, the law of war permits the delivery to be made to another neutral consignee by order of the enemy shipper.(f) But where the goods had been shipped by order and for the account and risk of neutral merchants, and after the ship had sailed, they signified that they would not accept the goods, and on this refusal, the enemy shipper wrote to another neutral merchant offering the goods to him on conditions of payment, which were accepted, and a claim was given for the second consignee, it was determined to be inadmissible. As the bills of lading were signed to the account and risk of the first consignees, and the goods sailed under that description, they were their goods, and the shipper had no right to stop them, but on the special contingency of an

(d) Per Washington J. The Venus, Supreme Court of the U. S. February Term, 1814. M. S.

(e) 1 *Robinson*, 336. The Vrow Margaretha.

(f) 6 *Robinson*, 321. The Constantia.

apprehension of non-payment. On that event the law gives him a proprietary lien for his security, and the right of stopping the goods. In this case it was asserted, that the first consignees actually refused to pay for the goods, and therefore the event had emerged on which the right of the consignor to stop is founded. The shipper might have forced the goods on the first consignees under the order, and might have compelled them to accept and pay. But he did not exercise that right, he took the goods to himself again, in order to sell them to another person, and by that act the goods became again the property of the shipper. Then comes the question which answers itself; whether the goods of an enemy can be transferred *in transitu*. In time of peace, when the rights of third parties do not intervene, there may be no objection to the validity of a transfer of this kind. But in time of war, it would open a door to fraud, against which courts of justice could never be effectually protected, and therefore it has been prohibited.(g)

In another case goods were shipped, and the bill of lading was in the name of the consignees, and the invoice purported to be on their account and risk. A letter from the shipper to the consignees, after describing the goods and the labour he had employed in the business, and stating that they were sent partly in the *Fanny* and partly in the *Frances*, says, "I have exceeded in some articles and have sent you others not ordered: I leave it with yourselves to take the whole of the two shipments, or none at all, just as you please. If you do not wish them, I will thank you to hand the invoices and letters over to Messrs. Falconer, Jackson & Co: I think twenty-four hours will allow you ample opportunity for you to make up your minds on this point, and if you do not hand them over within that time, I will of course consider that you take the whole!"

It was argued for the consignees and claimants, that by the invoice and bill of lading, and the true construction of the

(g) 6 *Robinson*, 329, The Twende Venner.

shipper's letter, the property was vested in them, liable to be divested by their rejecting the consignment within twenty-four hours after receiving the letters ; that the condition annexed to the transfer, was *subsequent*, not *precedent*.

But the court could not concur in this reasoning. To vest the property in the claimants, a contract is necessary; and to form a contract, the consent of two parties is indispensable. Had the shipper in execution of the consignees' order, consigned to them unconditionally such goods as they had directed, the contract would have been complete, and the goods would on being shipped have become the property of the consignees. But the shipper had not done this : with the goods which were ordered he consigned other goods, expressly stipulating that the consignees should not take the goods they had ordered, unless they consented to take the whole quantity put on board both vessels. This, then, was a new proposition, on which the consignees were at liberty to exercise their discretion. They might accept, or reject it, and until accepted, the property must remain in the shipper.

But the claimants prayed an order for further proof, and said that before the capture of the *Frances*, the *Fanny* had arrived, and they had consented to take both cargoes.

This application was opposed by the captors upon the principle, that were the fact true as alleged by the claimants, belligerent property cannot change its character *in transitu*.

Reserving any opinion upon the law, if this fact should be proved, further proof was ordered, *and* upon the production of the further proof the property was condemned,[h]

17. And contracts of purchase effected on the part of the belligerent, but left executory as to payment and contingent on a delivery at an ulterior port at the risk of the neutral merchant, are not allowed in time of war; the

[h] Per Marshall, C. J. The Frances, Supreme Court of the U. S. February T. 1814.

goods sailing under such a contract, and taken *in transitu*, are held to be the absolute property of the enemy. By the civil and common laws the nature of the contract of sale renders the thing sold at the risk of the vendee until delivered, unless the contrary is expressly stipulated by the parties.[i] It is the liberty of making this express stipulation which is taken away by this rule of the prize law, it being so liable to abuse for the purposes of fraud. When the contract is made in time of peace or without any contemplation of war, no such rule exists; but where the form of the contract is framed directly for the purpose of obviating the danger apprehended from approaching hostilities, it is a rule which unavoidably must take place. Where the goods are to become the property of the enemy on delivery, *capture* is considered as *delivery:* The captors by the rights of war stand in the place of the enemy, and are entitled to a condemnation of goods passing under such a contract, as of enemy's property.[k] The ordinary state of commerce is, that goods ordered and delivered to the master are considered as delivered to the consignee, whose agent the master is in this respect; but that general contract of the law may be varied by special agreement, or by a particular prevailing practice, that presupposes an agreement amongst such a description of merchants. In time of profound peace when there is no prospect of approaching war, there would unquestionably be nothing illegal in contracting, that the whole risk should fall on the consignor, till the goods came into possession of the consignee. In time of peace they may divide this risk as they please. In time of war this cannot be permitted, for it would at once put an end to all captures at sea; the risk would in all cases be laid on the consignor where it suited the purpose of protection; on every contemplation of war,

(i) *Pothier*, Des Obligations, No. 7. De Vente, No. 307, 2 *Johnson's Reports*, 13.

(k) 3 *Robinson*, 299. The Atlas, 4 *Robinson*, 107. The Anna Catharina.

this contrivance would be practised in all consignments from neutral ports to the enemy's country, to the manifest defrauding of all rights of capture ; it is therefore considered to be an invalid contract in time of war ; or to express it more accurately, it is a contract, which, if made in war, has this effect ; that the captor has a right to seize the property and convert it to his own use ; for having all the rights that belong to his enemy, he is authorised to have his taking possession considered as equivalent to an actual delivery to his enemy ; and the shipper who put it on board in time of war must be presumed to know the rule, and to secure himself in his agreement with the consignee against the contingency of any loss to himself that can arise from capture.(1)

18. By the prize codes of several nations, the want of papers found on board the captured vessel, and the suppression, concealment, or spoliation of papers, is considered as furnishing presumptive evidence of the existence of enemy interests, and unless rebutted by contrary proof of a satisfactory nature, as affording a ground of condemnation. Thus by the French ordinance of August, 1681, *Des Prises*, art. 6, all vessels on board of which no charter party, bills of lading, or invoices are to be found, are, together with their cargoes, declared good prize. And by the Ordinances of 1543, art. 43, and of 1584, art. 70, the throwing overboard of the charter party, or other papers concerning the lading of the vessel, is declared a sufficient cause of condemnation. Doubts having arisen as to the application of this rule of evidence, in cases where sufficient papers were found remaining on board to furnish proof of the proprietary interest, the ordinance of the 5th September, 1708, was rendered ; by which it was provided, That every captured vessel, from which papers have been thrown over board, shall be good prize together with the cargo, upon

(1) 2 *Robinson*, 133. The Packet de Bilboa.

proof of this single fact only, without its being necessary to examine into the nature of these papers, or by whom they were thrown overboard, nor whether sufficient papers were found remaining on board to furnish evidence that the vessel and the goods of her lading belonged to friends or allies. But this decision appearing too rigorous in practice, Louis the Fourteenth, in a letter of the 2d February, 1710, addressed to the Admiral of France, directed the Council of Prizes to apply the terms of this Ordinance according to the peculiar circumstances and the subsidiary proofs in each case. Valin is of opinion that, though this letter escaped the attention of the framers of the Regulation of the 21st October, 1744, of which the 6th article is entirely conformable to the Ordinance of the 5th September, 1708, yet it ought to be applied to temper the rigour of this article according to circumstances.

In the British courts of prize spoliation of papers is in all cases considered as a proof of *mala fides*; and where that appears, it is an universal rule to presume the worst against those who are convicted of it: it will always be supposed that such papers relate to the ship or cargo; and that it was of material consequence to some interests, that they should be destroyed.[m] And where there has been such a spoliation, or a suppression of papers, farther proof is always ordered.[n] But if the master, or other person concerned in the spoliation or suppression, be at the same time the owner of any part of the ship or cargo, it is considered as sufficient to effect the condemnation of his share; and the misconduct of the master in this respect is visited upon the neutral owner of the ship by refusing freight upon the goods condemned.[o]

[m] 1 *Robinson*, 131. The Two Brothers.

[n] 2 *Robinson*, 361. The Polly.

[o] 2 *Robinson*, 104. The Rising Sun.

19. The right of visitation and search is a right of belligerent powers consequent, not merely upon the right of capturing enemy's goods in neutral vessels, but upon that of capturing enemy's vessels and enemy's goods laden on board the same, contraband of war, and vessels committing a breach of blockade, or of detaining vessels transporting military persons or despatches in the service of an enemy. Even if the rule that *free ships make free goods* be adopted, the exercise of this right is essential in order to determine whether the ships themselves are neutral, and documented as such according to treaties and the law of nations. Indeed it seems that the practice of maritime captures could not exist without it. Accordingly the unanimous authority of the writers on public law establishes this right in the armed and commissioned vessels of belligerent states.(p)

Various treaties and ordinances of belligerent states prescribe the mode in which the right of visitation and search is to be exercised so as to prevent disorder and illegal violence. The earliest of these treaties is that of the Pyrenees of the 17th November, 1659. By the 17th article of this celebrated treaty, it is provided that, To avoid all disorder, the ships of the one power shall not approach those of the other nearer than within cannon-shot, and shall send their boat on board of the merchant vessel with two or three men only, to whom the master of the merchant vessel shall exhibit the passports by which shall be made to appear, not only the lading, but also the place of domicil or residence; the name of the master and that of the vessel, in order by these means to ascertain whether she carries any contraband goods, and that the character of the ship, as well as the quality of the master, may satisfactorily

(p) *Bynkershoek*, Q. J. P. L. 1. c. 14. *Vattel*, L. 3. c. 7. § 114. *Martens*, L. 8. c. 6 § 14. *Galliani*, De Doveri de Principi neutrali verso i Principi guerregianti, et de questi verso i neutrali. 458. *Lampredi*, Del Commercio de Popoli Neutrali in Tempo de Geurra. 185. *Azuni*, Part 2, c. 3. art. 4. § 2.

appear. The same rules are adopted by the prize laws of different nations, but are very irregularly observed in practice.

The penalty affixed to a violent resistance to the exercise of this right by the universal law and usage of nations, is confiscation.(q) Thus by the French Ordinance of August, 1681, it is provided, That every vessel which refuses to lower its sails, after being thereunto summoned by our ships of war, or the private armed vessels of our subjects, may be compelled by force; and in case of resistance and combat, shall be good prize. L. 3. tit. 9. art. 12. *Des Prises.* The same provision was contained in the Ordinance of 1584, art. 65; and is incorporated into the Spanish Ordinance of 1718. Notwithstanding the practice of the British courts of prize is in conformity with this rule,(r) there is a singularly anomolous case adjudged in the English common law courts, in which the right of search is not only denied, but the lawfulness of resisting its exercise is maintained. This was the case of an insurance in England on a ship belonging to subjects of Tuscany, then neutral between Great Britain and Spain, laden with neutral property, and captured by a Spanish cruizer and carried into a port of Spain, where she was condemned. The first ground of condemnation which appeared in the sentence was, that the ship had refused to be searched, and resisted with force, having fired on the Spanish cruizer, contrary to the above Ordinance. The ship was warranted neutral; and the payment of the loss resisted upon the ground of the forfeiture of her neutrality appearing by the

(q) *Vattel*, L. 3. c. 7. § 114. *Azuni*, Part 2, c. 3. art. 4. § 5. *Il diritto delle genti giustifica la forza contro di chiunque contrasta o appone impedimento all'esercizio dell'altrui diritto perfetto: dunque a tal riguardo potrà perseguitarsi la nave neutrale e sottoporla alla confisca dichiarandola buona preda, come ha giustamente stabilito il Gius' convenzionale dell' Europa, che in questa parte spiega il Diritto primitivo e generale della natura.* Ib. § 7.

(r) 1 *Robinson*, 340. The Maria.

sentence of condemnation. Upon these facts, the court of King's Bench were of opinion that the insured were entitled to recover, and gave judgment accordingly. As to the alleged cause of condemnation, the judges agreed that a ship, warranted neutral, must so conduct herself as not to forfeit her neutrality; and that if by the wilful act of the master, she do this, to the injury of the owners, it will amount to the offence of barratry: But in this case, it was said, nothing of that kind was imputable to him. That a neutral ship is not bound to submit to search, searching being an act of superior force, rather than the exercise of a right, which may always be resisted when the party is able; and the searcher who acts at his peril, always pays costs, unless he finds something on board to justify him, like the case of custom-house officers: That this was confirmed by the practice of the Admiralty, where costs are always given in cases of improper detention, which would not be done if neutral vessels were liable, at all events, to be stopped: That in the present case there was nothing to justify the search, the cargo being neutral: That a ship is only bound to take notice of the laws of the countries from which, and to which, she sails; but not the particular ordinances of other powers; and that a detention, therefore, under the authority of particular ordinances which do not make a part of the law of nations, was a risk within the policy.[s]

Although the doctrine of this case, so far, at least, as relates to the determination of the question of municipal law arising in it, was afterwards reversed by the same court in the case of *Garrels vs. Kensington*, 8 T. R. 23; yet as it has been cited by a celebrated writer on public law as a conclusive authority against the right of search for merchandize, it may not be useless briefly to examine its reasoning as affecting that right.[t]

([s]) *Marshall on Insurance*, B. 1. c. 8. § 5. Saloucci vs. Johnson.

([t]) *Schlegel on Neutral Rights*. In Appendix.

And this reasoning will be found to be extremely inconsequent. For though it is certainly true that the particular ordinances of belligerent powers have no binding force as a part of the law of nations, yet when they are only declaratory of that law, and are conformable therewith, a condemnation under their authority in a court of prize is not the less valid and legal. And though it is equally true that the law and practice of the admiralty condemn in costs and damages the captor, who has abused the right of search, by detaining and carrying in for adjudication neutral vessels against which no reasonable cause of suspicion exists, yet no instance can be found of costs and damages awarded against a captor for stopping and searching a neutral vessel on the high seas; much less does it depend upon the event of such search, whether the captor shall be thus condemned in costs and damages. For, as Bynkershoek has justly observed, it is lawful to detain a neutral vessel, in order to ascertain, not by the flag merely, which may be fraudulently assumed, but by the documents themselves which are on board, whether she is really neutral. If then search be a lawful act, how can it be said that it may always be resisted when the party is able? And how can it be said that the searcher acts at his peril, when the award of costs and damages against him does not depend upon the immediate event of the search, but upon that of the further detention and carrying in for adjudication?[u]

[u] When it is laid down that there is no right of search, because *the cruizer searches at the hazard of costs and damages if he find nothing*, it must equally occur that this very liability in costs and damages is itself the firmest security of the right of search, by engaging the neutral's submission to the exercise of it under the remedy of an indemnification. That the question of costs and damages should depend upon the result of a search is perfectly intelligible, it being a question of after-consideration; but that it should depend upon the result of a search whether that search can *in limine* be lawfully resisted, is a contradiction equally in terms and in meaning. The purpose of the resistance is to exclude the knowledge of the fact which the fact is to ascertain; and if the resistance is suc-

The question therefore returns, resistance to search being an unlawful act, what is the penalty affixed to it by the law of nations. And we have seen that this penalty is confis cation.

But in order to induce the infliction of this penalty, it must be shewn that the merchant vessel had reasonable grounds to be satisfied of the existence of war, otherwise there is no such thing as neutral character, nor any foundation for the several duties, which the law of nations imposes upon that character. In a case, therefore, where at the time of sailing no war was supposed to exist, in the knowledge or contemplation of the master, and he was consequently unconscious that he had any neutral duties to perform, a resistance to visitation and search was held to be no ground of condemnation.(v) So neither will the forcible resistance of the enemy master affect neutral property laden on board his vessel. For an attempt on his part to rescue his vessel from the possession of the captor is nothing more than the hostile act of a hostile person who has a perfect right to make such an attempt. If a neutral master attempts a rescue, or to withdraw himself from search, he violates a duty which is imposed upon him by the law of nations, to submit to search, and to be carried in for enquiry and adjudication as to the property of the ship or cargo; and if he violates this obligation by a recurrence to force, the consequence will undoubtedly reach the property of his owner; and it would, perhaps, extend also to the whole property entrusted to his care, and thus fraudulently attempted to be withdrawn from the operation of the rights of war. With an enemy master the case is very different: No duty is violated by such an act on his part—

cessful, the fact will remain unknown on which the legality of the resistance is itself to depend. *Croke's Answer to Schlegel.*

(v) 5 *Robinson*, 33. The St. Juan Baptista *et al.*

lupum auribus teneo, and if he can withdraw himself, he has a right so to do.(w)

The question how far a neutral has a right to lade his goods on board an armed enemy vessel, and how far his property is involved in the consequences of resistance by the enemy master, was agitated during the late war with Great Britain in a case celebrated on account of the importance of its principles, and the eloquence and ability with which they were discussed.(x) The claimant, a native and resident of Buenos Ayres in South America, chartered a British armed vessel for a voyage from London to Buenos Ayres and back again to London, and put his goods on board. The vessel sailed under convoy of two British frigates, but parted from them before her capture. In the prosecution of her voyage, and while in sight of Madeira, where she meant to stop in the expectation of joining the convoy she had parted from, she was captured by a private armed vessel of the United States, after having made resistance, in which the claimant did not participate. Under these circumstances, the district court condemned the goods claimed, as prize of war ;(y) a decree affirming the condemnation, was entered *pro forma* in the circuit court, and the cause was carried by appeal to the supreme court. Three of the judges of that court were of the opinion, that a neutral had a right to ship goods of his property on board a belligerent armed merchant ship without forfeiting his neutral character, unless he actually concurred and participated in the vessel's resistance to capture.(z) One judge

(w) 5 *Robinson*. The Catharina Elizabeth. *Nè il predatore può avere alcun diritto d'inseguire la preda, che non avea custodita ; mentre era la sola custodia quella, che poteva mantenerlo in possesso della nave predata, giusta i principi della ragion commune.* Azuni, Part 2, c. 4. art. 5. § 2.

(x) The Nereid. Supreme Court of the U. S. February T. 1815.

(y) Per Van Ness, J. District Court for the Southern District of N. Y. August 9th, 1814.

(z) Per Marshall, C. J. Washington and Livingston, J.

declined expressing any opinion on that point, as unnecessary; because he thought it sufficient to say that a merchant of Buenos Ayres, considering the situation of his country, the dangers of Carthagena cruizers, and the risks to which himself and his property would be subject in case of capture, was warranted by considerations in no way connected with the war between the United States and Great Britain, in availing himself of an armed belligerent merchant ship as the only adequate means of carrying on his trade, and which had been so prior to the declaration of war by the United States ;([a]) whilst the two other judges present dissented from the judgment of the court, reversing the condemnation decreed in the courts below, and restoring the property as claimed.([b])

But where the vessel was captured, and possession taken by sending three persons on board her, who being unable to navigate her, the neutral master continued to direct her course according to the instructions of his owners, refusing to carry the vessel into the belligerent port for adjudication, and she was carried in by another cruizer; it was determined that this was not a case of rescue that would subject the vessel to confiscation. The duty of navigating the captured vessel into port for adjudication is not imposed on the master and his crew. They owe no service to the captors, and are still to be considered answerable to the owners for their conduct. It is the duty as well as the interest of the captors to make the capture sure; if they neglect it from any anxiety to make other captures, or thinking the force already furnished sufficient, it is exclusively at their own peril.([c])

([a]) Per JOHNSON, J.

([b]) Per DUVAL and STORY, J.

([c]) *Acton*, 33. The Pennsylvania.

CHAPTER IV.

The property of persons resident, or having possessions, or a house of trade in the enemy's territory, considered as an object of capture.

1. The property of persons domiciled in the enemy's country, is liable to capture and condemnation, although such persons may be citizens or subjects of the belligerent state, or of neutral powers.([a])

2. The permanent character of an enemy arises from the party being under the allegiance of the power at war with the belligerent state. The allegiance being permanent, the character is permanent. But a neutral can be an enemy only with respect to what he is doing under a local or temporary allegiance to the power at war. When the allegiance determines, the character determines. He can have no fixed character of enemy who owes no fixed allegiance to our enemy, and has ceased to be in hostility against us; it being only in respect of his being in a state of actual hostility that he was even for a time an enemy at all. But a person who resides under the allegiance and protection of a hostile country for all commercial purposes is to be considered to all civil purposes as much an enemy as if he were born there.([b])

([a]) Robinson, passim. 2 Dallas, 42. Federal Court of Appeals in Prize Causes, 1787. Vantylenger, Claimant. 1 *Magens*, 525. Sir Leolyn Jenkins' letter, 17 September, 1666.

([b]) 1 *Bos.* & *Pul.* 168. Sparenburgh vs. Bannatyne. 3 *Ib.* 114. M'Connel vs. Hector.

Thus it has been determined in the courts of municipal law that a citizen residing in a foreign country might acquire the commercial privileges attached to his domicil, and thus be exempt from the operation of a law of his original country restraining commerce with another foreign country.(c)

So also it has been decided that a natural born subject might become the citizen of a foreign country for the purposes of commerce, and be entitled to all the advantages of trade conceded by treaty between his native country and that foreign country; and that the circumstance of his returning for a temporary purpose does not deprive him of those advantages.(d)

3. As the person who has a commercial inhabitancy in the hostile country has the benefits of his situation so also he must take its disadvantages. *Qui commodum sentit, sentire debet et onus*, is the maxim of the civil law; and as in the above cases, the party was held to acquire all the commercial privileges of a subject or citizen of a foreign power, it follows that he would be subjected to the correspondent disadvantages of his situation.

All the citizens or subjects of the enemy who are such from a permanent cause, that is to say, settled in the country, are liable to the law of reprisals, whether they be natives or foreigners; but not so, if they are only travelling or sojourning for a little time.(e) A residence in a foreign country, with an intention to make it a permanent place of abode is styled *domicil*, and is defined to be, a habitation fixed in any place with an intention of always staying there.

(c) 1 *Cranch*, 65. Murray vs. The Charming Betsey.

(d) 8 *T. R.* Wilson vs. Marryat.

(e) *Grotius* de J. B. ac P. 563. It is not the place of any man's *nativity*, but of his *domicil*; not of his *origination*, but of his *habitation*, that subjects him to reprize: The law doth not consider so much where he was born, as where he lives; not so much where he came into the world, as where he improves the world. *Molloy* de J. M. B. 1. c. 2. XVI.

Consequently a person does not establish his domicil in any place, unless he makes known, either tacitly, or by an express declaration, his intention to establish himself there. Nor does this declaration prevent him, in case he changes his intention, from removing his domicil elsewhere. The natural or original domicil is that which is given us by birth, where our father had his; and we are held to retain it, so long as we do not abandon it in order to choose another. The acquired domicil, *adscititium*, is where we establish ourselves by our own voluntary act.(f)

4. Questions of residence or domicil are of considerable difficulty, depending on a great variety of circumstances hardly capable of being defined by any general precise rules. The active spirit of commerce now abroad in the world still further increases this difficulty by increasing the variety of local situations, in which the same individual is to be found at no great distance of time; and by that sort of extended circulation, by which the same transaction communicates with different countries, without enabling us to assign the exact legal effect of the local character of every particular portion of this divided transaction. Of the few principles that can be laid down generally, it may be held that time is the grand ingredient in constituting domicil. In most cases it is unavoidably conclusive. It is not unfrequently said, that if a person comes only for a special purpose, *that* shall not fix a domicil. This is not to be taken in an unqualified latitude, and without some respect had to the time which such a purpose may or shall occupy; for if the purpose be of such a nature as *may*, *probably*, or *does actually* detain the person for a great length of time, a general residence might grow upon the special purpose. A special purpose may lead a man to a country, where it shall detain him the whole of his life. Against such a long residence, the plea of an original special pur-

(f) *Vattel*, l. 1. c. 19, § 218.

pose could not be averred; it must be inferred in such a case, that other purposes forced themselves upon him, and mixed themselves with his original design, and impressed upon him the character of the country where he originally resided. Suppose a man comes into a belligerent country at or before the beginning of a war; it is certainly reasonable not to bind him too soon to an acquired character, and to allow him a fair time to disentangle himself; but if he continues to reside during a good part of the war, contributing by payment of taxes and other means, to the strength of that country, he could not plead his special purpose with any effect against the rights of hostility. If he could, there would be no sufficient guard against the fraud and abuses of masked, pretended, original, and sole purposes of a long continued residence. There is a time which will estop such a plea; no rule can fix the time *a priori*, but such a time there *must* be. In proof of the efficacy of mere time, it is not impertinent to remark, that the same quantity of business, which would not fix a domicil in a certain space of time, would nevertheless have that effect, if distributed over a larger space of time. This matter is to be taken in a compound ratio of the time and the occupation, with a great preponderance on the article of time: be the occupation what it may, it cannot happen, but with few exceptions, that mere length of time shall not constitute a domicil.(g)

But on the other hand, mere length of time cannot of itself be decisive, where the purpose is clearly proved to have been temporary, and still continues so, without any enlargement of views. Therefore where the party merely went out to collect the debts due to his house of trade, and there was no part of the evidence which pointed to a distinct trade disconnected with those debts, and the whole transaction was in time of peace, the court thought that the

(g) 2 Robinson, 322. The Harmony.

presumption from length of time was not so forcible. Nor would the circumstance that the shipment was made in the character of an enemy's subject, but before knowledge of hostilities, affect him unfavourably. For a distinction has been taken in the authorities between a time of peace and of war. Much greater laxity is allowed to mercantile transactions in peace than in war. Disguises and covers are allowable in the former which would not be tolerated in the latter. The court did not know that a single case had been decided in which the assuming a national character in time of peace to avoid municipal duties or regulations, or to avoid the effects of impending war, had been held to bind the party where it had not been in fraud of the belligerent who made the capture. If the party had gone on after the war making shipments in the enemy character, the court had no doubt that he would have been affected with its penal consequences. But the question was, if the shipment made in the enemy character, without being engaged as a general merchant, and without the intention of evading any other but the municipal or belligerent rights of the enemy, should conclude the party as to his domicil? The court could not say that, where the proof is otherwise satisfactory, this circumstance alone ought to draw after it that consequence. It thought that great indulgence was usually granted to neutrals and to citizens, as to transactions in time of peace and at the commencement of a war, and if they contravened no municipal or national policy, it was not prepared to say that this indulgence is inconsistent with law. *Vide* Chap. V. § 1. [h]

5. The native character and natural or original domicil easily reverts, and it requires fewer circumstances to constitute domicil, in the case of a native citizen or subject,

[h] Per Story J. The Ann Greene. Circuit Court of the U. S. for the Massachusetts district, October T. 1812. MS.

than to impress the national character on one who is originally of another country.[i]

Thus by the French edicts of the 23d July, 1704, 21st October, 1744, and 26th July, 1788, it is provided that the passports granted by neutral or allied powers, to the subjects of states at war with France, who have obtained letters of naturalization from or transferred their domicil to the territories of such powers, shall not be valid in case they shall return to the dominions of the states at war with France for the purpose of there continuing their trade.[k]

6. Where the claimants were native British subjects, who came to the United States many years prior to the late war, and, after the regular period of residence, were admitted to the rights of naturalization.—Some time after this, but long prior to the declaration of war, they returned to Great Britain, settled themselves there, and engaged in the trade of that country, where they were found carrying on their commercial business at the time these shipments were made; and at the time of the capture, one of the claimants was yet in the enemy's country, but had, since he heard of the capture, expressed his anxiety to return to the United States, but had been prevented from so doing by various causes set forth in his affidavit. Another actually returned some time after the capture; and a third was still in the enemy's country.

This claim was resisted upon an objection to the national character of the claimants.

The great question involved in this case was, whether the property of claimants who were settled in the enemy's country, and engaged in the commerce of that country, shipped before they had a knowledge of the war, but which was captured, after the declaration of war, by a cruizer of the belligerent state, ought to be condemned as lawful

(i) 5 Robinson, 98. La Virginie.

(k) 1 *Code des Prises*, 92. 139. 303.

prize. It was contended by the captors, that as the claimants had gained a domicil in the enemy's country, and continued to enjoy it up to the time when war was declared, and when the capture was made, they must be considered as enemies, in reference to this property, and consequently, that it might legally be seized as prize of war, in like manner as if it had belonged to real enemy subjects. But if not so, it was then insisted, that these claimants having, after their naturalization, returned to the country of their birth, and there resettled themselves, they became redintegrated British subjects, and ought to be considered by the court in the same light as if they had never emigrated. On the other side it was argued, that citizens of the belligerent state settled in the country of the enemy, as these persons were, at the time war was declared, were entitled to a reasonable time to elect, after they knew of the war, to remain there, or to return home; and that, until such election was *bona fide* made, the courts of this country were bound to consider them as citizens of it, and their property shipped before they had an opportunity to make this election, as being protected against capture by its cruizers.

There being no dispute as to the facts upon which the domicil of these claimants was asserted, the questions of law to be considered were two—First, By what means, and to what extent, a national character may be impressed upon a person, different from that which permanent allegiance gives him?—and, Secondly, What are the legal consequences to which this acquired character may expose him, in the event of a war taking place between the country of his residence and that of his birth, or in which he had been naturalized?

I. The writers upon the law of nations distinguish between a temporary residence in a foreign country, for a special purpose, and a residence accompanied with an intention to make it a permanent place of abode. *Vide Supra.* §3.

The doctrine of the prize courts, as well as of the courts of common law in England, which, it was hinted in argument, had no authority of universal law to stand upon, is the same with what is stated by Grotius and Vattel, except that it is less general, and confines the consequences resulting from this acquired character to the property of *those persons engaged in the commerce of the country where they reside.* It is decided by those courts, that whilst an Englishman, or a neutral, resides in a hostile country, he is a subject of that country, and is to be considered (even by his own, or native country, in the former case) as having a native character impressed upon him.

In deciding whether a person has obtained the right of an acquired domicil, it is not to be expected that much, if any assistance should be derived from mere elementary writers on the law of nations. They can only lay down the general principles of law, and it becomes the duty of courts to establish rules for the proper application of those principles. The question, Whether the person to be affected by the right of domicil, had sufficiently made known his intention of fixing himself permanently in the foreign country, must depend upon all the circumstances of the case. If he had made no express declaration on the subject, and his secret intention is to be discovered, his acts must be attended to, as affording the most satisfactory evidence of his intention. On this ground it is, that the courts of England have decided, that a person who removes to a foreign country, settles himself there, and engages in the trade of the country, furnishes by these acts, such evidence of an intention permanently to reside there, as to stamp him with the national character of the state where he resides. In questions on this subject, the chief point to be considered, is the *animus manendi;* and courts are to devise such reasonable rules of evidence as may establish the fact of intention. If it sufficiently appears that the intention of removing was to make a permanent settlement, or for an indefinite time, the right of domicil is acquired by residence even of a few days. This is one of the rules of the British prize courts, and it appears to be perfectly reasonable. Another is, that a neutral or subject, found residing in a foreign country, is presumed to be there *animo manendi*; and if a state of war should bring his national character into question, it lies upon him to explain the circumstances of his residence.(1) As to some other rules of the prize courts of England, particularly those which fix a national character upon a person, on the ground of constructive residence, or the peculiar nature of his trade, the court was not called upon to give an opinion at that time; because in this case, it was admitted that the claimants had acquired a right of domicil in Great Britain at the time of the breaking out of the war between that country and the United States.

II. The next question is, What are the consequences to which this acquired domicil may legally expose the person entitled to it, in the event of a war taking place between the government under which he resides, and that to which he owes a permanent allegiance? A neutral, in this situation, if he should engage in open hostilities with the other belligerent, would be considered and treated as an enemy. A citizen of the other belligerent could not be so considered, because he could not, by any act of hostility, render himself strictly speaking an enemy, contrary to his permanent allegiance. But although he cannot be considered an enemy in the strict sense of the word, yet he is deemed such, with reference to the seizure of so much of his property concerned in the trade of the enemy, as is connected with his residence. It is found adhering to the enemy. He is himself adhering to the enemy although not criminally so, unless he engages in acts of hostility against his native country, or (probably) refuses, when required by

(1) 1 *Robinson*, 86. 102. The Bernon.

his country, to return. The same rule, as to property engaged in the commerce of the enemy, applies to neutrals, and for the same reason. The converse of this rule inevitably applies to the subject of a belligerent domiciled in a neutral country; he is deemed a neutral by both belligerents, with reference to the trade which he carries on with the adverse belligerent, and with all the rest of the world.

But this national character which a man acquires by residence, may be thrown off at pleasure, by a return to his native country, or even by turning his back on the country in which he resided, on his way to another. To use the language of Sir W. Scott, it is an adventitious character, gained by residence, and which ceases by non-residence; it no longer adheres to the party from the moment he puts himself in motion, *bona fide*, to quit the country *sine animo revertendi*. 3 *Robinson*, 17. 12. The Indian Chief.—The reasonableness of this rule can hardly be disputed. Having once acquired a national character by residence in a foreign country, he ought to be bound by all the consequences of it, until he has thrown it off, either by an actual return to his native country, or to that where he was naturalized, or by commencing his removal, *bona fide*, and without an intention of returning. If any thing short of actual removal be admitted to work a change in the national character acquired by residence, it seems perfectly reasonable that the evidence of a *bona fide* intention to remove should be such as to leave no doubt of its sincerity. Mere declarations of such an intention ought never to be relied upon, when contradicted, or at least rendered doubtful, by a continuance of that residence which impressed the character. They may have been made to deceive; or, if sincerely made, they may never be executed. Even the party himself ought not to be bound by them, because he may afterwards find reason to change his determination, and ought to be permitted to do so. But when he accompanies these declarations by acts which speak a language not to be mistaken, and can hardly fail to be consummated by actual removal, the strongest evidence is afforded which the nature of such a case can furnish. And is it not improper that the courts of a belligerent nation should deny to any person the right to use a character so equivocal, as to put it in his power to claim whichever may best suit his purpose, when it is called in question? If his property be taken trading with the enemy, shall he be called on to shield it from confiscation, by alleging that he had intended to remove from the country of the enemy to his own, then neutral, and therefore, that, as a neutral, the trade was lawful? If war exist between the country of his residence and his native country, and his property be seized by the former or by the latter, shall he be heard to say in the former case, that he was a domiciled subject of the country of the captor, and in the latter that he was a native subject of the country of that captor also, because he had declared an intention to resume his native character; and thus to parry the belligerent rights of both? It is to guard against such inconsistencies, and against the frauds which such pretensions, if tolerated, would sanction, that the rule above mentioned has been adopted. Upon what sound principle can a distinction be framed between the case of a neutral, and the subject of one belligerent domiciled in the country of the other at the breaking out of the war? The property of each, found engaged in the commerce of their adopted country, belonged to them, before the war, in their character of subjects of that country, so long as they continued to retain their domicil; and when a state of war takes place between that country and any other, by which the two nations and all their subjects become enemies to each other, it follows, that this property, which was once the property of a friend, belongs now, in reference to that property, to an enemy.

This doctrine of the common law and prize courts of England is founded like that mentioned under the first head, upon international law, and it is believed to be strongly supported by reason and justice. And why, it may be confidently asked, should not the property of enemy's subjects be exposed to the law of reprisals and of war, so long as the owner retains his acquired domicil, or, in the words of Grotius, continues a permanent residence in the country of the enemy? They were before, and continue after the war, bound, by such residence, to the society of which they are members, subject to the laws of the state, and owing a qualified allegiance thereto;—they are obliged to defend it, (with an exception in favour of such subject, in relation to his native country) in return for the protection it affords them, and the privileges which the laws bestow upon them as subjects. The property of such persons, equally with that of the native subjects in their totality, is to be considered as the goods of the nation, *in regard to other states.* It belongs, in some sort, to the state, from the right which the state has over the goods of its citizens, which make a part of the sum total of its riches, and augment its power.[m] In reprisals, continues the same author, we seize on the property of the subject, just as we would that of the sovereign; every thing that belongs to the nation is subject to reprisals, wherever it can be seized with the exception of [n] a deposit entrusted to the public faith. Now if a permanent residence constitutes the person a subject of the country where he is settled, so long as he continues to reside there, and subjects his property to the law of reprisals, as a part of the property of the nation, it would seem difficult to maintain that the same consequences would not follow in the case of an open and pub-

[m] Vattel, L. 1. c. 14. § 182.

[n] L. 2. c. 18. § 344.

lic war, whether between the adopted and native countries of persons so domiciled, or between the former and any other nation. If, then, nothing but an actual removal, or a *bona fide* beginning to remove, can change a national character, acquired by domicil, and if, at the time of the inception of the voyage, as well as at the time of capture, the property belonged to such domiciled person in his character of a subject, what is there that does, or ought to except it from capture by the privateers of his native country, if, at the time of capture, he continues to reside in the country of the adverse belligerent? It was contended that a native or naturalized subject of one country who is surprised in the country where he was domiciled, by a declaration of war, ought to have time to make his election to continue there, or to remove to the country to which he owes a permanent allegiance; and that, until such election be made, his property ought to be protected from capture by the cruizers of the latter. This doctrine is believed to be as unfounded in reason and justice, as it clearly is in law. In the first place, it is founded upon a presumption, that the person will certainly remove, before it can possibly be known whether he may elect to do so or not. It is said that the presumption ought to be made, because upon receiving information of the war, it will be his duty to return home. This position is denied. It is his duty to commit no acts of hostility against his native country, and to return to her assistance when required to do so; nor will any just nation, regarding the mild principles of the law of nations, require him to take arms against his native country, or refuse permission to him to withdraw whenever he wishes to do so, unless under peculiar circumstances, which, by such removal at a critical period, might endanger the public safety. The conventional law of nations is in conformity with these principles. It is not uncommon to stipulate in treaties, that the subjects of each party shall be allowed to remove with their property, or to remain unmolested. Such a stipulation does not coerce those subjects either to remove or to remain. They are left free to choose for themselves; and when they have made their election, they claim the right of enjoying it under the treaty—But until the election is made, their former character continues unchanged. Until this election is made, if his property found upon the high seas, engaged in the commerce of his adopted country, should be permitted by the cruizers of the other belligerent, to pass free under a notion that he may elect to remove, upon notice of the war, and should arrive safe, what is to be done in case the owner of it should afterwards elect to remain where he is? For, if captured and brought immediately to adjudication, it must, upon this doctrine, be acquitted until the election to remain is made and known. In short, the point contended for would apply the doctrine of relation to cases, where the party claiming the benefit of it, may gain all, and can lose nothing. If he, after the capture, should find it his interest to remain where he is domiciled, his property embarked before his election was made, is safe. And if he finds it best to return, it is safe of course. It is safe whether he goes or stays. This doctrine producing such contradictory consequences, is not only unsupported by any authority but it would violate principles long and well established in the prize courts of England, and which ought not, without strong reasons which may render them inapplicable to this country, to be disregarded by the court. The rule there, is, that the character of property, during war, cannot be changed *in transitu*, by any act of the party subsequent to the capture. The rule indeed goes further; as to the correctness of which in its greatest extension, no opinion needed then be given; but it might safely be affirmed, that the change cannot, and ought not to be effected by an election of the owner and shipper of it, made subsequent to the capture, and more especially, after a knowledge of the capture is obtained by the owner. Observe the consequences which would result from it. The capture is made and known. The owner is allowed to deliberate whether it is his interest to remain a subject of his adopted, or of his native country. If the capture be made by the former, then he elects to be a subject of that country;—if by the latter, then a subject of that. Can such a privileged situation be tolerated by either belligerent? Can any system of law be correct, which places an individual, who adheres to one belligerent, and, to the period of his election to remove, contributes to increase her wealth, in so anomalous a situation as to be clothed with the privileges of a neutral, as to both belligerents? This notion about a temporary state of neutrality impressed upon a subject of one of the belligerents, and the consequent exemption of his property from capture by either, until he has had notice of the war and made his election, is altogether a novel theory, and seemed, from the course of the argument, to owe its origin to a supposed hardship to which the contrary doctrine exposes him. But if the reasoning employed on the subject be correct, no such hardship can exist. For if, before the election is made, his property on the ocean is liable to capture by the cruizers of his native and deserted country, it is not only free from capture by those of his adopted country, but is under its protection. The privilege is supposed to be equal to the disadvantage, and is therefore just. The double privilege claimed seems too unreasonable to be granted.

It will be observed that in the foregoing opinion respecting the nature and consequences of domicil, very few cases have been referred to. It was thought best not to interrupt the chain of argument, by stopping to examine cases; but faithfully to present the essential principles to be extracted from those which were cited at the bar, or which have otherwise come under the view of the court, and which applied to the subject, that the national character of the owner at the time of capture must decide his right to claim, and that a subject is concluded by it, even in the court of his native country, without time being allowed him to elect to remove.(o)

The case first cited is somewhat stronger than the present in that, the state of hostility, alleged to have existed at the time of capture, was made out by considering the subsequent declaration of war as relating back to the time of seizure under the embargo, by which reference it was decided to be a hostile embargo, and of course tantamount to an actual state of war. But this case also proves, not only that the hostile character of the property at the time of capture establishes the legality of it, but that no future circumstance changing the hostile character of the claimant to that of a friend or a subject, can entitle him to restitution. Whether the claimant in this case was a neutral or a British subject, does not appear. But if the former, it would not, it was presumed, be contended that he is, upon the principles of national law, less to be favoured in the courts of the belligerent, than a subject of that nation domiciled in the country of the adverse belligerent. *Mr. Whitehill's* case, however, referred to frequently in Robinson's Reports, comes fully up to the present, because he was a British subject, who had settled but a few days in the hostile country, but before he knew or could have known of the declaration of war; yet, as he went there with an intention to settle, this, connected with his residence, short as it was, fixed his national character, and identified him with the enemy of the country he had so recently quitted. The want of notice, and of an opportunity to extricate himself from a situation to which he had so recently and so innocently exposed himself, could not prevail to protect his property against the belligerent rights of his own country, and to save it from confiscation.(p)

(o) 5 *Robinson*, 230. Boedes Lust. 1 *Robinson*, 115. Herstelder, 107. Dankebaar Africaan.

(p) Per WASHINGTON, J. The Venus. Supreme Court of the U. S. February T. 1814. M. S.

The opinion of the court in the above case was dissented from by two of the judges,(q) the first of whom stated, that he entirely concurred in so much of the opinion delivered in this case, as attaches a hostile character to the property of a citizen continuing, after the declaration of war, to reside and trade in the country of the enemy; and subscribed implicitly to the reasoning urged in its support. But from so much of that opinion as subjects to confiscation the property of a citizen shipped before a knowledge of the war, and which disallowed the defence founded on an intention to change his domicil and to return to the United States, manifested in a sufficient manner, and within a reasonable time after knowledge of the war, although it be subsequent to the capture, he felt himself compelled to dissent.

The question was undoubtedly complicated and intricate. It was difficult to draw a line of discrimination, which should be, at the same time, precise and equitable. But the difficulty did not appear to him to be sufficient to deter courts from making the attempt.

A merchant residing abroad for commercial purposes, may certainly intend to continue in the foreign country, so long as peace shall exist, provided his commercial objects shall detain him so long, but to leave it the instant war shall break out between that country and his own. This intention it is not necessary to manifest during peace, and when war shall commence, the belligerent cruizer may find his property on the ocean, and may capture it before he knows that war exists. The question, whether this be enemy's property or not, depends, not exclusively on the residence of the owner at the time, but on his residence taken in connexion with his national character as a citizen; and with his intention to continue or discontinue his commercial domicil in the event of war.

The evidence of this intention, will rarely, if ever, be given during peace. It must, therefore, be furnished, if

(q) MARSHALL, C. J. and LIVINGSTON, J.

at all, after the war shall be known to him; and that knowledge may be preceded by the capture of his goods. It appeared then, to be a case in which, as in many others, justice requires that subsequent testimonies shall be received to prove a pre-existing fact. Measures taken for removal immediately after a war may prove a previous intention to remove in the event of war, and may prove that the captured property, although, *prima facie*, belonging to an enemy, does, in fact, belong to a friend. In such case, the citizen has a right, in the nature of the *jus post liminii*, to claim restitution.

As this question was not only decisive of many claims then depending before the court, but also of vast importance to our merchants generally, he might be excused for stating at some length, the reason on which his opinion was founded.

The whole system of decisions applicable to this subject, rests on the law of nations as its base. It is, therefore, of some importance to enquire how far the writers on that law consider the subjects of one power residing within the territory of another, as retaining their original characters, or partaking of the character of the nation in which they reside.

Vattel, who, though not very full to this point, is more explicit and more satisfactory on it than any other which had fallen into his hands, says, "The citizens are the members of the civil society; bound to this society by certain duties and subject to its authority; they equally participate in its advantages. The *natives*, are those born in the country, of parents who are citizens. Society not being able to subsist and perpetuate itself but by the children of the citizens, those children naturally follow the condition of their father, and succeed to all his rights."

"The inhabitants, as distinguished from citizens, are strangers who are permitted to settle and stay in the country. Bound by their residence to the society, they are subject to the laws of the state, while they reside there, and they are obliged to defend it, because it grants them protection, though they do not participate in all the rights of citizens. They enjoy only the advantages which the laws, or custom gives them. The *perpetual inhabitants* are those who have received the right of perpetual residence. These are a kind of citizens of an inferior order, and are united and subject to the society, without participating in all its advantages."

A domicil, in the sense in which this term is used by *Vattel*, requires not only actual residence in a foreign country, but "an intention of always staying there," actual residence without this intention, amounts to no more than "simple habitation."

Although this intention may be implied without being expressed, it ought not to be implied, to the injury of the individuals from acts entirely equivocal. If the stranger has not the power of making his residence perpetual; if circumstances, after his arrival in a country, so change, as to make his continuance there disadvantageous to himself, and his power to continue doubtful, "an intention always to stay there" ought not, to be fixed upon him, in consequence of an unexplained residence previous to that change of circumstances. Mere residence, under particular circumstances, would seem, at most, to prove only an intention to remain so long as those circumstances continue the same, or equally advantageous. This does not give a domicil. The intention which gives a domicil is an unconditional intention "to stay always."

The right of the citizens or subjects of one country to remain in another, depends on the will of the sovereign of that other; and if that will be not expressed otherwise than by general hospitality which receives and affords security to strangers, it is supposed to terminate with the relations of peace between the two countries. When war breaks out, the subjects of one belligerent in the country of the other, are considered as enemies, and have no right to remain there.

Vattel says, "Enemies continue such wherever they happen to be. The place of abode is of no account here. It is the political ties which determine the quality, while a man remains a citizen of his own country, he remains the enemy of all those with whom a nation is at war."

It would seem to require very strong evidence of an intention to become the permanent inhabitants of a foreign country, to justify a court in presuming such intention to continue, when that residence must expose the person to the inconvenience of being considered and treated as an enemy. The intention to be inferred solely from the fact of residence during peace, for commercial purposes is necessarily conditional, and dependent on the continuance of the relations of peace between the two countries.

So far is the law of nations from considering residence in a foreign country in time of peace, as evidence of an intention "always to stay there," even in time of war, that the very contrary is expressed. *Vattel* says, "The sovereign declaring war can neither detain those subjects of the enemy who are within his dominions at the time of the declaration, nor their effects. They came into his territory on the public faith. By permitting them to enter his territory and to continue there, he tacitly promised them liberty and security for their return. He is therefore to allow them a reasonable time for withdrawing with their effects; and if they stay beyond the term prescribed, he has a right to treat them as enemies, though as enemies disarmed."

The stranger merely residing in a country during peace, however long his stay, and whatever his employments, provided it be such as strangers may engage in, cannot, on the principles of international law, be considered as incorporated into that society, so as immediately on a declaration of war, to become the enemy of his own. "His property," says *Vattel*, "is still a part, of the totality of the wealth of his nation." "The citizen or subject of a state, who absents himself for a time, without any intention to abandon the society of which he is a member, does not lose his privilege by his absence; he preserves his rights, and remains bound by the same obligations. Being received in a foreign country, in virtue of the natural society, the communication, and commerce, which nations are obliged to cultivate with each other, he ought to be considered there as a member of his own nation and treated as such."

The subject of one power inhabiting the country of another ought not to be considered as a member of the nation in which he resides, even by foreigners; nor ought he, on the first commencement of hostilities, to be treated as an enemy by the enemies of that nation.

Burlamaqui says, "as to strangers, those who settle in the enemies country after a war is begun, of which they had previous notice, may justly be looked upon as enemies and treated as such. But in regard to such as went thither before the war, justice and humanity require that we should give them a reasonable time to retire; and if they neglect that opportunity, they are accounted enemies."

If this rule be obligatory on foreign nations, much more, ought it, to bind that, of which the individual is a member.

He thought he could not be mistaken when he said that, in all the views taken of this subject by the most approved writers on the law of nations, the citizens of one country residing in another, is not considered as incorporated in that other, but is still considered as belonging to that society of which he was originally a member: And if war break out between the two nations, he is to be permitted, and is expected, to return to his own. He did not perceive in those writers any exception with regard to merchants.

It must, however, be acknowledged, that the great extention of commerce has had considerable influence on national laws. Rules have been adopted, perhaps by general consent; principles have been engrafted on the originals tock of public law, by which merchants, while belonging politically to one society, are considered commercially as the members of another. For commercial purposes, the merchant is considered as a member of that society in which he has his domicil; and less conclusive evidence than would seem to be required in general cases, by the law of nations, has been allowed to fix the domicil for commercial purposes. But he could not admit that the original meaning of the term is to be entirely disregarded, or the true nature of this domicil to be overlooked. The effects of the rule ought to be regulated by the motives which are presumed to have induced its establishment, and by the convenience it was intended to promote.

The policy of commercial nations receives foreign merchants into their bosoms; and permits their own citizens to reside abroad for the purposes of trade, without injury to their rights or character as citizens. This free intercommunication must certainly be believed, by the nations who allow it, to be promotive of their interests. Nor is this opinion ill founded. Nothing can be more obvious than that the affairs of a commercial company will be transacted to most advantage by being conducted, as it respects both purchase and sale, under the eye of a person interested in the result. The nation which takes an interest in the prosperity of its commerce, can feel no inclination to restrain its citizens from residence abroad, for the purposes of commerce; nor will it hastily construe such residence into a change of national character, to the injury of the individual. It is not the policy of such a nation, nor can it be its wish, to restrain its citizens from pursuing abroad, a business, which tends to enrich itself. It ought not, therefore, to consider them as enemies in consequence of their having engaged in such pursuit in the country of a friend, who before their removal, becomes an enemy.

If, indeed, it be the real intention of the citizen permanently to change his national character; if it be his choice to remain in the country of the enemy during war, there can be no harshness, no injustice, in treating him as an enemy. But if, while prosecuting his business in a foreign country, he contemplates a return to his own; if, in the prosecution of that business, he is promoting rather than counteracting the interests and policy of the country of which he is a member, it would seem to be pressing the principles too far, and to be drawing conclusions which the premises will not warrant, to infer conclusively, an intention to continue in a country which has become hostile, from a residence and trading in that country while it was friendly; and to punish him by the confiscation of his goods, as if he was fully convicted of that intention.

It was admitted to be a general rule, that, while the state of things remains unaltered; while the motives which carried the citizen abroad continue; while he still prosecutes a business of uncertain duration, his capacity to prosecute which, is not impaired, his mercantile character is confounded with that of the country in which he resides, and his trade is considered as the trade of that country.

It will require but a slight examination of the subject, to perceive the reason of this rule; and that, to a certain extent, it is convenient without being unjust.

In times of universal peace, the question of national character can arise only when some privilege or some disability is attached to it, or in cases of insurance. A particular trade may be allowed or be prohibited to the merchants of a particular nation, or property may be warranted to be of a particular nation. If, in such cases, the residence of the individual be received as evidence of his national mercantile character, the subjects of inquiry are simplified; the questions are reduced to a plain one; and the various complex enquiries, which might otherwise arise, are avoided. There is therefore much convenience in adopting this principle in such a state of things; and it is not perceived that any injustice can grow out of it; since the individual to whom the rule is applied, is not surprized by any new or unlooked for event.

So if war exists between two nations, each belligerent having a right to capture the property of the other found on the ocean, each being intent on destroying the commerce of the other, and on depriving it of every cover under which it may seek to shelter itself, will certainly not allow the advantages of neutrality to a merchant residing in the country of his enemy. Were this permitted, the whole trade of the enemy could assume, and would assume a neutral garb.

There is in general no reason for supposing that a merchant residing in a foreign country, and carrying on trade, means to withdraw from it, on its engaging in war with any other country to which he is bound by no obligation. By continuing during war the domicil acquired in peace, he violates no duty, offends against no generally acknowledged principle, and retains all his rights of residence and commerce. The war then furnishes no motive for presuming that he is about to change his situation, and to resume his original national character.

These reasons appear to require the rule as a general one, and to justify its application to general cases, but, they do not justify its application to the case of a merchant whom war finds engaged in trade in a country which becomes the enemy of his own; this country ought not to bind him by his residenee during peace, nor to consider him as precluded by it from showing an intention that it should terminate with the relations of peace.

When it is considered that his right to remain and prosecute that trade in which he had been engaged during peace is forfeited; that, his duty and most probably his inclinations, call him home; that he has become the enemy of the country in which he resides; that his continuance in it exposes him to many and serious inconveniences; that his person and property are in danger; it is not going too far to say, that this change in his situation may be considered as changing his intention on the subject of residence, and as affording a presumption of intending to return.

Let it be remembered that, according to the law of nations, domicil depends on the intention to reside permanently in the country to which the individual has removed; and that a change of this intention is, at any time, allowable. If upon grounds of general policy and general convenience, while the circumstances under which the residence commenced continue the same residence and employment; if permanent trade be considered as evidence of an intention to continue permanently in the country, and as giving a commercial national character; may not a total change in circumstances, a loss of the capacity to carry on the trade, be received, in the absence of all conflicting proof, as presumptive evidence of an intention to leave the country; as extricating the trade, carried on in the time of supposed peace, from the national character, so far as to protect it from the perils of war? At any rate, do not reason and justice require that this change of circumstances should leave the question open to be decided on such other evidence as the war must produce?

The great object for which an American merchant fixes himself in a foreign country, is, most generally, to carry on trade between that country and his own. In almost every case of this description before the court, the claimant was a member of a commercial house established in the United States; and his business abroad subservient to the business at home. This trade is annihilated by the war.

If, while peace subsists between the United States and Great Britain; while the American merchant possesses there all the commercial rights allowed to the citizens of a friendly nation, and may carry on uninterruptedly his trade to his own country, he is presumed, his intentions being unexplained, to intend remaining there always, and may for general convenience, be cloathed with the commercial character of the nation in which he resides, ought this presumption to be extended by his own government, beyond the facts out of which it grows, if the interest of the individual be materially affected by that extention? Do not reason and justice require that we should consider his original intention as being only coextensive with the causes which carried him to and detained him in the country—as being, in its nature, conditional and dependent on the continuance of those causes?

If such a person were required, on his arrival in a foreign country, to declare his real intention on the subject of residence, he would most probably say, if he spoke honestly, "I come for the purpose of trade; I shall remain while the situation of the two countries permits me to carry on my trade lawfully, securely, and advantageously; when that situation so changes, as to deprive me of these rights, I shall return." His intention then, to reside in the country, his domicil in it, and consequently his commercial character, unless he continued his trade after war, would be clearly limited by the duration of peace. It would not be unreasonable to say, that the intention, to be implied from his conduct, ought to have the same limitation.

To him it seemed that a mere commercial domicil acquired in time of peace, necessarily expires on the commencement of hostilities. Domicil supposes rights incompatible with a state of war. If the foreign merchant be not compelled to abandon the country, it is not because his commercial character confers on him a legal right to stay, but because he is specially permitted to stay. If in this he was correct, it would seem to follow, that if all the legal consequences of a residence in time of peace do not absolutely terminate with the peace, yet the national commercial character which that residence has attached to the individual, is not so conclusively fixed upon him as to disqualify him from showing, that, within a reasonable time after the commencement of hostilities, he made arrangements for returning to his own country. If a residence and trading after the war be not indispensably necessary to give the citizen merchant or his property a hostile character, yet removal, or measures showing a determination to remove within a reasonable time after the war, may retroact upon property shipped before a knowledge of the war, and rescue that property from the hostile character attached to the property of the nation in which the individual resided.

The law of nations is a law founded on the great and immutable principles of equity and natural justice. To draw an inference against all probability, whereby a citizen, for the purpose of confiscating his goods, is clothed, against his inclination, with the character of an enemy, in consequence of an act which, when committed, was innocent in itself, was entirely compatible with his political character as a citizen, and with the political views of his government, would seem to subvert those principles. The rule which, for obvious reasons, applies to the merchant in time of peace or in time of war; the national commercial character of the country in which he resides, could not, without subverting those principles, apply a hostile character to his trade carried on during peace, so conclusively as to prevent his protecting it by changing that character within a reasonable time after a knowledge of the war.

His opinion then was, that a mere commercial domicil acquired by an American citizen in time of peace, especially if he be a member of an American house, and is carrying on a trade auxiliary to his trade with his own country, ought not to be considered positively as continuing longer than the state of peace. The declaration of war is a fact which removes the causes that induced his residence in the foreign country: they no longer operate upon him. When they cease, their effects ought to cease. An intention which they produced, ought not to be supposed to continue. The character of his property, shipped before a knowledge of the war, ought not to be decided absolutely by his residence at the time of shipment or capture, but ought to depend on his continuing to reside and trade in the enemy country, or on his taking prompt measures for returning to his own.

This is the conclusion to which his mind would certainly be conducted, might he permit it to be guided by the lights of reason and the principles of national justice. But it was said, that a course of adjudication has settled the law to be otherwise; that the court could not, without overturning a magnificent system, bottomed on the broad base of international law, and of which the parts are admirably adjusted to each other, yield to the dictates of humanity on this particular question. Sir William Scott, it was agreed at the bar, had, by a series of decisions, developed the principles of law on this subject, with a perspicuity and precision which mark plainly the path they ought to tread.

He respected Sir William Scott, as he did every truly great man, and he respected his decisions; nor should he depart from them on light grounds. But it was impossible to consider them attentively, without perceiving that his mind leans strongly in favour of the captors. Residence, for example, in a belligerent country, will condemn the share of a neutral in a house trading in a neutral country; but residence in a neutral country will not protect the share of a belligerent or neutral in a commercial house established in a belligerent country. In a great maritime country, depending on its navy for its glory and its safety, the national bias is perhaps so entirely in this direction, that the judge, without being conscious of the fact, must feel its influence. However this might be, it was a fact of which he was fully convinced; and, on this account, it appeared to him to be the more proper to investigate rigidly the principles on which Sir William Scott's decisions have been made, and not to extend them where such extension may produce injustice.

While he made this observation, it would betray a want of candor not to accompany it with the acknowledgment, that he perceived in the opinions of this eminent judge, no disposition to press *this principle* with peculiar severity against neutrals. He had certainly not mitigated it when applying it to British subjects.

With this impression respecting the general character of British admiralty decisions, he proceeded to examine them so far as they bear on the question of domicil.

The case of the *Vigilantia*(r) does not itself involve the point: but in delivering his opinion, the judge cited two cases of capture which had been quoted and relied on at bar. In each of these, the share of the partner residing in the neutral country was restored, and that of the partner residing in the belligerent country was condemned. But these decisions applied to a trade continued to be carried on during war,

In a subsequent case, the share of the partner residing in the neutral country also was condemned; and the Lords Commissioners said, that the principle on which restitution was decreed in each of the first mentioned cases, was, "That they were merely at the commencement of a war." They said, that "a person carrying on trade habitually in the country of the enemy, though not resident there, should have time to withdraw himself from that commerce; that it would press too heavily on neutrals to say, that immediately on the first breaking out of a war, their goods would become subject to confiscation."

On these cases it is to be observed, that although the two first happened at the commencement of the war, yet they happened during a war; and the partners whose interest was condemned, do not appear to have discontinued their residence and trading in the country of the enemy after war had taken place. The declaration "that it would

(r) 1 *Robinson*, 1.

press too heavily on neutrals to say, that immediately on the first breaking out of a war, their goods would become subject to confiscation," though applied to a neutral not residing in the belligerent country, clearly discriminates, in a case of capture, between the rights of parties at the commencement of a war, and at a subsequent period. But it was sufficient to say, that neither the case itself, nor the cases and opinions cited in it, applied directly to the question before the court.

In the case of the *Harmony*,(s) the property of Mr. Murray, an American citizen residing in France, was condemned on account of that residence. But Mr. Murray had removed to France during the war, and had continued there for four years.

The scope of the argument of Sir William Scott goes to show, that the single circumstance of residence in the enemy country, if not intended to be permanent, will not give the enemy character to the property of such resident captured in a trade between his own country and that of the enemy. It is material that the conduct of Mr. Murray, subsequent to the capture, had great influence in determining the fate of his property. Had he returned to the United States immediately after that event, much was not hazarded in saying, that restitution would have been decreed.

In the case of the *Indian Chief*,(t) Mr. Johnson, an American citizen domiciliated in England, had engaged in a mercantile enterprize to the British East Indies; a trade allowed to an American citizen, but prohibited to a British subject. On its return the vessel came into Cowes, and was seized for being concerned in illicit trade. Mr. Johnson had then left England for the United States. He was considered as not being a British subject at the time of capture, and restitution was decreed.

(s) 2 *Robinson*, 322. (t) 3 *Robinson*, 12.

In delivering his opinion in this case, Sir William Scott said, "Taking it to be clear that the national character of Mr. Johnson, as a British merchant, was founded in residence only, that it was acquired by residence, and rested on that circumstance alone, it must be held, that, from the moment he turns his back on the country where he has resided, on his way to his own country, he was in the act of resuming his original character, and is to be considered as an American. The character that is gained by residence ceases by non-residence. It is an adventitious character, that no longer adheres to him from the moment that he puts himself in motion, *bona fide*, to quit the country *sine animo revertendi.*"

This case undoubtedly proves, affirmatively, that the national character gained by residence ceases with that residence; but he could not admit it to prove, negatively, that this national character can be laid down by no other means. I cannot, for instance, admit, that an American citizen, who had gained a domicil in England during peace, and was desirous of returning home on the breaking out of war, but was detained by force, could, under the authority of this opinion, be treated as a British trader, with respect to his property embarked before a knowledge of the war.

In the case of *La Virginie*,(u) the property of Mr. Lapierre, who was probably naturalized in the United States, but who had returned to St. Domingo, and had shipped the produce of that island to France, was condemned. But he was considered as a Frenchman, was residing at the time in a French colony, and was engaged in a trade between that colony and the mother country. The case, the judge observed, might have been otherwise decided, had the shipment been made to the United States.

In tne case of the *Jonge Klassina*,(v) Mr. Ravie had a license to make certain importations as a British subject,

(u) 5 *Robinson*, 11?   (v) 5 *Robinson*, 265.

he had a house in Amsterdam, went there in person during the war, and made the shipments under his own inspection and control. It was determined that, in this transaction, he acted in his character as a Dutch merchant, and was not protected by his license. This was a trading with the enemy.

In the case of the *Citto*,(x) the property of Mr. Bowden, a British subject residing in Holland, was condemned. It appeared that he had settled in Amsterdam, where he had resided, carrying on trade for six years. In 1795, when the French troops took possession of that country, he left it, and settled in Guernsey. The *Citto* was a Danish vessel, captured in April, 1796, on a voyage from a Spanish port to Guernsey, where Mr. Bowden then resided. In June 1796, after the capture of the *Citto*, he returned to Holland. In argument it was contended that it appeared that British subjects might reside in Holland, without forfeiting their British character, from the proclamation of the 3d of September 1796, which directs the landing of goods imported, uuder that order, into the United Provinces, to be certified by British merchants resident there.

The judge was desirous of knowing the nature of Mr. Bowden's residence in Holland, whether he had confined himself to the object of withdrawing his property, or had been engaged in the general traffic of the place. If the former, " he may," said the judge, " be entitled to restitution, more especially adverting to the order in council, which is certainly so worded as not to be very easy to be applied."

The cause stood for further proofs.

It is plain that, in this opinion, the residence of the claimant at the time of the capture, was not considered as conclusive, had it been so, restitution must have been decreed, because Mr. Bowden was a British subject, and at that

(x) 3 *Robinson*, 38.

time resided in Guernsey. It is equally apparent, that, had his subsequent residence in an enemy country been for the sole purpose of withdrawing his property, the law was not understood to forbid restitution. The language of Sir William Scott certainly ascribes considerable influence to the proclamation, but does not rest the rights of the claimant altogether on that fact.

On the 17th of March 1800, an affidavit of Mr. Bowden, made the 6th of August 1799, was produced, in which he stated his residence in Holland previous to the invasion by the French—That he quitted Holland and landed in England, the 20th of January 1795, whence he proceeded to Guernsey, where he resided with his family—That, in the month of June 1796, he was under the absolute necessity of returning to Holland, for the purpose of recovering debts due, and effects belonging to the partnership, his partner remaining in Guernsey.

The affidavit then proceeded to state many instances of his attachment to his own government, and concluded with averring that he was still under the necessity of remaining in Holland, for the purpose of recovering part of the said debts and effects, which would be impossible were he to leave the country; but that it was his intention to return to his native country, so soon as his affairs would permit, where his mother and his relations resided.

The court observed, that it appeared from the affidavit, that Mr. Bowden was at that time in Holland; and added, "It would be a strange act of injustice, if, while we are condemning the goods of persons of all nations resident in Holland, we were to restore the goods of native British subjects resident there. An Englishman residing and trading in Holland, is just as much a Dutch merchant as a Swede or a Dane would be."

This case was decided in 1800; Mr. Bowden had returned to Holland in 1796, during the war, and had continued in the country of the enemy. It is not denied that he continued his trade, and the fact that he did continue it, is fairly to be inferred, not only from his omitting to aver the contrary, but from the language of Sir William Scott, "an Englishman residing and trading in Holland," says that judge, "is just as much a Dutch merchant as a Swede or a Dane would be." The case of Mr. Bowden then, is the case of a British subject who continued to reside and trade in the country of an enemy, four years after the commencement of hostilities. His property must have been condemned on one of two principles. Either the judge must have considered his residence in Guernsey, from January 1795 to June 1796, as a temporary interruption of his permanent residence in Holland, and not as a change of domicil, since he returned to that country, and continued in it as a trader, to the rendition of the final sentence, or he must have decided, that, although Mr. Bowden remained, and intended to remain, in fact, a British subject, yet the permanent national commercial character which he acquired after this capture, retroacted on a trade which, at the time of capture, was entirely British, and subjected the property to confiscation. On whichsoever of these principles the case was decided, it is clear that the hostile character attached to the property of Mr. Bowden, in consequence of his residing and trading in the country of the enemy during the war. This case is materially variant from one in which the residence and trading took place during peace, and the capture was made before a change of residence could be conveniently effected.

The *Diana*,(y) was also a case of considerable interest, which contains doctrines entitled to attentive consideration.

During the war between Great Britain and Holland, which commenced in 1795, the island of Demarara surrendered to the British arms. By the treaty of Amiens, it was restored to the Dutch. That treaty contained an article, allowing the inhabitants, of whatever country they might

(y) 5 *Robinson*, 58.

be, a term of three years, to be computed from the notification of the treaty, for the purpose of disposing of their property acquired and possessed before or during the war, in which term they might have the free exercise of their religion, and enjoyment of their property.

Previous to the declaration of war against Holland in 1803, the *Diana* and several other vessels loaded with colonial produce, were captured on a voyage from Demarara to Holland, immediately after the declaration of war; and before the expiration of three years from the notification of the treaty of Amiens, Demarara again surrendered to Great Britain. Claims to the captured property were filed by original British subjects, inhabitants of Demarara, some of whom had settled in the colony while it was in possession of Great Britain, others before that event. The cause came on after the island had again become a British colony.

Sir William Scott decreed restitution to those British subjects who had settled in the colony while in British possession, but condemned the property of those who had settled there before that time. He held, that their settling in Demarara while belonging to Great Britain, afforded a presumption of their intending to return, if the island should be transferred to a foreign power, which presumption, recognized in the treaty, relieved those claimants from the necessity of proving such intention. He thought it highly reasonable that they should be admitted to their *jus post liminii*, and be held entitled to the protection of British subjects.

But the property of those claimants who had settled before it came to the possession of Great Britain, was condemned. "Having settled without any faith in British possession, it cannot be supposed," he said, "that they would have relinquished their residence, because that possession had ceased. They had passed from one sovereignty to another with indifference; and if they may be supposed to have looked again to a connexion with this country, they must have viewed it as a circumstance that was in no degree likely to affect their intention of continuing there."

"On the situation of persons settled there previous to the time of British possession," I feel myself, said the judge, "obliged to pronounce that they must be considered in the same light as persons resident in Amsterdam. It must be understood, however, that if there were among these any who have been actually removing, and that fact is properly ascertained, their goods may be capable of restitution. All that I mean to express is, that there must be evidence of an intention to remove, on the part of those who settled prior to British possession, the presumption not being in their favour."

This having been a hostile seizure, though made before the declaration of war, the property was held equally liable to condemnation as if captured, the instant of that declaration.

So much of the case as relates to those claimants who had settled during British possession, proves that other circumstances than an actual getting into motion for the purpose of returning to his own country, may create a presumption of intending to return; and may put off that hostile commercial character which a British subject residing and trading in the country of an enemy, is admitted to acquire. The settlement having been made in a country which, at the time, was in possession of Great Britain, though held only by the right of conquest, a tenure known to be extremely precarious, and rarely to continue longer than the war in which the acquisition is made, is sufficient to create this presumption. But the case does not declare negatively, that no other circumstances would be sufficient.

He was aware that the part of the case which applies to claimants who had settled previous to British possession, would at first view, appear to have a strong bearing on the question before the court. The shipment was in time of peace, and the seizure was made before the declaration of war. The trade was one in which a British subject, in time of peace, might lawfully engage. However strong his intention might be to return to his native country in the event of war, he could not be expected to manifest that intention before the actual existence of war. The reconquest of the island followed the declaration of war so speedily, as scarcely to leave time for putting the resolution to return in execution, had one been formed. Taking these circumstances into view, the condemnation would seem to be one of extreme severity. Yet even this case, admitting the decision to be perfectly correct, did not, when accurately examined, go so far as to justify a condemnation under such circumstances as belonged to some of the cases at bar.

The island having surrendered during war, such of its inhabitants as were originally British subjects were not allowed to derive, from this reannexation to the dominions of Great Britain, the advantages to which a voluntary return to their own country, of the same date, would have entitled them. They were considered as if they had been "residents of Amsterdam."

But Sir William Scott observes, that "if there are among these any who have been actually removing, and that fact is properly ascertained, their goods may be capable of restitution." *Actually removing*—when? Not surely before the seizure; for that was made in time of peace. Not before the declaration of war, when the original seizure was converted into a belligerent capture; for until that declaration was known, a person whose intention to remain or return was dependant on peace or war, would not be *actually removing*. On every principle of equity then, the time to which these expressions refer, must be the surrender of Demarara, or a reasonable time after the declaration of war was known there. The one period or the other would be subsequent to that event which was deemed equivalent to capture.

It was not unworthy of remark, that *Sir William Scott*, adds explanatory words which qualify and control the words, "actually removing," and show the sense in which he used them. "All" says the judge, "that I mean to express is, that there must be evidence of an *intention* to remove, on the part of those who settled prior to British possession, the presumption not being in their favour."

It would then, be rejecting a part, and a material part of the opinion, to say, that an intention to remove, clearly proved, though not accompanied by the fact of removal, would have been deemed insufficient to support the claim for restitution.

Were there no other circumstances of real importance in this case, did it rest solely on the sentiments expressed by the judge, unconnected with those circumstances, he should certainly consider it as leaving open to the claimants before this court, the right of proving an intention to return within a reasonable time after the declaration of war, by other acts than an actual removal.

But there are other circumstances which he could not deem immaterial; and, as the opinions of a judge are always to be taken with reference to the particular case in which they are delivered, he must consider these expressions in connexion with the whole case.

The probability is, that the claimants were not merely British merchants. Though the fact is not expressly stated, there is some reason to believe that they had become proprietors of the soil, and were completely incorporated with the Dutch colonists. They are not denominated merchants. They are spoken of, through the case, not as residents, but as settlers. "They had passed," said *Sir William Scott*, "from one sovereignty to another with indifference." This mode of expression appears to me to indicate a more permanent interest in the country, a more intimate connexion with it, than is acquired by a merchant removing to a foreign country, and residing there in time of peace, for the sole purpose of trade, and in another of the same class of cases, it is said, that, previous to the last war, the principal plantations of the island were in possession of British planters from the three British islands.

The voyage, too, in making which the *Diana* was captured, was a direct vòyage between the colony and the mother country. The trade was completely Dutch, and the property of any neutral, wherever residing, if captured in such a voyage during war, would be condemned.

But it is still more material, that those who settled in Demarara before British possession, must have settled during the war, which was terminated by the treaty of Amiens; or, if they settled in time of peace, must have continued there while the colony was Dutch, and while Holland was at war with Great Britain. Whichever the facts might be, whether they had settled in an enemy country during war, or had continued through the war a settlement made in time of peace, they had demonstrated that war made no change in their residence. In their cases then, it might be correctly said, "that war created no presumption of an intention to return."—"That they passed from one sovereign to another with indifference."

He could not consider claims under these circumstances as being in the same equity with claims made by persons who had removed into a foreign country in time of peace, for the sole purpose of trade, and whose trade would be annihilated by war.

The case of the *Boedes Lust* [1] differs from the *Diana* only in this—the claimants are not alleged to have been originally British subjects. Restitution was asked, because the property did not belong to an enemy at the time of shipment, not at the time of seizure, nor at the time of ad-

[1] 5 *Robinson*, 207.

judication. These grounds were all declared to be insufficient. The original seizure was provisionally hostile; and the declaration of war consummated the right to condemn the property to the crown, as enemy's property. The subsequent change in the character of the claimants, who become British subjects by the surrender of Demarara, could not divest it. "Where property is taken in a state of hostility," said *Sir William Scott*, "the universal practice has been to hold it subject to condemnation, although the claimants may have become friends and subjects prior to adjudication." "With as little effect," he added "can it be contended that a *postliminium* can be attributed to these parties. Here is no return to the original character, on which only a *jus postliminii* can be raised. The original character at the time of seizure and immediately prior to the hostility which has intervened was Dutch. The present character, which the events of war have produced, is that of British subjects; and although the British subject might, under circumstances, acquire the *jus postliminii* upon the resumption of his native character, it never can be considered that the same privilege accrues upon the acquisition of a character totally new and foreign."

This opinion is certainly not decisive; but it appears rather to favour than oppose the idea, that a merchant residing abroad, and taking measures to return on the breaking out of war, may entitle himself to the *jus postliminii*, with respect to property shipped before knowledge of the war.

The *President* (a) was captured on a voyage from the Cape of Good Hope to Europe. Mr. Elmslie, the claimant was born a British subject, but claimed as a citizen of the United States. He had removed to the Cape of Good Hope, during the preceding war, and still resided there. The property was condemned. In delivering his opinion,

(a) 5 Robinson, 248.

Sir William Scott observed. "It is said the claimant is entitled to the benefit of an intention of removing to Philadelphia, in a few months. A mere intention to remove, has never been held sufficient without some overt act, being merely an intention residing secretly and undistinguishably in the breast of the party, and liable to be revoked every hour. The expressions of the letter in which this intention is said to be found, are, I observe, very weak and general of an intention merely *in futuro*. Were they even much stronger than they are, they would not be sufficient. Something more than mere verbal declaration—some solid fact showing that the party is in the act of withdrawing, has always been held necessary in such cases."

It is to be held in mind, that this opinion is delivered in the case of a person who had fixed his residence in an enemy country, during war, and that he claimed to be the subject of a neutral state. For both these reasons, the war afforded no presumption of his intending to return either to his native or adopted country. To the vague expression of an intention to return at some future indefinite time, no influence can be ascribed. When the judge says that "something more than mere verbal declaration, some solid fact showing that the party is in the act of withdrawing, has always been held necessary in such cases."—I do not understand him to say, the person must have put himself in personal motion to return; must have commenced his voyage homeward, in order to be considered as in "the act of withdrawing;"—Many other overt acts, as selling a commercial establishment; stopping business; making preparations to return, accompanied by declarations of the intent, and not opposed by other circumstances, may be considered as acts of withdrawing.

In the case of the *Ocean* (b) *Sir William Scott* said, "This claim relates to the situation of British subjects

(b) 5 Robinson, 91.

settled in a foreign state, in time of amity, and taking early measures to withdraw themselves, on the breaking out of war, the affidavit of claim states, that this gentleman had been settled as a partner in a house of trade in Holland, but that he had made arrangements for the dissolution of the partnership, and was only prevented from removing personally, by the violent detention of all British subjects who happened to be within the territories of the enemy, at the breaking out of the war. It would, I think, under these circumstances, be going further than the principle of law requires, to conclude this person by his former occupation, and by his present constrained residence in France, so as not to admit him to have taken himself out of the effect of supervening hostilities, by the means which he had used for his removal."

If other means for removal were taken, than arrangements for the dissolution of the partnership, they are not stated; and it is fairly to be presumed, that these arrangements were the most prominent of them, since that fact is alone selected and particularly relied upon. In his statement of the case, the reporter says that the claimant had actually made his escape and returned to England, in July, 1803; (the trial was in January, 1804) but this must be a mistake, or is a fact not adverted to by the judge, since he says his opinion is, that the claimant is, at the time, "a constrained resident of France."

He should notice two other cases frequently cited, though he had seen no full report of either of them.

The first is the case of Mr. *Curtisses*.(c) This gentleman, who was a British subject, had gone to Surinam in 1766, and from thence to St. Eustatius where he remained till 1776. He then went to Holland to settle his accounts, and with an intention, "*as was said*," of returning afterwards to England to take up his final residence. In December,

(c) 3 Robinson, 20. In Notis.

1780, orders of reprisal were issued by England against Holland. On the first of January, 1781, *The Snelle Zeylder* was captured, and, on the 5th of March, and 10th of April, 1781, the vessel and cargo were condemned as Dutch property. On the 27th of April, 1781, Mr. *Curtisses* returned to England; and on an appeal, the sentence of condemnation was reversed by the Lords of Appeals, and restitution decreed.

Other claims of Mr. *Curtisses* were brought before the court of admiralty; and, on a full disclosure of these circumstances, restitution was decreed, before the decree of the Lords in the case of the *Snelle Zeylder* was pronounced.

The principle of this decree is said to be, that Mr. *Curtisses* was *in itinere*, and had put himself in motion, and was in pursuit of his original British character.

He did not mean to find fault with this decision; but certainly it presents some strong points more unfavourable to the claimant than would be found in some of the cases before the court. Mr. *Curtisses* had obtained a commercial domicil in the country of the enemy. At the time of the sailing, capture and condemnation of *The Snelle Zeylder*, he still resided in the country of the enemy. But, it is said, he was *in itinere*, he was in motion in pursuit of his original British character, what was this journey he is said to have been performing in pursuit of his original character? He had passed from one part of the dominions of the United Provinces to another. He had moved his residence from St. Eustatius to Holland, where he remained from the year 1776, till 1781—a time of sufficient duration for the acquisition of a domicil, had he not previously acquired it. This change of residence, to make the most of it, is an act too equivocal in itself, to afford a strong presumption that it was made for the purpose of returning to England. Had his stay in Holland even been short, a colonial merchant trading to the mother country, may so frequently be carried there on the business of his trade, that the fact can afford but weak evidence of an intention to discontinue that trade: but an interval of between four and five years elapsed between his arrival in Holland and his departure from that country, during which time he is not stated to have suspended his commercial pursuits or to have made any arrangements, such as transferring his property to England, or making an establishment there, which might indicate, by overt acts, the intention of returning to his native country. This journey to Holland connected with this long residence would seem to be made as a Dutch merchant for the purpose of establishing himself there, rather than as preparatory to his return to England. But it was said that he intended to return to England. How was this intention shown? If not by his journey to Holland and his long residence there, it was only shown by his being employed in the settlement of his accounts while a merchant at St. Eustatius, a business in which he would of course engage, whatever his future objects might be. This equivocal act does not appear to have been explained, otherwise than by his own declarations; nor does it appear that these declarations were made previous to the capture.

But could it be even admitted that the journey from St. Eustatius to Holland was made with a view of passing ultimately from Holland to England, yet the intention was not to be immediately executed. The time of carrying it into effect, was remote and uncertain,—subject to so many casualties, that, had not the war supervened, it might never have been carried into effect.

But laying aside these circumstances, the case proves only that being *in itinere*, in pursuit of the native character, divests the enemy character acquired by residence and trading; it is not insinuated that this character can be divested by other means.

Mr. *Whitehill's* case, though one of great severity, did not, he thought, overturn the principle, he was endeavouring to sustain. Mr. W. went to St. Eustasia but a few days before Admiral Rodney and the British forces made their appearance before that place. But it was proved that he went for the purpose of making a permanent settlement there. No intention to return appears to have been alleged, the recency of his establishment seems to have been the point on which his claim rested.

This case, in principle, bore on that before the court, so far only as it proves that war does not, under all circumstances, necessarily furnish a presumption, that the foreigner residing in the enemy country, intends to return to his own. The circumstances of this case, so far as we understand them, were opposed to the presumption, that war could effect Mr. *Whitehill's* residence. War actually existed at the time of his removal; and had that fact been known to him, there would have been no hardsnip in his case. He would have voluntarily taken upon himself the enemy character, at the same time that he took upon himself the Dutch character. There is reason to believe that the court considered him in equal fault with a person removing to a country known to be hostile. St. Eustatius was deeply engaged in the American trade, which, from the character of the contest, was, at that time, considered by England as cause of war, and was the fact which drew on that island the vengeance of Britain. Mr. *Whitehill* could have fixed himself there only for the purpose of prosecuting that trade. "He went," says *Sir William Scott*, "to a place which had rendered itself particularly obnoxious by its conduct in that war." This was certainly a circumstance which could not be disregarded, in deciding on the probability of his intending to remain in the country in the event of war.

These were the cases which appeared to him to apply most strongly to the question before the court. No one of them decides, in terms, that the property of a British subject residing abroad in time of amity, which was shipped before a knowledge of war, and captured by a British cruiser, shall depend, conclusively on the residence of the claimant at the time of capture, or on his having, at that time, put himself in motion to change his residence. In no case, which he had had an opportunity of inspecting, had he seen a *dictum* to this effect, the cases certainly required an intention, on the part of the subject residing and trading abroad, to return to the subject's own country, and that this intention should be manifest by overt acts; but they did not, according to his understanding of them, prescribe any particular overt act, as being exclusively admissible; nor did they render it indispensable that the overt act should, in all cases, precede the capture. If a British subject, residing abroad for commercial purposes, takes decided measures, on the breaking out of war, for returning to his native country, and especially if he should actually return, his claim for the restitution of property shipped before his knowledge of the war, would, he thought, be favourably received in a British court of admiralty; although his actual return, or the measures proving his intention to return, were subsequent to the capture. Thus understanding the English authorities, he did not consider them as opposing the principle he had laid down.

An American citizen, having merely a commercial domicil in a foreign country is not, he thought, under the British authorities, concluded, by his residence and trading in time of peace, from averring and proving an intention to change his domicil on the breaking out of war, or from availing himself of that proof in a court of admiralty. The intrinsic evidence arising from the change in his situation, produced by war, renders it extremely probable that, in this new state of things, he must intend to return home, and will aid in the construction of any overt act by which such intention is manifested. Dissolution of partnership; discontinuance of trade in the enemy country; a settlement of accounts, and other arrangements obviously preparatory to a change of residence, were, in his opinion, such overt acts as might under circumstances showing them to be made in good faith, entitle the claimant to restitution.

He did not perceive the mischief or inconvenience that could result from the establishment of this principle. Its operation is confined to property shipped before a knowledge of the war. For if shipped afterwards, it is clearly liable to condemnation, unless it be protected by the principle that it is merely a withdrawing of funds. Being confined to shipments made before a knowledge of the war, the evidence of an intention to change or continue a residence in the country of the enemy, must be speedily given. A continuance of trade after the war, unless perhaps under very special circumstances, and for the mere purpose of closing transactions already commenced, would fix the national character and the domicil previously acquired. An immediate discontinuance of trade and arrangements for removing followed by actual removal within a reasonable time, unless detained by causes which might sufficiently account for not removing, would fix the intention to change the domicil and show that the intention to return had never been abandoned; that the intention to remain always, had never been formed. It was a case, in which, if in any that can be imagined, justice required that the citizen, having entirely recovered his national character by his own act, and by an act which shows that he never intended to part with it finally, should, by a species of the *just postliminii*, be allowed to aver the existence of that character at the instant of capture. In the establishment of such a principle, he could perceive no danger. In its rejection, he thought he perceived much injustice. An individual whose residence abroad is certainly innocent and lawful, perhaps advantageous to his country, who never intended that residence to be permanent, or to continue in time of war, finds himself against his will, clothed with the character of an enemy, so conclusively that not even a return to his native country can rescue from that character and from confiscation, property shipped in the time of real or supposed peace. His sense of justice revolted from such a principle.

In applying this opinion to the claimants before the court, he should be regulated by their conduct after a knowledge of the war. If they continue their residence and trade, after that knowledge; at any rate, after knowing that the repeal of the orders in council was not immediately followed by peace, their claim to restitution would be clearly unsustainable. If they took immediate measures for returning to this country, and had since actually returned, or had assigned sufficient reasons for not returning, their property, he thought, might be capable of restitution. Some of the claimants would come within one description, some within the other. It would, under the opinion given by the court, be equally tedious and useless to go through their cases.

His reasoning has been applied entirely to the case of native Americans. This course has been pursued for two reasons. It presents the argument in what he thought its true light; and the sentence of condemnation makes no discrimination between native and other citizens.

The claimants were natives of that country with which we were at war, who have been naturalized in the United States. It was impossible to deny that many of the strongest arguments, urged to prove the probability that war must determine the native American citizen to abandon the country of the enemy and return home, are inapplicable, or apply but feebly to citizens of this description. Yet he thought it was not for the United States, in such a case as this, to discriminate between them. He would not pretend to say what distinctions may or may not exist between these two classes of citizens, in a contest of a different description. But in a contest between the United States, and the naturalized citizen, in a claim set up by the United States to confiscate his property, the citizen might, he thought, protect himself by any defence which would protect a native American. In the prosecution of such a claim, the United States were, if he might be excused for borrowing from the common law a term peculiarly appropriate, *estopped* from saying that they have not placed this adopted son on a level with those born in their family.([d])

7. Wherever even a mere factory is founded in the eastern parts of the world, European persons trading under the shelter and protection of those establishments, are conceived to take their national character from that association under which they live and carry on their commerce. It is a rule of the law of nations applying peculiarly to those countries, and is different from what prevails ordinarily in Europe and the western parts of the world, in which men take their present national character of the country in which they are resident; and this distinction arises from the nature and habit of the countries: In the western parts of the world alien merchants mix in the society of the natives; access and intermixture are permitted, and they become incorporated to almost the full extent. But in the east, from the oldest times, an immiscible character has been kept up; foreigners are not admitted into the general body and mass of the society of the nation; they continue strangers and sojourners as all their fathers were.—*Doris amara suam non intermiscuit undam*; not acquiring any national character under the general sovereignty of the country, and not trading under any recognized authority of their own original country, they have been held to derive their present character from that of the association or factory, under whose protection they live and carry on their trade.

Thus with respect to establishments in Turkey, it was declared that a merchant carrying on trade at Smyrna under the protection of the Dutch consul at Smyrna, was to be considered a Dutchman, and his property was condemned as Dutch property. The same in China, and generally

([d]) Per Marshall, C. J. The Venus. Supreme Court of the U. S. February T. 1814. M. S.

throughout the East, persons admitted into a factory, are not known in their own peculiar national character; and being not admitted to assume the character of the country, they are considered only in the character of that association or factory.

But these principles are considered not to apply to the territories occupied by the British in Hindostan; because, though the sovereignty of the Mogul is occasionally brought forward for purposes of policy, it hardly exists otherwise than as a phantom: It is not applied in any way for the regulation of their establishments. Great Britain exercises the power of declaring war and peace, which is among the strongest marks of actual sovereignty, and if the high, and empyrean sovereignty of the Mogul is sometimes brought down from the clouds, as it were, for purposes of policy, it by no means interferes with the actual authority which that country, and the East India company, a creature of that country, exercises there with full effect. The law of treason would apply, to Europeans living there, in full force. It is nothing to say that some particular parts of the English civil code are not applicable to the religious or civil habits of the Mahomedan or Hindoo natives; and that they are, on that account, allowed to live under their own laws. This is no exception; for with respect to internal regulations, there is in Great Britain, a particular sect, the Jews, that in matters of legitimacy, and on other important subjects, are governed by their own particular regulations, and not by all the municipal laws of that country, some of which are totally inapplicable to them. It is, besides, observable, that the British acts of parliament and treaties have been by no means scrupulous in later times, in describing the country in question as the territory of Great Britain.(e)

(e) 3 *Robinson*, 12. The Indian Chief.

In a case which occurred during the late war with Great Britain, it was contended by the American captors that the privileges granted to British subjects in the Portuguese dominions by the treaty of 1810, between Great Britain and Portugal, completely recognized the exclusive national character of these subjects; and the case was likened to those above cited in the eastern parts of the world. But it is now settled by the lords of appeal, that a British born subject resident in the English factory at Lisbon, so far possesses the Portuguese character as that his trade with the enemies of his native country is not illegal.[f] Upon the footing of authority, therefore, the case for the captors was not made out.

And upon principle it is as difficult to maintain—the 8th and 10th articles of the treaty secure no more than the freedom of trade and the right to have all causes tried by a special tribunal, according to the laws and customs of Portugal. Still however, it is an incorporation of British residents into the general commerce of the country. They are still subject to the general laws respecting revenues and taxes; to the general duties of qualified allegiance, and to the general regulations of social and domestic, as well as commercial intercourse. Far different is this from the case of eastern factories, where the laws of the factory govern the parties who claim protection under it, and no general *amenability* to the laws of the country, is either claimed or exercised. It was therefore decided that British residents in the dominions of Portugal take the character of their domicil, and as to all third parties, are to be deemed Portuguese subjects.[g]

8. Where goods were shipped by a house of trade in the enemy's country to a house of trade in a neutral country,

[f] 4 *Robinson*, 255. Note. The Danaos.

[g] Per Story, J. The St. Indiano. Circuit Court of the U. S. for the Massachusetts district, October T. 1814. M. S.

both consisting of the same partners, all native subjects of the enemy, two of whom were domiciled in the enemy's country, and one in the neutral country—the captors contended that the share of the latter was liable to condemnation, as being the property of a person connected in a house of trade in the enemy's country, and continuing that connexion after and during the war, the property having been purchased and shipped on the account and risk of the same house.

In this case, the learned judge, by whom it was determined, observed that in general the national character of a person is to be decided by that of his domicil: If that be neutral, he acquires the neutral character; if otherwise, he is affected with the enemy character. But the property of a person may acquire a hostile character, altogether independent of his own peculiar character, derived from residence. In other words, the origin of the property, or the traffic in which it is engaged, may stamp it with a hostile character, although the owner may happen to be a neutral domiciled in a neutral country. Thus the produce of an estate belonging to a neutral in an enemy's colony, is impressed with the character of the soil, notwithstanding a neutral residence.(h) So, if a vessel purchased in the enemy's country, is by constant and habitual occupation employed in the trade of that country during the war, she is deemed a vessel of the country from which she is so navigating, whatever may be the domicil of the owner.(i) He

(h) 5 *Robinson*, 20. The Phœnix.

(i) *Vide Supra*, Chap. III. § 6. And analogous, though more remotely, are the cases of property condemned for resistance to search, (Chap. III. § 19.) for breach of blockade, (Chap. VI. § 11.) as contraband of war, (*Ib.* § 2.) and for sailing under the flag and pass or license of the enemy, (Chap. V.) So also the property of citizens or subjects of the belligerent state engaged in trade with the enemy, is confiscated upon the ground that it is taken adhering to the enemy, and therefore the proprietor is, *pro hac vice* to be considered as an enemy. 1 *Robinson*, 196. The Nelly, *in notis* to the Hoop. These are all cases of an adoption of the enemy therefore agreed that it was a doctrine supported by strong principles of equity and propriety, that there is a traffic which stamps a national character on the individual independent of that character, which mere personal residence may give him.

And he thought the case then before the court clearly within the range of the principle stated. Here was a house of trade composed entirely of British subjects established in the enemy's country, and habitually and continually carrying on its trade, with all the advantages and protection of British subjects. It was true one partner is domiciled in the neutral country—but for what purpose? For ought that appeared, for purposes exclusively connected with the enemy establishment. At all events the whole property embarked in its commercial enterprises centered in that house and received its exclusive management and direction from it. Under such circumstances, the house was as purely hostile in its domicil (if he might use the expression) and in its commerce, as it could be if all the partners resided in the enemy's territory. If the case, therefore, were new, he did not perceive how it could be extracted from the grasp of confiscation on account of its thorough

character, rendering the property liable to capture and condemnation, without regard to the personal domicil of its owner. The principle upon which is founded the British rule of the war of 1756, is quite different, and proceeds upon the doctrine that a neutral has no right to carry on a trade in time of war, from which he was excluded in time of peace. Even that rule, itself, in its origin, was supported upon the sound and true principle of adoption, by means of special licenses or passes granted by the French (then at war with Great Britain) to the Dutch, (then neutral) permitting them to engage in the colonial trade of France. There is all the difference between this principle and the modern British doctrine, (invented during the war of the French revolution, to justify a revival and undue extension of the rule of the war of 1756) that there is between the granting by the enemy of a special license to the subjects of the belligerent state to trade with a neutral country, (*vide infra*, Chap. V. § 3.) and a general exemption of such trade from capture by the enemy. (*Vide Ib.* § 5.)

incorporation into the enemy character. But how stood the case upon the footing of authority? It was agreed that no decision comes up to the point, and that the court was called upon by the captors to promulgate a novel doctrine. If, however, he was not greatly deceived, it would be found on an attentive examination, that there is a strong current of authority all setting one way. From the cases of the Jacobus Johannes and the Osprey, an erroneous notion had been adopted that the domicil of the parties was that alone to which the court had a right to resort in prize causes. But in the case of Coopman, those cases were put upon their true foundations, as cases merely *at the commencement of a war* in reference to persons who, during peace, had habitually carried on trade in the enemy's country, though not resident there, and were therefore entitled to have time to withdraw from that commerce. But the Lords of Appeal in that case expressly laid it down, that if a person entered into a house of trade in the enemy's country in time of war, or continued that connexion during the war, he should not protect himself by mere residence in a neutral country.[k] Now he was utterly at a loss to know how terms more appropriate could be employed to embrace the present case, which was that of a connexion in a house of trade in the enemy's country *continued during the war*. This doctrine held by the highest authority known in the English prize law has been repeatedly recognized and enforced by the same learned court.[l] The very exception was taken in the cases of the Portland, &c.[m] as to Mr. Ostermeyer, who, though domiciled at Blankanese (in a neutral country) was alleged to be engaged in the trade of Ostend (in the enemy's country), either as a partner or as a sole trader. In those cases the general principle was explicitly

(k) 1 *Robinson*, 1. The Vigilantia.

(l) 2 *Robinson*, 251. The Susa.

(m) 3 *Robinson*, 41.

admitted, and one vessel, the Jonge Amelia, eventually condemned on that ground. It was a mistake of the learned counsel for the claimant, that the court in those cases confined the further proof to the fact whether Mr. Ostermeyer was sole trader at Ostend; it will appear on a careful examination that further proof was also required as to the alleged partnership, and particularly as to a letter in the Frau Louisa pointing to that partnership. In the Jonge Klassina, which was a very strong case of the application of the same doctrine, Sir William Scott avows it, and declares that, a man may have mercantile concerns in two countries, and if he acts as a merchant of both, he must be liable to be considered as a subject of both, with regard to the transactions originating respectively in those countries.(n) The case of the Herman, so far from impugning the principles, evidently proceeds upon the admission of it; and he thought it might be affirmed without rashness that not a single authoritative *dictum* exists which can shake its force. It had been attempted to distinguish those cases from that before the court, by alleging that none of them present the fact of a shipment made from a house in the enemy country to its connected house in the neutral country. But it did not seem to him that this difference presented any solid ground on which to rest a favourable distinction.

On the whole, he was of opinion that the shipment in this case being made by a house in the enemy's country for their own account, in a voyage originating in that country must be deemed enemy's property, and that the share of the partner residing in the neutral country must follow the fate of the shares of his co-partners.(o)

(n) 5 *Robinson* 302.

(o) Per STORY, J The St. Indiano. Circuit Court for the Massachusetts district, October T. 1814. M. S.

The captors had further contended in reference to other claimants before the court, that the same principle applies in cases where a house in the enemy's country ships goods to one of its partners domiciled in a neutral country, either in his single name, or to a neutral house there, of which he is also a partner; and *e converso* where a partner of a neutral house is domiciled in the enemy's country, and ships to such house goods, the manufactures of that country.

In respect to the two former cases, the learned judge agreed at once to the position, if the shipment be really made on the account and for the benefit of the house in the enemy's country. For in such case the neutral partner or house acts but as their agent, and the whole property and profits of every enterprize rest in the hostile house; and indeed, it is wholly immaterial to whom the consignment may be, whether to a partner or a stranger; the property in its origin, transit and return, is thoroughly imbued with the enemy character. And the same might be affirmed of the third case, if the party so domiciled in the enemy's country be really engaged in the general commerce of that country for the exclusive benefit of his neutral house. For although in general, the residence of a stationed agent in the enemy's country will not affect the trade of the neutral principal with a hostile character, yet this is true only as to the ordinary trade of a neutral, as such carried on in the ordinary manner. But the principles contended for by the captors spread over a wider surface, and extend to cases where a shipment has originated in a house of trade in the enemy's country, consigned either to a partner, or to a house, in a neutral country, of which such partner is a member, although the shipment be *bona fide* exclusively on account and risk of such neutral partner or house. And the declaration of Sir William Scott in the Jonge Klassina, already quoted, was relied on as an authority which supports the argument. But the learned judge did not think that the language of Sir William Scott, correctly considered, admitted of this interpretation. The latter is merely alluding to the origin of transactions which exclusively regard the interests of a house of trade established in a particular country, and not of transactions where it acts merely as an agent or shipper for other persons. To shew this the more distinctly, in the Portland, he says, I know of no case, nor of any principle that could support such a position as this, that a man, having a house of trade in the enemy's country, as well as in a neutral country, should be considered in his whole concerns as an enemy merchant, as well in those which respected solely his neutral house, as in those which belonged to his belligerent domicil. The only light in which it could affect him would be, as furnishing a suggestion that the partners in the house in one place were also partners in the other. And in the Herman, where a shipment was actually made from an enemy's port, by order of the neutral house to the belligerent house, but on account of the former, the property was adjudged to be restored.

These cases did, as he thought, assign and establish the true and reasonable limits of the doctrine; and he had no difficulty in maintaining that shipments made by an enemy house, on account and risk *bona fide*, and exclusively, of a neutral partner or house are not subject to confiscation as prize of war. And the same principle must apply in the converse case of a partner or agent domiciled in the enemy's country, and making shipments to his neutral house or principal on the exclusive account of the latter.(p)

(p) Per STORY, J. *Ib.*

CHAPTER V.

Of the liability to capture of property, sailing under the flag and pass, or license of the enemy.

1. It is an established rule with respect to a vessel, that if she is navigating under the pass of a foreign country, she is to be considered as bearing the national character of that country under whose flag she sails: she makes a part of its navigation, and is in every respect liable to be considered as a vessel of that country. For ships have a peculiar character impressed upon them by the special nature of their documents, and are always held to the character, with which they are so invested, to the exclusion of any claims of interest that persons resident in neutral countries may actually have in them.(a) But where the cargo was laden on board in time of peace, and documented as foreign property in the same manner with the ship, with the view of avoiding alien duties, the sailing under the foreign flag and pass was not held conclusive as to the cargo. A distinction was made between the ship, which was held bound by the character imposed upon it by the authority of the government from which all the documents issued, and the goods, whose character had no such dependence upon the authority of the state. In time of war a more strict principle might be necessary; but where the transaction took place in peace, and without any expecta-

(a) 1 *Robinson*, 13. The Vigilantia, 5 *Robinson*, 2. The Vrow Elizabeth, ib. In Appendix. Additional Notes, No. II.

tion of war, the cargo should not be involved in the condemnation of the vessel, which under these circumstances was considered as incorporated into the navigation of that country whose flag and pass she bore.[b]

And where the ship was sailing under a special pass or license of adoption, entitling her to engage in the colonial trade of the enemy, being in all other respects undoubtedly and avowedly a neutral vessel, and documented as such, she was restored to the neutral claimant.[c]

2. By the law of war, all intercourse between the subjects or citizens of the belligerent powers is prohibited. No commercial, or other intercourse can therefore be lawfully carried on between the citizens or subjects of the hostile states, but by the special permission and license of their respective governments, who are alone competent to decide on all the considerations of expediency, by which such an exception from the ordinary consequences of war must be controlled. Such licenses are of antient invention and use. Thus in the Black Book of the English admiralty, p. 76, we find a prohibition of all intercourse with the enemy, laid down with the exception of a *special license from the king or his admiral.* And by the French Ordinances of the 5th August, 1676, and the 7th December, 1689, confirmed by that of the 18th March, 1705, the French ships of war are forbidden from detaining any vessel bearing the passport of the king, to whatever nation the same may belong. As such intercourse can only be legalized in the citizens or subjects of the belligerent state, by a license from their own government, it is evident that the use of a license for such a purpose from the enemy only must be illegal, and affect the property with confiscation. For, as has been before observed, it is the sovereign power of the state that

(b) 5 *Robinson*, 5. *In Notis.* The Vreede Scholtys. *Vide supra*, Chapter IV. § 8. note i.

(c) The Clarissa, cited in 5 *Robinson*, 4.

is alone competent to decide on all the considerations of expediency, by which such an intercourse may be permitted to its citizens or subjects.

But though this principle may be considered as applicable to a license protecting a direct commercial intercourse with the enemy, yet the question how far it may be applicable to an indirect intercourse, by a voyage to a neutral country, or a country in alliance with the enemy, may be thought more doubtful.

Valin, speaking of the reason for requiring *the name and domicil of the assured* in the policy, as well as a specification of the *goods insured*, *the name of the ship*, *and the place where the cargo is to be laden and unladen*, says, That the intention of the ordinance in requiring this, is, to discover in time of war, if notwithstanding the interdiction of commerce included in every declaration of war, the subjects of the king are not engaged in trade with the enemies of the state, or with friends or allies, *by whose interposition*, *munitions of war*, *provisions*, *and other prohibited articles*, *may be handed over to the enemy:* for a trade in these articles, being forbidden as prejudicial to the state, they would be subject to confiscation and to be declared good prize, being found either on board French vessels, or those of friends and allies. *Sur l'Ordonnance*, L. 3. tit. 6. *des Assurances*, art. 3.([d]) If it be said that the commentator is here speaking only of contraband trade, it is answered, that by this ordinance the munitions of war are alone considered as contraband, whilst provisions are deemed inno-

([d]) L'intention de l'ordonnance, en exigeant que la police contienne, &c. est encore de connoître en temps de guerre, si malgré l'interdiction de commerce qu'emporte toujours toute déclaration de guerre, les sujets du roi ne font point commerce avec les ennemis de l'etat, ou avec des amis ou alliés, *par l'interposition desquels on ferait passer aux ennemis des munitions de guerre et de bouche, ou d'autres effets prohibés :* car tout cela étant défendu, comme préjudiciable à l'état, serait sujet à confiscation, et à être déclaré de bonne prise, étant trouvé, soit sur les navires de la nation, soit sur ceux des amis et alliés.

cent articles. Besides, Valin immediately proceeds to observe that, This interdiction of commerce with the enemies of the state, comprehends also of right a prohibition against insuring their goods, whether laden on board their own vessels, or the vessels of allies and neutrals. For to insure the goods of the enemy, or *to send them to him directly or indirectly*, is at bottom the same thing. It is true that the law 11, *Ff. de Publicanis*, which is cited on this subject, speaks only of munitions of war and provisions, which are prohibited from being sent to the enemy on account of the nature of the things themselves; but the Ordinance of 1543, art. 42. and that of 1584, art. 69. which is likewise cited, *absolutely proscribes all commerce direct or indirect with the enemy*, as well as the transportation of the munitions of war on board the vessels of allies or neutrals to the enemy.(e)

If it be said that the principles relative to trading with the enemy are not applicable to the case of a license granted by the enemy to protect a voyage to a neutral port, unless it appears that the goods were to be sent on to the enemy; it may in return be asked if all intercourse with the enemy be prohibited by the law of war, how can the purchase or acceptance of a license from that enemy be lawful? If the license be an article of sale, in what respect can it be distinguished from a sale of merchandize? If purchased

(e) Cette interdiction de commerce avec les ennemis, comprend aussi de plein droit la défense d'assurer les effets qui leur appartiennent, qu'ils soit chargés, sur leurs propres vaisseaux, ou sur des navires amis, alliés ou neutres. Car assurer les effets de l'ennemi, ou *les lui envoyer directement ou indirectement*, c'est au fond la même chose. Il est vrai que la loi 11, *Ff. de Publicanis*, que l'on cite á ce sujet, ne parle que des munitions de guerre et de bouche, qu'il est defendu de nature de chose de faire passer à l'ennemi; mais l'ordonnance de 1543, art. 42, et celle de 1584, art. 69, que l'on cite aussi, *proscrivent absolument tout commerce direct ou indirect avec les ennemis*, aussi bien que le transport que les navires amis ou neutres pourraient faire des munitions de guerre aux ennemis.

directly from the enemy government, would it not be a trading with the enemy? If purchased indirectly can it change the nature of the transaction? Nor can it be said, that if purchased of a neutral, the trade in licenses is no more illegal than the purchase of goods of enemy fabric *bona fide* conveyed to neutrals. For the purchase of goods of enemy manufacture, and avowedly belonging to an enemy is not legalized by the mere fact of the sale being made in a neutral port. The goods must have been incorporated into the general stock of neutral trade, before a subject of the belligerent state can lawfully become the purchaser. If such licenses be a legitimate article of sale, will they not enable the enemy government to raise a revenue from the citizens of the belligerent state, and thereby add to the enemy's resources of war? Admit, however, that they are not so sold, but that they are a measure of policy adopted by the enemy government, to favour its own interests, and ensure a supply of necessary articles, either in or through neutral countries; can it be asserted that a citizen of the belligerent state is wholly blameless, who enters into stipulations and engagements to effect these purposes of the enemy? Is not the enemy thereby relieved from the pressure of the war, and enabled to wage it more successfully against other branches of the same commerce, not protected by this indulgence. The case of a personal license is very distinguishable from a general order of the enemy government, authorising and protecting all trade to a neutral country. The first presupposes a personal communication with the enemy, and an avowed intention of furthering his objects to the exclusion of the general trade by other merchants to the same country. It has a direct tendency to prevent such general trade, and relieves the belligerent from the necessity of resorting to a general order of protection. It contaminates the commercial enterprizes of the favoured individual with purposes not reconcileable with the general policy of his country; exposes him to extraordinary temptations to succour the enemy by intelligence, and separates him from the general character of his country, by clothing him with all the effective interests of a neutral. These are some of the leading principles upon which a trade with the enemy has been adjudged illegal by the law of nations. On the other hand, a general order opens the whole trade of the neutral country to every merchant. It presupposes no incorporation in enemy interests. It enables the whole mercantile enterprize of the country to engage upon equal terms in the traffic, and it separates no individual from the general national character. It relaxes the rigour of war, not only in that particular trade, but collaterally opens a path to other commerce. There is all the difference between the cases that there is between an active personal co-operation in the measures of the enemy, and the merely accidental aid afforded by the pursuit of a fair and legitimate commerce. In the purchase or gratuity of a license for trade, there is an implied agreement that the party shall not employ it to the injury of the grantor—that he shall conduct himself in a perfectly neutral manner, and avoid every hostile conduct. Can a citizen of the belligerent state be permitted in this manner to carve out for himself a neutrality on the ocean when his country is at war? Can he justify himself in refusing to aid his countrymen who have fallen into the hands of the enemy on the ocean, or decline their rescue? Can he withdraw his personal services when the necessities of the nation require them? Can an engagement be legal which imposes upon him the temptation or necessity of deeming his personal interest at variance with the legitimate objects of the government? The principles of international law, which formerly considered the lives and properties of all enemies as liable to the arbitrary disposal of their adversary, cannot be so far relaxed, that a part of the people may claim to be at peace, while the residue are involved in the desolations of war. There are many acts which inflict upon neutrals the penalty of confiscation, from the subserviency which they are supposed to indicate to enemy interests,—the carrying of enemy despatches,—the transportation of military persons. The ground of these decisions is the voluntury interposition of the party to further the views and interests of one belligerent power at the expense of the other. If then the property of a neutral is condemnable, for lending himself to the views and interests of the enemy in those cases, *a fortiori* is that of a citizen or subject liable to condemnation for thus lending himself in the present case.

By the French ordinance of August, 1681, it is provided that every vessel fighting under any other flag than that of the state whose commission she bears, or having commissions from two different princes or states, shall be good prize; and if armed for war, the commander and officers shall be punished as pirates. *Liv. 3. tit. 9. Des Prises, Art. 5.* And Valin, in his *Traité des Prises*, 53, says, that in respect to the vessel on board of which are found commissions from two different princes or states, it is also just that they should be declared good prize, either because they could not have accepted those commissions unless for fraudulent and deceptive purposes, in case they were both from friendly or neutral princes: or because they could not use the flag of the one in consequence of bearing his commission, without injuring the other. Besides this applies to French *subjects*, as well as to *foreigners*.(f)

In what consists the substantial difference, between navigating under the commission of our own and also of an-

(f) A l'egard du vaisseau, ou se trouveront des commissions de deux differens princes ou etats, il est egalement juste qu'il soit declaré de bonne prise, soit parce qu'il ne peut avoir pris ces commissions que dans un esprit de fraude et de surprise, furent elles toutes deux de princes amis ou neutres: soit parcequ'il ne peut arborer le pavillon de l'un en consequence de sa commission, sans faire injure à l'autre. Ceci au reste regarde *les Francais* comme *les etrangers*.

other sovereign, and navigating under the protection of the passport of such sovereign which confer or compel a neutral character?

Valin also declares in his Commentary upon the Ordinance, if on board a French vessel there be found a foreign commission together with that of France, the vessel will be prize; although she may have used no other flag than the French. *Liv.* 3. *tit.* 9. *art.* 4. *p.* 241. (g) It is true that he just before observes that this circumstance of two clearances or passports, or two bills of lading, of which one is French, and the other of an enemy country, is not alone sufficient to pronounce the *enemy* vessel good prize, and this must depend upon the circumstances which may serve to indicate her real destination.(h) But it is evident that Valin is here referring to the case of an *enemy ship*, having a passport of trade from the sovereign of France. It may be inferred from his language, that a French vessel sailing under the passport, *congé*, or license of its enemy, without the authority of its own sovereign, would have been lawful prize.(i)

3. Where the vessel in question, the property of a citizen of the belligerent state, laden with a cargo of flour and bread, and bound from Baltimore to Lisbon, was captured on the voyage thither, and brought in for adjudication, the ship was claimed by the owner, and the cargo by him and other citizens. Among the documentary evidence was a

(g) Si sur un navire Français il y a une commission d'un prince etranger avec celle de France, il sera de bonne prise, quoiqu'il n'ait aboré que le pavillon Français.

(h) Que la circonstance de deux congés ou passports, ou de deux connoisements, dont l'un est de France et l'autre d'un pays ennemi, ne suffit pas seul pour faire déclarer le *navire ennemi* de bonne prise, et que cela doit dependre des circonstances capables de faire découvrir sa véritable destination.

(i) Per STORY J. The Julia. Supreme Court of the U. S. February T. 1814. M. S.

letter from the enemy's Admiral Sawyer, of the 5th August, 1812, directed to Andrew Allen, jun. (as British consul at Boston) stating, that being aware of the importance of ensuring a constant supply of flour and other dry provisions to Spain and Portugal, and to the West Indies, he should give directions to the officers of his Britannic majesty's squadron under his command, not to molest American vessels unarmed and so laden, *bona fide* bound to Portuguese and Spanish ports, whose papers should be accompanied by a certified copy of that letter under Allen's consular seal. Also a letter from Allen, addressed to all the officers of his said majesty's ships of war or privateers belonging to his subjects, reciting that it is of vital importance to continue a full and regular supply of flour and other dry provisions to the ports of Spain and Portugal, or their colonies, and that in consequence thereof, it had been thought expedient by his majesty's government, that every degree of protection and encouragement should be given to American vessels, so laden and destined, with a copy of his letter certified under his consular seal, which documents were intended as a perfect safeguard and protection to such vessel in the prosecution of her voyage; and that in compliance with such instructions, he had granted to the vessel in question a copy of the said Admiral Sawyer's letter, certified under his consular seal, requesting all officers of his majesty's ships of war, and of private armed vessels belonging to his subjects, not to offer any molestation to the said vessel, but, on the contrary, to grant her all proper assistance and protection in her passage to Lisbon, and on her return from thence to her port of departure, laden with salt or in ballast only. The purchase of the license, and the price paid, were proved; also that the license was in blank, for inserting the names of any vessel and master, and that these licenses formed an article of traffic in the market as much as any species of merchandize.

It was contended that the facts in this case differed so materially from those which appeared in the case above cited, that the principles of law which ruled that case, were inapplicable to this.

There certainly are some differences in the two cases. The important circumstance which seems to have influenced the decision in the former case was, that the license contemplated the ensuring a constant supply of dry provisions *to the allied armies* in Spain and Portugal, and consequently an unlawful connexion with the enemy to supply his armies, and a subserviency to the interests of that enemy. In the latter case no such views were expressed in the license of Sawyer; yet the court must have been wilfully blind not to see that this was, in reality, the object of Sawyer and of Allen, and that it must have been so understood by those who sailed under it. In both cases the allied armies were to be supplied, not by sales to be made to their agents, (for this is not required by either) but by carrying supplies to the Peninsula, which would indirectly come to their use. The license, as well as the letter of Allen accompanying it, pointed out the great importance of such supplies being sent to Spain and Portugal; and the latter added, that in furtherance of *these views of his Majesty's government*, he had been directed, by Admiral Sawyer, to furnish a copy of his letter to vessels so laden and destined. Can it be said that a citizen, sailing under the protection of papers professing such to be the views of the enemy's government, does not act in such a manner as to subserve the views and interest of the enemy? Upon the whole, the court was of opinion, that there was no substantial difference between this case and the former one; and that this was fully within the principle laid down by the court in deciding that.

It was stated in behalf of the claimants of the cargo, that they ought not to be bound by the illegal act of the owner of the vessel. It is a sufficient answer to this argument to observe, that, in this case, it must be presumed that the license was known to the owners of the cargo, if it was not the joint property of all. It is inconceivable that the owner of the vessel should expend about sixteen hundred dollars for the protection of a cargo in which it appeared that he was not largely concerned, without communicating such an advantage to his shippers, and even requiring some reimbursement, either by demanding higher freight, or compensation in some other way. But what is conclusive on this point was, that an order for further proof in relation to this license was made, and yet no affidavit or proof was offered by any of the owners, denying knowledge of these documents being on board.[k]

4. The same principle was applied to the following case. The vessel and cargo in question were captured during the late war. From the documentary evidence and preparatory examinations it appeared, that the vessel sailed from Norfolk with a cargo of dry provisions, was consigned to the supercargo, obtained a clearance for St. Bartholomews, and was ostensibly bound thither. At the time of capture she was to the leeward of that island, and enemy licenses were found on board of a description similar to those in the last mentioned case. The court found it difficult to discriminate between this case and the preceding ones.—All had licenses of the same character, and substantially for the same purpose, except only that the object of the first vessel was to supply the allied armies in Portugal, and the original intention of the vessel in this case was to go to the enemy's West India islands. It is by no means clear that this intention was ever changed; but admitting that, from an apprehension of seizure on her return to the

(k) Per Washington, J. The Hiram. Supreme Court of the United States, February Term, 1814. M. S.

belligerent state, after touching at an enemy's port, she in fact sailed on a voyage to St. Bartholomews, a neutral port, this could make no substantial difference in her favour. The object in going there was equally criminal, and subserved the views of the enemy nearly, if not quite, as well as if her cargo had been landed in an enemy's island. Of the real intent of the voyage there could remain no doubt; for it abundantly appeared from the license itself, that the professed object of Admiral Sawyer, at least in granting it, was to obtain a supply of provisions for the enemy; and the court would not easily lend its ear to a suggestion that, notwithstanding the vessel was found with an enemy's protection on board of so obnoxious a character, yet her owners intended to deceive the enemy, either by going to a port not mentioned in it, or by disposing of her cargo in a way that would not have promoted his views. Without meaning to say that such conduct might, under no circumstances whatever, be explained, the court thought that there was no proof in this case to shew that it was not the intention of the claimants to carry into effect the original understanding between them and Mr. Allen. For though a destination to the neutral port be conceded, it is evident that Mr. Allen, who acted as British Consul, supposed the views of Admiral Sawyer might be answered as well in that way as any other; nor is it clear, as was said at the bar, that the documents received from Mr. Allen, and which varied more in form than in substance from the Admiral's passport, would not have protected the vessel from enemy capture on a voyage to the neutral port.—The protection of the British Admiral extended to unarmed American vessels, laden with dry provisions, and *bona fide* bound to British, Portuguese, or Spanish ports. The only modification or extension introduced by Mr. Allen, was a permission to go to a Swedish island, equally neutral with Spain and Portugal, in the vicinity of the British possessions. Whether all or any of these papers would have saved the vessel from confiscation in an enemy's court of prize, the court was not bound to assert; it is sufficient, if that was the reasonable expectation of the parties, as it certainly was; and it is more than probable that such expectation would have been realized, considering the very important advantages the enemy was to derive from them.— In case of capture, there can be no doubt that the claimants would have interposed those very papers, which were supposed to have emanated from unauthorized agents, as a shield against forfeiture; and probably with success. Why then should they be permitted to allege, in a court of the belligerent state, that these documents would have been ineffectual for that purpose?

It was also insisted, that in this case no illicit intercourse had taken place; that the whole offence, if any, consisted in intention; and that, if a capture had not intervened, there was still a *locus penitentiæ*, and no one could say that even the project of going to the neutral port might not have been abandoned.

In this reasoning the court did not concur, but was of opinion, that the moment the vessel started on the voyage for the neutral port with the license in question, and a cargo of provisions, she rendered herself liable to capture by the public or private armed vessels of the belligerent state, who were not bound to lay by, and see how she would conduct herself during the voyage; the consequence of which would be, that no right of capture would exist until all chance of making it was at an end.(1)

5. Where the vessel in question had been exempted from condemnation on the return voyage by the enemy on account of her producing a certificate of having landed her outward

(1) Per Livingston, J. The Aurora. Supreme Court of the United States, February Term, 1814. M. S.

cargo in Portugal, the captors contended that the vessel and return cargo were subject to condemnation, because the voyage must have been performed under the protection of a British license, and upon any other supposition it was impossible to account for the exemption from British condemnation. But the learned judge by whom the case was determined, did not think that under the circumstances so pregnant a suspicion would arise of subserviency to enemy interests as the captors supposed. All knew that soon after the commencement of the war, with a view to facilitate the supply of the British armies in Portugal, licenses were granted by the British government to protect from capture, vessels with cargoes destined to those countries. It had been decided in the case of the Julia, that the acceptance and use of such license on the part of an American citizen, constituted such an avowed adoption of the policy of the enemy as stamped the property engaged in the traffic with all the penal consequences of hostile character.[m] He looked back upon that decision without regret, and after much subsequent reflection could not doubt that it had a perfect foundation in the principles of public law. To the many authorities there stated, he might have added the pointed language of the court in the Jonge Pietre. That without the license of the government, *no communication direct or indirect* can be carried on with the enemy;[n] and the rule strongly illustrative of the principle, which is acknowledged as early as the year books, Per Brian, J. 19. Edw. 4. 6;[o] and has been sanctioned down to the present times,[p] that every contract and engagement made with the enemy pending war, is utterly void. But to return—It was well

[m] *Supra*, § 2.

[n] 4 *Robinson*, 79.

[o] Cited in *Hool. Dig.* L. 1. c. 6. § 71.

[p] 13 *Vezey June.* 71.

known that long before the decision of the above case, doubts had existed as to the legality of such licenses, doubts which must soon have become known to the enemy; and as the policy of maintaining the supply continued the same, it was not extraordinary that the British government should give every encouragement to such shipments as its necessities required, by prohibiting its cruizers from the capture of vessels engaged in this trade. Under such circumstances, it was not incredible that a mere certificate of the landing of the outward cargo at Lisbon, signed by a person in whom it had confidence, a person (as the captors alleged) acting as a British commissary, should exempt the vessel and cargo from capture on the return voyage. He did not assert that any such general exemption had been authorized by any orders of the British government, but when the master and crew directly and positively denied any British license to have been used during the voyage, he could not feel himself at liberty to set aside their testimony upon mere suspicions, arising from facts which admitted of a fair interpretation in their favour. The evidence of enemy connexion was drawn exclusively from the certificate of the landing of the cargo, which it was said operated virtually as a license. For himself he could not see any very noxious quality in that certificate. Suppose it was known at Lisbon (and the fact must undoubtedly have been believed, or the present cargo would not have been shipped) that the British government would not molest American vessels returning with cargoes, if they could prove that they had landed outward cargoes of provisions at Lisbon, would there be any thing illegal in taking such certificate from a respectable merchant sanctioned by the American consul? He did not perceive the illegality. If the certificate were false in point of statement, he supposed that such an attempt to deceive the enemy's cruizers would not have been deemed unjustifiable. Why should its truth render it more so? The argument seemed to suppose that if the British government had by a general order exempted all American vessels from capture, bound to Lisbon with provisions, that the mere sailing on such a voyage would constitute an illegal subserviency to the interest of the enemy; and could not be distinguished from the case of sailing with a special British license. The same argument was used in the Julia for the opposite purpose, viz. to shew that both proceedings were legal and innocent; and the answer given in that case, he was still disposed to consider as sufficient to establish the fallacy of the reasoning. The trade to Lisbon on neutral or domestic account, was a commerce authorized by the laws of the United States, and growing out of that amity which subsisted with the Portuguese government. Provisions might be lawfully exported and sold there, and if thereby the British interests were aided, or the British policy enforced, it was a mere incidental effect which no more infected the transaction with hostility, than the trade of a Portuguese merchant with the United States would constitute a violation of his neutrality, merely by adding to the revenue of this country. If the mere chance that a trade may assist the resources or aid the enterprizes of an enemy through indirect channels, were a sufficient proof of hostile attachment and interest, he knew not how in the present state of the world, any neutral commerce could exist. While therefore the trade was by the laws left open to citizens of the United States, it could not acquire an illegal character unless carried on expressly for British account, or shipped under British contracts, or destined for British use—or voluntarily incorporated into British service by licenses which give the immunity of British navigation. In other words, where the trade is carried on *bona fide* on neutral or domestic account for general sale in a neutral market, the voyage is not contaminated, although the enemy obtain his supplies from the general stock of that market.(q)

(q) Per STORY, J. The Liverpool Packet. Circuit Court of the U. S. for Massachusetts district, 1813. M. S. *Vide supra*, Chapter IV. § 8. note i.

CHAPTER VI.

Of neutral property considered as a legal object of capture.

1. Not only is enemy's property, and that of persons resident or having possessions in the enemy's country, and property sailing under the flag and pass or license of the enemy, liable to capture; but neutral property is also, under certain circumstances, a legal object of capture and condemnation as prize of war.

2. It is the duty of neutrals to observe an exact impartiality between the belligerent parties, and to afford no assistance to either, to the prejudice of the other. *Pacem utrique paci quod medios deceat amicos; optent bello se non interponant.*[a] Their commerce with the belligerent powers is generally free and unrestrained by the war. But to this general freedom there are several exceptions. Among these is included the trade *with the enemy*,[b] in certain articles denominated contraband of war. The almost unanimous authority of elementary writers, of the ordinances of belligerent powers, and of treaties, agrees to enumerate among these, all warlike instruments, or materials by their own nature fit to be used in war. But beyond

[a] *Liv.* L. 35. c. 48.

[b] *Dunque la proibizione introdotta dal diritto convenzionale dell' Europa sul commercio dei generi detti di contrabbando di guerra non può cadere, che sul preciso trasporto di essi ai paesi nemici, non mai però sulla loro vendita imparziale nel territorio, o porti dei pacifici e neutrali; giacchè ivi, nè sono, nè possono chiarmarsi merci di contrabbando.* Azuni, Part 2, c. 2. § 3.

this enumeration, there is some difficulty in reconciling the different authorities, which are extremely discordant, and at variance with reason and justice. Grotius, in considering this subject, makes a distinction between those things that are useful for the purposes of war, those which are not so, and those which are susceptible of indiscriminate use in war and in peace. The first he agrees with all other writers in prohibiting neutrals from carrying to the enemy; as well as in permitting the second to be so carried; the third class he sometimes prohibits, and sometimes permits.(c) Vattel makes somewhat of a similar distinction; though he includes timber and naval stores among those articles that are useful for the purposes of war, and always contraband; whilst he considers provisions as such, only in certain circumstances, when there are hopes of reducing the enemy by famine.(d) But the learned and judicious Bynkershoek strenuously contends against admitting into the list of contraband articles, those things which are of promiscuous use. He considers the limitation of the right of intercepting them, to the case of necessity, and under the obligation of restitution or indemnification, as insufficient to justify the exercise of the right itself. He concludes that the materials out of which contraband goods are formed, are not themselves contraband; because if all the materials are prohibited, out of which something may be made that is fit for war, the catalogue of contraband goods will be immense, since there is hardly any kind of material, out of which something, at least, fit for war, may not be fabricated. The interdiction of so many articles, would amount to a total interdiction of commerce, and might as well be so expressed.(e) Indeed, when we once go beyond the line of warlike instruments or materials, *by themselves* fit to be

(c) *Grotius*, De J. B. ac P. L. 3. c. 1. § 5.

(d) *Vattel*, L. 3. c. 7. § 112.

(e) Q. J. P. L. 1. c. 10.

used in war, we know not where to stop until we come to the entire proscription of neutral trade. As to the distinction by which provisions are forbidden to be carried to a blockaded or besieged place of the enemy, it is evident that this prohibition is not on account of their contraband nature, but in consequence of the blockade or siege itself, which excludes all commercial intercourse whatsoever with the place.

3. As little foundation is there for the distinction raised by the British courts of prize, by which articles of promiscuous use are considered as contraband, when destined to a port of naval equipment;([f]) since the trade to such ports must be as free as any other, unless they are actually besieged or blockaded. Nor is the nature of the port material, as Sir William Scott has himself observed, since naval stores, if they are to be considered as contraband, are so without reference to the nature of the port, and equally, whether bound to a mercantile port only, or to a port of naval military equipment. The consequences of the supply may be nearly the same in either case. If sent to a mercantile port, they may then be applied to immediate use in the equipment of privateers, or they may be conveyed from the mercantile to the naval port, and there become subservient to every purpose to which they could have been applied if going directly to a port of naval equipment. ([g]) Another distinction which has been adopted by these courts, considers certain articles as contraband only so far as to give the belligerent power the right of taking them to his own use, paying the neutral a suitable indemnification; and it is said the practice of pre-emption has been substi-

([f]) 1 *Robinson*, 26. The Staadt Embden. *Ib.* 22. The Endraught. *Ib.* 189. The Jonge Margaretha. 3 *Robinson*, 108. The Neptunus. 4 *Robinson*, 68 The Edward 5 *Robinson*, 97 The Nostra Signora de Begona. 6 *Robinson*, 92. The Frau Margaretha, *Ib.* 93. The Zeldea Rust. *Ib.* 125. The Ranger.

([g]) 5 *Robinson*, 305. The Charlotte.

tuted, in certain cases, in the place of confiscation, by the modern law of nations.(h) But this practice appears to have been derived from the principle laid down by Grotius, which restrains the right of intercepting things of promiscuous use to the case of necessity, and under the obligation of restitution or indemnification. And unless it can be shown that by the ancient law of nations these articles were deemed contraband, this practice, so far from being regarded as a mitigation of the rights of war, can be considered in no other light than an unlawful innovation. Now as to bread corn and provisions, *commeatus*, they are not declared contraband by any writer of authority, except on certain occasions, when there are hopes of reducing the enemy by famine. And as to naval stores, Sir William Scott, laying down the doctrine of their liability to be seized as contraband in their own nature, when going to the enemy's use, under the modern law of nations, observes, that formerly, when the hostilities of Europe were less naval than they have since become, they were of a disputable nature, and perhaps continued so at the time of making the treaty between England and Sweden in 1661, or at least at the time of making the treaty which is the basis of it, that of 1656. And Valin, in his commentary, says, That in the war of 1700, pitch and tar were comprehended in the list of contraband, because the enemy treated them as such, except when found on board Swedish ships, these articles being of the growth and produce of their country. In the treaty of commerce concluded with the King of Denmark, the 23d August, 1742, pitch and tar were also declared contraband, together with rosin, sail cloth, hemp and cordage, masts and ship timber. Thus, as to this matter, there is no fault to be found with the conduct of the English, except where it contravenes particular treaties; for in law

(h) 1 *Robinson*, 237. The Sarah Christina. *Ib.* 237. The Maria. 2 *Robinson*, 174. The Haabet.

these things are now contraband, and have been so since the beginning of the present century, *which was not the case formerly*, as it appears by ancient treaties, and particularly that of St. Germain concluded with England in 1677; the fourth article of which expressly provides, that the trade in all these articles shall remain free, as well as in every thing necessary to human nourishment; with the exception of places besieged or blockaded. *Sur l'ordonnance, L. 3. tit. 9. Des Prises, art. 11.* It is difficult to discover how the above revolution in the law of contraband mentioned by Valin took place, since he has informed us, that pitch and tar were declared such in consequence of the enemies of France having set the example. And not only he more ancient French ordinances, but that of 1681, upon which he was commenting, had declared munitions of war only to be contraband. The same declaration is also confirmed by the regulation of 1744; and with the exceptions mentioned in the third chapter of this work, relative to the total prohibition of neutral commerce with the enemy, has ever since continued to be the law of France. It is true that the stipulations of the above treaty between France and Denmark, were afterwards adopted in the convention of the 4th July, 1780, explanatory of the treaty of 1670, between England and Denmark. But this was done in order to preserve the impartiality of Denmark in her neutral character, by conceding to England what she had already conceded to France, the other belligerent power. No inference can therefore be drawn from it of any change during the last century, by which naval stores, which had formerly been deemed exempt from seizure, were declared contraband of war.

By the treaty of navigation and commerce of Utrecht between Great Britain and France, renewed and confirmed by the treaty of Aix la Chapelle in 1748, by the treaty of Paris in 1763, by the treaty of Versailles in 1783, and by the commercial treaty between Great Britain and France of 1786, the list of contraband is confined to munitions of war; and naval stores, provisions, and all other goods which have not been worked into the form of any instrument or furniture for warlike use, by land or by sea, are expressly excluded from this list. So also by all the treaties between Great Britain and Russia, down to that of 1801, munitions of war only are considered as contraband. This last treaty is the more important as a precedent, because, as has been before shown, it is declaratory of the primitive and pre-existing law of nations, forming a permanent rule between the parties, not only to govern their conduct towards each other, but towards all the rest of the world; and this is peculiarly the case with the third section of the third article, relative to contraband, which is literally copied from the conventions of armed neutrality of 1780 and 1800.(i) By the eighteenth article of the Swedish ordinance of 1715, all goods applicable to the purposes of war, *(qui peuvent être employées pour la guerre)* are declared contraband. And by the treaties of 1656, 1661, 1664 and 1665, between Sweden and England, munitions of war only are declared contraband. We shall therefore seek in vain in the ordinances of belligerent powers, or in treaties, for any evidence of that change in the law of contraband, which is supposed to have taken place during the last century. Indeed if any change took place in this respect during the course of that century, it may with truth be affirmed to have more accurately defined the list of contraband, so as to confine it strictly to such articles as are of immediate use in war.

4. Upon the same principle which is applied to other munitions of war, ships built for war, and going to the enemy's country for sale, are subject to condemnation as contraband. But the application of this rule is restricted to cases, in which no doubt exists as to the character of the

(i) *Vide Supra*, c. 3. § 12.

vessels, or the purpose for which they are intended to be sold.([k])

5. There is reason to believe, that the ancient law of prize did not subject contraband articles to confiscation, but only gave the captor a right of appropriating them to his own use, paying the owner a reasonable compensation for the same. For the French ordinance of 1584, art. 69, permits the capture of neutral vessels laden with munitions of war, destined for the enemy, and the retention of the cargoes, *according to a reasonable estimation to be made thereof by the Admiral, or his Lieutenant.* To this right of pre-emption, if it formerly existed, has succeeded the penalty of confiscation, which is applied to contraband goods captured on their destination to the enemy. And as they are thus condemned *ex delictu*, the carrier master is not entitled to his freight upon them, as he is upon innocent articles which are condemned as enemy's property. For though the master has an implied lien upon the goods for his freight, and though they may be expressly bound for its payment, and it is a maxim of the civil law, that if the pledge is forfeited, the *jus pignoris* is not thereby consequently extinguished; yet, as Bynkershoek has justly observed, what is condemned is to be considered as if it had perished by inevitable accident, whereby the *jus pignoris* is extinguished.([l])

A question arises whether the vessel, on board of which the contraband articles are laden, and the other goods of her cargo are also subject to confiscation. This question is determined in the negative by the French Ordinance of August, 1681, L. 3. tit. 9. Des Prises, Art. 11, the Regulation of the 23d July, 1704, and of the 21st October, 1744.

([k]) 5 *Robinson*, 325. The Richmond. *Ib.* Additional Notes, No. I.

([l]) Q. J. P. L. 1. c. 10. 1 *Robinson*, 91. The Ringende Jacob. *Ib.* 242. The Sarah Christina. *Ib.* 288. The Mercurius. 4 *Robinson*, 200. The Oster Risoer.

The regulation of the 26th July, 1778, provides that if three fourths in value of the cargo consists of contraband articles the remainder of the cargo and the vessel shall be included in the confiscation. The authority of other ordinances and treaties generally concurs in subjecting to confiscation the contraband articles. As to the *vessel*, Bynkershoek distinguishes whether she belongs to the master himself, or to others. But this circumstance does not appear to afford any just foundation for a distinction, since by the municipal law the master is the agent of the owners in respect to the management and employment of the vessel. Nor is his further distinction, whether the master knew that the contraband goods had been shipped on board or was ignorant of it, any better founded; since, as Bynkershoek has himself observed, according to the present usage the master is in the habit of signing bills of lading of the merchandize shipped on board his vessel, and as the revenue laws of all countries presume the master to be conusant of what goods are laden on board his vessel. As to the *goods*, he also makes the distinction whether all the goods belong to one and the same owner or to several. If to one and the same owner, he thinks the whole may be justly confiscated, as by the Roman law in revenue cases if any one carries at the same time lawful and unlawful merchandize, and declares the one and conceals the other, both are confiscated on account of the fraud of the carrier, as the commentators on the title of the Digest *De Publicanis et Vectigalibus* have collected from the text of that law itself, and from the third law of the code *De Nautico Fœnore.*(m) This last distinction is better founded, and is followed in practice both as to the vessel and the goods. Thus where the ship and the cargo do not belong to one and the same person, the carriage of contraband under the frau-

(m) *Omnino distinguendum putem an licitæ et illicitæ merces ad eundem dominum pertineant, an ad diversos; si ad eundem omnes recte publicabuntur, ob continentiam delicti.* Q. J. P. L. 1. c. 12.

dulent circumstances of false papers or false destination will work a condemnation of the ship as well as the cargo.(n) The same effect is likewise produced by the carriage of contraband articles in a ship, the owner of which is bound, by the express obligation of the treaties subsisting between his own country and the belligerent state, to refrain from carrying such articles to the enemy. In such a case, the ship throws off her neutral character, and is liable to be treated at once as an enemy's vessel, and as a violator of the solemn compacts of the country to which she belongs.(o) Excepting in these instances, the remainder of the cargo and the ship, unless they belong to the owner of the contraband articles, are not involved in the confiscation of the latter. But where the ship and the innocent articles of the cargo belong to the owner of the contraband they are all involved in the same penalty.(p)

7. This penalty has lately been attempted to be extended to the return voyage by the British courts of prize in cases where contraband had been carried outward with false papers. But it is evident that this innovation is not founded upon principle ; for in order to sustain the penalty there must be a *delictum* at the moment of seizure. To subject the property to confiscation whilst the offence no longer continues, would be to extend it indefinitely, not only to the return voyage, but to all future voyages of the same vessel, which could never be purified from the contagion communicated by the contraband articles. From the moment of quitting port, indeed, the offence is complete, and it is not necessary to wait, till the goods are actually endeavouring to enter the enemy's port ; but beyond that, if the

(n) 3 *Robinson*, 217. The Franklin. 4 *Robinson*, 69. The Edward. 6 *Robinson*, 125. The Ranger.

(o) 3 *Robinson*, 295. The Neutralitet.

(p) 1 *Robinson*, 31. The Staadt Embden *ib.* 238. The Mercurius, 288. In Notis. *ib.* 330. The Jonge Tobias.

goods are not taken *in delicto*, and in the actual prosecution of such a voyage, the penalty is not held to attach.(q)

8. Of the same nature with the carrying of contraband is the transportation of military persons or despatches in the service of the enemy.

9. A neutral vessel which is used as a transport for the enemy's forces is subject to confiscation. Nor will the fact of her being impressed by duress and violence into that service exempt her from this penalty. The master cannot be permitted to aver that he was an involuntary agent in the matter. Were an act of force exercised by one belligerent power on a neutral ship or person, to be deemed a sufficient justification for any act done by him, contrary to the known duties of the neutral character, there would be an end of any prohibition under the law of nations to carry contraband, or to engage in any other hostile act. If any loss is sustained in such a service, the neutral yielding to such demands, must seek redress against that government which has imposed the restraint upon him. And the forfeiture is not extinguished, until the vessel has receded from, and shaken off, her belligerent character. So long as she remains under the command and control of the enemy, she continues liable to capture and condemnation.(r)

And where a neutral vessel was taken, with a few goods of small bulk and little value, and a number of officers and mariners in the military service of the enemy on board, she was held subject to condemnation, notwithstanding her partial commercial character. There is no precise technical definition of transport vessels, more than this, that they are vessels hired by the government to do such acts as shall be imposed upon them, in the military service of the country; and it is by no means essential to the character of a transport, that she should be chartered in a particular

(q) 3 *Robinson*, 167. The Imina.

(r) 4 *Robinson*, 256. The Carolina.

manner, or in any particular form of words, or by any particular department of the government. The form is of no importance. The substance of the thing is, whether they are vessels hired by the agents of the government, for the purpose of conveying soldiers in the service of the state? That is the substance; and it signifies nothing, whether the men so conveyed, are to be put into action on an immediate expedition or not. The mere shifting of drafts in detachments, is an ordinary employment of transport vessels, and it is a distinction totally unimportant, whether this or that case may be connected with the immediate active service of the enemy. In removing forces from distant settlements, there may be an intention of immediate action: but still the general importance of having troops conveyed to places where it is convenient that they should be collected, either for present, or future use, is what constitutes the object and employment of transport vessels. Different is the character and the case of a vessel carrying only a few individual *invalid* soldiers, or discharged sailors, taken on board by chance, and at their own charge.(8) What is the number of military persons that shall affect the vessel with confiscation, it may be difficult to define. In the above case there were many; but number alone is an insignificant circumstance in the considerations, on which the principle of law on this subject is built; since fewer persons of high quality and character may be of more importance than a much greater number of persons of lower condition. To carry a veteran general, under some circumstances, might be a much more noxious act than the conveyance of a whole regiment. The consequences of such assistance are greater, and therefore it is what the belligerent state has a stronger right to prevent and punish. Nor is it material whether the master be ignorant of the character of the service on which he is engaged, nor necessary that there should be

(8) 6 *Robinson*, 420. The Friendship, Collard.

some proof of delinquency in him, or his owner, in order to support the penalty. It is sufficient if there has been an injury arising to the belligerent state from the employment in which the vessel is found. If imposition be practised, it operates as force; and if redress is to be sought against any person, it must be against those, who have, by means either of compulsion or deceit, exposed the property to danger; otherwise such opportunities of conveyance would be constantly used, and it would be almost impossible, in the greater number of cases, to prove the knowledge and privity of the immediate offender.(t)

10. The fraudulent carrying the despatches of the enemy will also subject the neutral vessel in which they are transported, to capture and confiscation. The consequence of such a service is indefinite, infinitely beyond the effect of any contraband that can be conveyed. The carrying of two or three cargoes of military stores is necessarily an assistance of a limited nature; but in the transmission of despatches, may be conveyed the entire plan of a campaign, that may defeat all the projects of the other belligerent in that quarter of the world. It is true, as it has been said, that *one ball* might take off a Charles the XIIth, and might produce the most disastrous effects in a campaign; but that is a consequence so remote and accidental, that in the contemplation of human events it is a sort of evanescent quantity of which no account is taken; and the practice has been *accordingly*, that it is in considerable quantities only that the offence of contraband is contemplated. The case of despatches is very different; it is impossible to limit a letter to so small a size, as not to be capable of producing the most important consequences in the operations of the enemy: it is a service therefore, which, in whatever degree it exists, can only be considered in one character, as an act of the most noxious and hostile nature. The

(t) 6 *Robinson*, 430. The Orozembo.

offence of fraudulently carrying despatches in the service of the enemy, being then greater than that of carrying contraband under any circumstances, it becomes absolutely necessary, as well as just, to resort to some other penalty than that inflicted in cases of contraband. The confiscation of the noxious article, which constitutes the penalty in contraband, where the vessel and cargo do not belong to one and the same person, would be ridiculous when applied to *despatches.* There would be *no* freight dependent on their transportation, and therefore this penalty could not, in the nature of things, be applied. The vehicle in which they were carried must therefore be confiscated.[u]

But carrying the despatches of an ambassador or other public minister of the enemy, resident in a neutral country, is an exception to the reasoning on which the above general rule is founded. They are despatches from persons who are, in a peculiar manner, the favourite objects of the protection of the law of nations, residing in the neutral country for the purpose of preserving the relations of amity between that state and their own government. On this ground a very material distinction arises, with respect to the right of furnishing the conveyance. The neutral country has a right to preserve its relations with the enemy, and you are not at liberty to conclude, that any communication between them can partake, in any degree, of the nature of hostility against you. The enemy may have his hostile projects to be attempted in the neutral state; but your reliance is on the integrity of that state, that it will not favour nor participate in such designs, but as far as its own councils and actions are concerned, will oppose them. And if there should be private reason to suppose that this confidence in the good faith of the neutral state has a doubtful foundation, that is matter for the caution of the government, to be counteracted by just measures of preventive

(u) 6 *Robinson*, 440. The Atalanta.

policy, but is no ground on which a prize court can pronounce that the neutral master has violated his duty by bearing despatches, which, as far as he can know, may be presumed to be of an innocent nature, and in the maintenance of a pacific connexion. The limits assigned to the operations of war against ambassadors, by writers on public law, are, that the belligerent may exercise his right of war against them, wherever the character of hostility exists: he may stop the ambassador of his enemy on his passage; but when he has arrived in the neutral country, and taken on himself the functions of his office, and has been admitted in his representative character, he becomes a sort of *middle*-man, entitled to peculiar privileges as set apart for the protection of the relations of amity and peace, in maintaining which all nations are, in some degree, interested. If it be argued, that he retains his national character unmixed, and that even his residence is considered as a residence in his own country; it is answered, that this is a fiction of law, invented for his further protection only, and as such a fiction, it is not to be extended beyond the reasoning on which it depends. It was intended as a *privilege;* and cannot be urged to his disadvantage. Could it be said that he would on that principle, be subject to any of the *rights of war* in a neutral territory? Certainly not: he is there for the purpose of carrying on the relations of peace and amity, for the interest of his own country primarily, but, at the same time, for the furtherance and protection of the interests, which the neutral country also has in the continuance of those relations. It is to be considered also, with regard to this question what may be due to the convenience of the neutral state; for its interests may require that the intercourse of correspondence with the enemy's country should not be altogether interdicted. It might be thought to amount almost to a declaration, that an ambassador from the enemy shall not reside in the neutral state, if he is declared to be debarred from the only means of communicating with his own. For to what useful purpose can he reside there, without the opportunities of such a communication? It is too much to say that all the business of the two states shall be transacted by the minister of the neutral state, resident in the enemy's country. The practice of nations has allowed to neutral states the privilege of receiving ministers from the belligerent powers, and the use and convenience of an immediate negociation with them. This exception may be liable to great abuses, and so perhaps will any rule that can be laid down on this subject:—

——Mille adde catenas;
Effugiet tamen hæc—

Opportunities of conveying intelligence may always exist in some form or other. (v)

And it is the *general rule*, that the master is not at liberty to aver his ignorance of the nature of the papers taken on board, but that if he is made the victim of imposition practised on him by his private agent, or by the government of the enemy, he must seek for his redress against them. It is considered as a proof of fraud, if dispatches, being on board, are not produced voluntarily in the first instance.(w) But where the commencement of the voyage is in a neutral country, and it is to terminate at a neutral port, or at a port to which, though not neutral, an open trade is allowed, in such a case there is less to excite his vigilance, and therefore it may be proper to make some allowance for any imposition that may be practised upon him: and where the despatches come to the master among a variety of other letters from private persons where they are concealed in an envelope, addressed to a private person; and were taken on board in a neutral country—these are

(v) 6 *Robinson*, 461. The Caroline. 1 *Edwards*, 224. The Madison.

(w) 6 *Robinson*, 461. *In Notis.*

circumstances which would induce a court of prize to consider the case as excepted from the general rule.(x)

11. Another exception to the general freedom of neutral commerce in time of war is to be found in the trade to blockaded ports.

12. The right of blockade has been, at various periods of history, abused by belligerent powers to the total prohibition of neutral commerce with the enemy, or for the purpose of obtaining a commercial monopoly for the private advantage of the state imposing the blockade. Thus by the Convention concluded at London on the 22d August, 1689, between England and Holland, the contracting parties state in the preamble.—That having declared war against the Most Christian king, it behoves them to do as much damage as possible to the common enemy, in order to bring him to agree to such conditions as may restore the repose of Christendom: and that, for this end it was necessary to interrupt all trade and commerce with the subjects of the said king; and that, to effect this, they had ordered their fleets to block up all the ports and havens of France: and in the second and third articles of the same convention it is agreed, that they would take any vessel, whatever king or state it may belong to, that shall be found sailing into or out of the ports of France, and condemn both vessel and merchandize as legal prize; and that this resolution should be notified to all neutral states.(y) And by the several conventions and treaties of the 25th March, 1793, between Great Britain and Russia; of the 25th May, 1793, between Great Britain and Spain; of the 14th July, 1793, between Great Britain and Prussia; and of the 30th August, 1793, between Great Britain and Austria, it was stipulated by the several contracting parties, that they would unite their efforts to prevent other powers, not implicated in

(x) 1 *Edwards*, 228. The Rapid.

(y) *Lord Liverpool's Discourse*, 36.

the war, from giving, on this occasion of common concern to every civilized state, any protection whatever, directly or indirectly, in consequence of their neutrality, to the commerce or property of the French, on the sea, or in the ports of France. So also by the declaration of the British government of the 16th May, 1806, the coasts, rivers and ports from the river Elbe to Brest inclusive, were declared in a state of blockade, excepting that the blockade should not extend to prevent neutral vessels, laden with goods not being the property of his Britannic Majesty's enemies, and not being contraband of war, from approaching the said coasts, and entering into and sailing from said rivers and ports, (saving the coast, rivers and ports from Ostend to the river Seine, already then in a state of strict and rigorous blockade, and which were to be considered as so continued) provided the said vessels so approaching and entering (save as aforesaid) should not have been laden at any port belonging to or in the possession of his said Majesty's enemies; and that the said vessels should not be destined to any port belonging to or in the possession of his said Majesty's enemies, nor have previously broken the blockade. And by the British Order in Council of the 7th January, 1807, it was declared, that no vessel should be permitted to trade from one port to another, both which ports should belong to or be in the possession of France or her allies, or should be so far under her control as that British vessels might not freely trade thereat. And by the British Orders in Council of the 11th November, 1807, it was declared, that all ports and places of France and her allies, or of any other country at war with his Britannic Majesty, and all other ports or places in Europe, from which, although not at war with his said Majesty, the British flag was excluded, and all ports or places in the colonies belonging to his said Majesty's enemies, should be subjected to the same restrictions in trade and navigation as if actually blockaded in the most strict and rigorous manner; excepting the direct trade between the countries not included in the order and said colonies, and also excepting any vessel and cargo belonging to any country not at war with his said Majesty, clearing out under certain regulations, and proceeding direct from some British port, or from Gibraltar or Malta, or from any port belonging to the allies of his said Majesty, to the port specified in her clearance, or coming from any port or place in Europe included in the order, and destined to some port or place in Europe belonging to his said Majesty, and which should be on her voyage direct thereto. And also by the French Decree, issued at Berlin on the 21st November, 1806, the British islands were declared in a state of blockade, and all commerce and correspondence with them were prohibited. And by the Decree issued at Milan, on the 17th December, 1807, the same declaration was renewed, and every vessel of whatsoever nation, or whatsoever the nature of its cargo might be, proceeding from the ports of England, or her colonies, or the countries occupied by English troops, and going to England, or her colonies, or countries occupied by English troops, was declared good and lawful prize.

But such blockades are wholly illegal and void. Nor can they be justified upon the principle of retaliation; for retaliation can only be exercised upon the party who has committed the injury, and not against a friendly and neutral power. *Retorsio non est nisi adversus eum, qui ipse damni quid dedit, ac deindè patitur, non verò adversus communem amicum.*(1) And as we have before observed, in the words of Sir William Scott, the true mode of correcting the irregular practice of a nation is by protesting against it, and by inducing that country to reform it; it is monstrous to suppose, that because one country has been guilty of an irregularity, every other country is let loose

(1) *Bynkershoek*, Q. J. P. L. 1. c. 4.

from the law of nations, and is at liberty to assume as much as it thinks fit.[a]

13. By the law of nations, the denomination of a blockaded port is given only to that where there is, by the disposition of the power which attacks, or invests it, with ships stationary, or sufficiently near to occasion an evident danger in entering.[b] And even where there is such an actual investment of the port, if any of the blockading ships should not have enforced it, the blockade is so far relaxed. If the blockade has not been duly carried into effect by the ships stationed on the spot for the purpose, it is impossible for a court of prize to enforce it.[c]

To a violation of blockade thus legally constituted and continued, two things are necessary—1st, The knowledge of the party; and, 2dly, Some act of violation, either by going in, or by coming out with a cargo, after the commencement of the blockade.[d]

14. As a proclamation, or general public notification, is not of itself sufficient to constitute a legal blockade, so neither can a knowledge of the existence of such a blockade be imputed to the party *merely* in consequence of such a proclamation or notification. Not only must an actual blockade exist, but a knowledge of it must be brought home to the party, in order to shew that it has been violated.[e] As on the one hand, a declaration of blockade which is not supported by the fact cannot be deemed legally to exist, so on the other hand, the fact, duly notified to the party on the spot, is of itself sufficient to affect him with a knowledge of it; for public notifications between governments can be

(a) 1 *Robinson*, 142. The Flad Oyen.

(b) *Vide* Appendix, No. III.

(c) 3 *Robinson*, 147. The Jaffrow Maria Schroeder.

(d) 1 *Robinson*, 93. The Betsey.

(e) 1 *Robinson*, 93. The Betsey.

meant only for the information of individuals: but if the individual is personally informed, that purpose is still better obtained than by a public declaration.(f) Where the vessel sails from a country lying sufficiently near to the blockaded port to have constant information of the state of the blockade, whether it is continued or is relaxed, no special notice is necessary; for the public declaration in this case implies notice to the party *after sufficient time has elapsed to receive the declaration at the port from whence the vessel sails.*(g) But where the country lies at such a distance that the inhabitants cannot have this constant information, they may send their vessels conjecturedly, upon the expectation of finding the blockade broken up, after it has existed for a considerable time. In this case, the party has a right to make a fair enquiry whether the blockade be determined or not, and consequently cannot be involved in the penalties affixed to a violation of it, unless upon such enquiry he receives notice of the existence of the blockade.(h)

Where the blockade has been declared by a public notification from the government of the belligerent country to neutral governments, it is the duty of the belligerent country, which has thus declared the existence of the blockade, to notify, in the same way, and immediately, the discontinuance of it: to suffer the fact to cease, and to apply the notification again, at a distant time, would be a fraud on neutral nations. In such a case the blockade must be supposed to exist until it has been publicly repealed.(i) For it is to be presumed, that the notification will be formally revoked, and that due notice will be given of

(f) 1 *Robinson*, 83. The Mercurius.

(g) 2 *Robinson*, 131. The Jonge Petronella. *Ib.* 298. The Calypso. 3 *Robinson*, 173. The Neptunus.

(h) 1 *Robinson*, 332. The Betsey, Goodhue.

(i) 1 *Robinson*, 170. The Neptunus.

it: till that is done, the blockaded port is to be considered as closed up; and from the moment of quitting port to sail on such a destination, provided the country in which the port is situated be sufficiently near the blockaded port to have constant information of the state of the blockade, the offence of violating the blockade is complete. It is different in a blockade existing *de facto* only; there no presumption arises as to the continuance, and the ignorance of the party may be admitted as an excuse for sailing on a doubtful and provisional destination. The effect of such a notification to neutral governments, is to include all the individuals of that nation, after a sufficient time has elapsed to communicate the information to them. After that period, a neutral master cannot be heard to aver against a notification of blockade, that he was ignorant of it. If he is really ignorant of it, it may be a subject of representation to his own government, and may raise a claim of compensation from them, but it can be no plea in a prize court of the belligerent.[k] But the penal consequences of a notification given to one power, will not affect the subjects of another state from the same time, and in the same manner, as it would affect the subjects of those states to whom it was directly made. To say that it does not affect at any time, would be going too far; because, if a notification is made to the principal neutral states, a time would come when it would affect the rest; not *proprio vigore*, or by virtue of the direct act, but in the way of evidence. The knowledge of it would spread, and after the lapse of a reasonable time, must be considered as a reasonable ground of evidence.[l]

The fact of clearing out for a blockaded port, is in itself innocent, unless it be accompanied with knowledge of the blockade. The right to treat the vessel as an enemy is de-

(k) 2 *Robinson*, 110. The Neptunus.

(l) 2 *Robinson*, 111. The Adelaide. *In Notis.*

clared by Vattel, b. 3. § 177. to be founded on the *attempt* to enter; and certainly this attempt must be made by a person knowing the fact. The law of nations does not admit of the condemnation of the neutral vessel for the intention to enter a blockaded port, unconnected with any fact. Sailing for a blockaded port, knowing it to be blockaded, was in the above cases construed into an attempt to enter that port, and was therefore adjudged a breach of blockade, from the departure of the vessel. It may be observed, that in these cases the fact of sailing is coupled with the intention, and the condemnation is founded on an actual breach of blockade.(m) But in the case of the blockade of Martinique and Guadaloupe, in 1804, the British government sent orders to its naval commanders and judges of the vice admiralty courts in the West Indies, not to consider any blockade of these islands as existing, unless in respect of particular ports which may be actually invested, and then not to capture vessels bound to such ports, unless they shall previously have been warned not to enter them.(n) The import of these orders is, that a vessel cannot be placed in the situation of one having a notice of the blockade, until she is warned off. It gives her a right to enquire of the blockading squadron, if she has not previously received this warning from one capable of giving it, and consequently, dispenses with her making that enquiry elsewhere. While this order was in force, a neutral vessel might lawfully sail for a blockaded port, knowing it to be blockaded, and being found sailing towards such port, would not constitute an attempt to break the blockade, until she should be warned off.(o)

The municipal laws of certain countries have laid down very precise rules for determining questions of presump-

(m) Fitzsimmons vs. Newport Ins. Comp. 4 *Cranch*, 199.

(n) *Vide* Appendix, No. III.

(o) Marine Ins. Comp. vs. Woods. 6 *Cranch*, 49.

tive notice. Thus in cases of insurance made on property at a remote distance, lost or not lost, where the legality of the contract depends upon the supposition that no intelligence had been received of any accident, at the time when the insurance was made, they determine the question by a minute rate of travelling. Thus the *Consolato del Mare* reckons an hour as a league. So also the French *Code de Commerce* reckons an hour of time as equivalent to a league and a half of distance. Art. 336. But it considers this rate as *prima facie* evidence only, and does not exclude a resort to other proofs of the same fact. Our own municipal law determines this presumption by the particular circumstances of each case, taking into consideration not merely the distance, but referring also to the accidents by which the intercourse is likely to be affected, and information conveyed with more or less rapidity. So also in the law of blockades, the question as to the length of time proper to be allowed for notice is determined upon equitable considerations. It is not to be taken merely on a calculation of the distance; but with reference also to the accidents by which the general intercourse, even after the allowance of distance, is liable to be retarded.(p)

Where an enemy's port was declared in a state of blockade by notification, and at the same time when notification was issued, news arrived that the blockading squadron had been driven off by the superior force of the enemy, the blockade was held to be null and defective, from the beginning, in the main circumstance that is required as essentially necessary to give it legal operation, and that it would be highly unjust to hold neutral vessels to the observance of a notification, so accompanied by a circumstance that defeated its effect. This case was, therefore, considered as altogether independent of the presumption arising from notifications in other instances; the notification being de-

(p) 3 *Robinson*, 281. The Adelaide. *Ib.* 324. The Hurtige Hane.

feated, it must have been shewn that the actual blockade was again resumed, and the vessel would have been entitled to a warning, if any such blockade had existed when she arrived off the port. The mere act of sailing for the port under the dubious state of the actual blockade at the time was deemed insufficient to fix upon the vessel the penalty of breaking the blockade.(q)

In the above case, a question was raised, whether the notification which had issued was not still operative. But the court was of the opinion, that it could not be so considered, and that a neutral power was not obliged, under such circumstances to presume the continuance of a blockade, nor to act upon a supposition that the blockade would be resumed by any other competent force. It was argued that neutrals were bound to act on such presumptions, that when a blockading squadron is driven off by the superior force of the enemy, they are bound to presume that it will return, and that there is no discontinuance of the blockade. To which it was answered, that when a squadron is thus driven off, a new course of events arises, which may tend to a very different disposition of the blockading force. In such a case, the neutral merchant is not bound to foresee or to conjecture that the blockade will be resumed; and therefore, if it is to be renewed, it must proceed *de novo*, by the usual course, and without reference to the former state of facts, which had been thus effectually interrupted. On this principle it was that the former blockade was held in the above case to have become extinct. But in a subsequent case, where it was suggested that the blockading squadron had returned to its former station off the port, in order to renew the blockade, a question arose whether there had been that notoriety of the fact, arising from the operation of time or from other circumstances, which must be taken to have brought the existence of the blockade to the

(q) 6 *Robinson*, 62. The Triheten.

knowledge of the parties. Among other modes of resolving this question, a prevailing consideration would have been the length of time, in proportion to the distance of the country from which the vessel sailed. But as nothing more came out in evidence than that the squadron appeared off the port on a certain day, it was held that this would not restore a blockade which had been thus effectually raised, but that it should be renewed again, by notification, before foreign nations could be affected with an obligation of observing it. The squadron might return off the port with very different and new intentions. It might arrive there as a fleet of observation merely, or for the purpose of a qualified blockade only. On the other hand, the commander might attempt to connect the two blockades together, but this is what could not be done; and in order to revive the former blockade, the same form of communication must have been observed *de novo* that is necessary to establish an original blockade.([r])

15. Besides the knowledge of the party, some act of violation is essential to a breach of blockade, as either by going in or by coming out of the port with a cargo laden after the commencement of the blockade.([s])

Thus by the edict of the States General of Holland, of 1630, relative to the blockade of the ports of Flanders, it was ordered, that the vessels and goods of neutrals which should be found going in or coming out of the said ports, or being so near thereto as to shew beyond a doubt that they were endeavouring to run into them; or if from the documents on board, it should appear that they were bound

([r]) 6 *Robinson*, 112. The Hoffnung. Wherever the question has arisen in our courts of municipal law in cases of insurance respecting the legality of a blockade, it has been determined that a mere notification, without a blockade in fact, amounts to nothing. 2 *Caines*, 11. Williams v. Smith. *Caines' Cases in Error*, 7. Voss v. the United Insurance Company.

([s]) 1 *Robinson*, 93. The Betsey.

to the said ports, although they should be found at a distance from them, should be confiscated; unless they should, voluntarily, before coming in sight of or being chased by the Dutch ships of war, change their intention, while the thing was yet undone, and alter their course. Bynkershoek, in commenting upon this part of the decree, supports the reasonableness of the provision which subjects vessels to the penalty of confiscation *found so near to the blockaded ports as to shew beyond a doubt that they were endeavouring to run into them*, upon the ground of legal presumption, with the exception of extreme and well proved necessity only. Still more reasonable is the infliction of this penalty, where the intention expressly appears by the papers found on board. The third article of the same edict also subjects to confiscation such vessels and their cargoes as should come out of said ports, not having been forced into them by stress of weather, although they should be captured at a distance from them, unless they had, after leaving the enemy's port, performed their voyage to a port of their own country, or to some other neutral or free port, in which case they should be exempt from condemnation; but if in coming out of the said ports of Flanders they should be pursued by the Dutch ships of war, chased into another port, such as their own, or that of their destination, and found on the high sea coming out of *such* port, in that case they might be captured and condemned. Bynkershoek considers this provision as distinguishing the case of a vessel having broken the blockade, and terminated her voyage by proceeding voluntarily to her destined port, and that of a vessel chased and compelled to take refuge, which latter might still be captured after leaving the port in which she had taken refuge. And in conformity with these principles is the modern law and practice.[t]

(t) 1 *Robinson*, 154. The Columbia. 2 *Robinson*, 128. The Welvaart Van Pillaw.

With respect to violating a blockade by coming out with a cargo, the time of shipment is very material, for although it might be hard to refuse a neutral liberty to retire with a cargo already laden, and by that act already become neutral property; yet, after the commencement of a blockade, a neutral cannot be allowed to interpose in any way to assist the exportation of the property of the enemy. After the commencement of a blockade, a neutral is no longer at liberty to make any purchase in that port.(u) A neutral ship departing, can only take away a cargo *bona fide* purchased and delivered before the commencement of the blockade: if she afterwards take on board a cargo, it is a violation of the blockade. But where a ship was transferred from one neutral merchant to another in a blockaded port, and sailed out in ballast, she was determined not to have violated the blockade.(v) So where goods were sent into the blockaded port before the commencement of the blockade, but reshipped by order of the neutral proprietor, as found unsaleable, during the blockade, they were held entitled to restitution. For the same rule which permits neutrals to withdraw their vessels from a blockaded port, extends also, with equal justice, to merchandize sent in before the blockade, and withdrawn *bona fide* by the neutral proprietor.(w) Where a ship which had been purchased by a neutral of the enemy in a blockaded port, and sailed on a voyage to the neutral country, had been driven by stress of weather into a port of the belligerent state, where she was seized, she was held liable to condemnation under the general rule. That the vessel had been purchased out of the proceeds of the cargo of another vessel, was considered as an unavailable circumstance on a question of blockade. If the ship has been *purchased* in a blockaded port, *that* alone is the

(u) 1 *Robinson*, 93. The Betsey.

(v) 1 *Robinson*, 150. The Vrouw Judith.

(w) 4 *Robinson*, 89. The Potsdam.

illegal act, and it is perfectly immaterial out of what funds the purchase was effected. Another distinction taken was, that the vessel had terminated her voyage, and therefore that the penalty would no longer attach. But this was also overruled, because the port into which she had been driven was not represented as forming any part of her original destination. It was therefore impossible to consider this accident as any discontinuance of the voyage, or as a defeasance of the penalty which has been incurred.(x)

And where the vessel was captured on a voyage to the blockaded port, in ballast, she having sailed for the purpose of bringing away goods which had become the property of merchants in the neutral country before the date of the blockade, she was held liable to condemnation. The rule of blockade permits an *egress* to ships innocently in the port before the restriction was imposed, and even with cargoes, if previously laden; but in the case of *ingress*, there is not the same reason for indulgence, there can be no surprize upon the parties, and therefore nothing short of a physical necessity is admitted as an adequate excuse for making the attempt of entry. Generally where a neutral ship is proceeding to a blockaded port, it must be supposed that she is going there for the purposes of trade.—If she goes in ballast, it cannot be with the intention of being laid up for an indefinite time, in a foreign port, until the blockade is raised. It is a presumption which a court of prize, acting on reasonable principles, is bound to entertain and apply, that she has no other errand there than to keep alive that commercial intercourse with the interdicted port which it is the object of the blockade to prevent.(y)

A maritime blockade is not violated by sending goods to the blockaded port, or by bringing them from the same, through the interior canal navigation or land carriage of

(x) 4 *Robinson. In Notis.* The Juffrow Maria Shroeder.

(y) 6 *Robinson*, 61. The General Hamilton.

the country. A blockade may be of different descriptions. A mere maritime blockade, effected by a force operating only at sea, can have no operation upon the interior communications of the port. The legal blockade can extend no farther than the actual blockade can be applied. If the place be not invested on the land side, its interior communications with other ports cannot be cut off. If the blockade be rendered imperfect by this rule of construction, it must be ascribed to the physical impossibility of the measure, by which the extent of its legal pretensions is unavoidably limited.(z) But goods shipped in a river, having been previously sent in lighters along the coast from the blockaded port, and under charter party with the ship proceeding also from the blockaded port in ballast to take them on board, were held liable to confiscation. This case is very different from those above mentioned, because there the communication had been by inland navigation, which was in no manner, and in no part of it, subject to the blockade.(a)

6. The appropriate penalty for a breach of blockade is the confiscation of the vessel and cargo.(b) But where the owners of the cargo are not at the same time owners of the vessel, the confiscation cannot be extended to the cargo, unless its owners were, or might have been, conusant of the blockade, before they shipped their goods. Although the master is the agent of the owners of the vessel, and can bind him by his contracts or misconduct, he is not the agent of the owners of the cargo, unless expressly so constituted by them. In cases of insurance, and in revenue cases, where by the municipal law, the act of the master will affect the cargo, it is to be observed that the ground upon which they stand is wholly different. In the former it is in vir-

(z) 1 *Edwards*, 32. The Comet.

(a) 3 *Robinson*, 297. The Ocean. 4 *Robinson*, 65. The Stert.

(b) *Bynkershoek*, 2. J. P. L. 1. c. 11.

tue of an express contract which governs the whole case: and in revenue cases it proceeds from positive laws and the necessary strictness of all fiscal regulations.(c) And where goods are shipped in pursuance of orders from a distant country, if it appears that they were given after the time, when the notification of blockade could by a fair possibility be supposed to have been known to a person giving the orders, he would be bound directly by his own act; or, if the orders were sent *previous* to the notification, two questions might arise; 1st, whether sufficient time had intervened since the notification, to have given him an opportunity of counter-ordering the shipment; for if so, he would be legally answerable for the consequences of his own negligence; or, 2dly, if sufficient time had not intervened, whether, though personally free from all imputation of offence, he might not be bound by that powerful general principle of the municipal law, which holds the employer responsible for the acts of his agent, and thus be held by those of the shipping merchant in the blockaded port. It would perhaps be holding the party too rigorously to the strict principle of the law, to say, that it is his duty to write even with a hope, and under the chance of countermanding the order *in time,* because, in some cases, the party might naturally conceive from the time which had elapsed, that the order had been already executed, and that if he had written to countermand it, the letter would not be received till the shipment had been actually made. The abstract rule as to the principal being bound by the acts of his agent is undoubtedly just; but the agents of foreign merchants in the enemy's country, and in a blockaded port, do not stand in the same situation as other agents; they have not only a distinct, but even an opposite interest from that of their principals, to fulfil the commission at all risks as rapidly as

(c) 1 *Robinson,* 80. The Mercurius. *Ib.* 154. The Columbia.

possible, for their own private advantage, and for the public interest of their country, which at such a time must be under particular pressure as to the exportation of its produce.(d)

If it be objected, that to exempt the cargo from responsibility for the acts of the master will open the door to fraud, in allowing neutrals to trade to blockaded ports with impunity, by throwing the blame upon the carrier master; it is answered, that if such an artifice could be proved, it would establish the *mens rea* in the neutral merchant which would expose his property to confiscation, and it would at the same time be sufficient to cause the master to be considered in the character of agent, as well for the cargo as for the ship. Thus where a ship had been condemned for deviating into a blockaded port, under the fraudulent pretence of being in want of provisions, the cargo was likewise included in the condemnation, the inference being that she was going in with an intention of disposing of the cargo. It would be impossible to maintain blockades which are directed more against the cargo, than against ships, if a court of prize did not draw the inference, that a ship going in fraudulently, is going in the service of the cargo, with the knowledge, and by the direction of the owner. If any inconvenience arise to the owners of the cargo, from this necessary conclusion, the owners of the vessel or the master, are the persons to whom they must look for indemnification. (e) And where also the vessel had been condemned for a fraudulent deviation under the pretence of a mistake in navigation, it was inferred that the deviation had been resorted to in the service of the cargo. It was held that in other blockade cases, where excuses had been set up for want of water and provisions, or from other occasions, and

(d) 3 *Robinson*, 173. The Neptunus.

(e) 1 *Robinson*, 85. The Mercurius.

these excuses had been pronounced to be not real, a presumption *necessarily* arose that it was for the delivery of the cargo that such a fraud had been attempted; since there is scarcely any other adequate motive which can be supposed to induce a master to hazard the interests of his vessel; the motives assigned being demonstrated to be false. There is a presumption also in such cases, that this is done with the knowledge, and at the instigation, of the owner of the cargo; because although it is not an impossible thing that masters may be guilty of barratry, it is not a natural conduct, nor what is gratuitously to be supposed. The only question, therefore, must be as to the effect of the presumption arising from these inferences, whether it shall exclude all contrary averment, or whether it shall operate only as matter of evidence, in concurrence with other proof as to the guilt of the intention. It must undoubtedly *bind* the owner; but the question is whether it shall do so *presumptively*, or *conclusively*; and whether the party shall be let in to prove a contrary intention. And although the fact may exist that a master should commit a barratry in a case of this kind, yet the owner cannot be admitted to go into proof on this point, on account of the fraudulent abuse to which such a liberty must inevitably lead, since it would be perfectly easy at any time, to set up the pretence, and equally impossible on the other side, to detect it. For what would be the ordinary test? Letters sent to correspondents elsewhere, and insurances—measures wholly in the power of the parties, and capable of being made at their pleasure, a complete *recipe* for a safe traffic with a blockaded port. When this consequence is duly weighed on one side, and when it is considered on the other, what few inducements a master can have to go to any other port than that, at which his charter party binds him to deliver his cargo, and particularly to a blockaded port, less injustice will be done by adopting this rule than by permitting the freighter to distinguish, by external and collateral evidence, the destination of his cargo from that of the master. The master is not the representative of the owner of the cargo to that extent, and in the same direct manner, in which he is held to be the representative of the owner of the ship. On that account, where facts shew the intention of the owner to be pure, the benefit of this distinction is given to the party; for instance, where the voyage begins before the knowledge of the blockade, and where the master on being warned, appears to be actuated only by a personal obstinacy and perverseness, in pursuing his course to his place of original destination. That is a case where the intention of the owner is admitted to be pure, where nothing stands against it *in limine*, where there is no question of fact, whether he was consentient to the fraud; and where, if he was affected at all, it could only be by the application of the strict legal principle, that affects the principal by the conduct of his agent. But where the blockade was known to all, the parties at the time of shipment, and therefore the question is raised, whether the owner was not consentient at first, and whether the conduct of the master is not demonstrative evidence that he was so, the effect of all just presumption is against the owner; since there is scarcely any inducement to lead the master to commit such a fraud, contrary to the instructions and intentions of the owner of the cargo. Upon these grounds the cargo in the above case was involved in the condemnation of the ship. (f)

Where the blockade has been raised between the time of sailing and the capture, the penalty does not attach; because the blockade being gone, the necessity of applying the penalty to prevent future transgression no longer exists. The offence incurred by a breach of blockade generally remains during the voyage. But that must be understood as subject to the condition, that the blockade itself con-

(f) 4 *Robinson*, 93. The Alexander. 1 *Edwards*, 39. The Exchange.

tinues. When the blockade is raised, a veil is thrown over every thing that has been done, and the vessel is no longer taken *in delicto*. The *delictum* may have been completed at one period, but it is by subsequent events entirely done away.(g)

(g) 6 *Robinson*, 387. The Lisette.

CHAPTER VII.

Of the property of subjects of the belligerent state, or its allies, engaged in trade with the enemy, or of subjects taken in violation of a municipal law, considered as an object of capture.

1. In a state of war between two nations, declared by the authority in whom the municipal constitution vests the power of making war, the two nations, and all their citizens or subjects, are enemies of each other. The consequence of this state of hostility is, that all intercourse and communication between them is unlawful.

This principle of public law forms a part of the municipal jurisprudence of every country.

2. Thus in England, there exists a general rule in the maritime jurisprudence of that country, by which all trading with the public enemy, unless with the permission of the sovereign, is interdicted. It is not a principle peculiar to the maritime law of England; it is laid down by Bynkershoek as an universal principle of law—*Ex natura belli commercia inter hostes cessare non est dubitandum. Quamvis nulla specialis sit commerciorum prohibitio, ipso tamen jure belli commercia esse vetita, ipsæ indictiones bellorum satis declarant*, &c. He proceeds to observe that the interests of trade, and the necessity of obtaining certain commodities, have sometimes so far overpowered this rule, that different species of traffic have been permitted, *prout e re suâ, subditorumque suorum esse censent principes.* But it is in all cases the act and permission of the sovereign. Wherever that is permitted, it is a suspension of

the state of war *quo ad hoc*. It is, as he expresses it, *pro parte sic bellum, pro parte pax inter subditos utriusque principis*.(a) It appears from these passages to have been the law of Holland; Valin states it to have been the law of France, whether the trade was attempted to be carried on in national(b) or in neutral vessels:(c) and it appears from the case cited, to have been the law of Spain; and it may without rashness be affirmed to be a general principle of law in most of the countries of Europe.

By the law and constitution of Great Britain, the sovereign alone has the power of declaring war and peace—He alone therefore, who has the power of entirely removing the state of war, has the power of removing it in part, by permitting, where he sees proper, that commercial intercourse which is a partial suspension of the war. There may be occasions on which such an intercourse may be highly expedient. But it is not for individuals to determine on the expediency of such occasions on their own notions of commerce merely, and possibly on grounds of private advantage not very reconcilable with the general interest of the state. It is for the state alone, on more enlarged views of policy, and of all circumstances that may be connected with such an intercourse, to determine when it shall be permitted, and under what regulations. No principle ought to be held more sacred than that, this intercourse cannot subsist on any other footing than that of the direct permission of the state. Who can be insensible to the consequences that might follow, if every person in time of war had a right to carry on a commercial intercourse with the enemy, and under colour of that, had the means of carrying on any other species of intercourse he might think fit? The inconvenience to the

(a) Q. J. P. L. 1. c. 3.

(b) The Fortuna, cited in the Hoop.

(c) *Sur l'Ordonnance, L.* 3. *tit.* 6. *art.* 3.

public might be extreme; and where is the inconvenience on the other side, that the merchant should be compelled in such a situation of the two countries, to carry on his trade between them, (if necessary) under the eye and control of the government charged with the care of the public safety?

Another principle of law, of a less politic nature, but equally general in its reception and direct in its application, forbids this sort of communication as fundamentally inconsistent with the relation existing between the two countries; and that is, the total inability to sustain any contract by an appeal to the tribunals of the one country, on the part of the subjects of the other. In the law of almost every country, the character of alien enemy carries with it a disability to sue, or to sustain, in the language of the civilians a *persona standi in judicio.* The peculiar law of England applies this principle with great rigour. The same principle is received in its courts of the law of nations; they are so far *British* courts, that no man can sue therein who is a subject of the enemy, unless under particular circumstances that *pro hâc vice* discharge him from the character of an enemy; such as his coming under a flag of truce, a cartel, a pass, or some other act of public authority that puts him in the king's peace *pro hâc vice.* But otherwise he is totally *ex lex;* even in the case of ransoms which were contracts, but contracts arising *ex jure belli*, and tolerated as such, the enemy was not permitted to sue in his own proper person for the payment of the ransom bill; but the payment was enforced by an action brought by the imprisoned hostage in the courts of his own country, for the recovery of his freedom. A state in which contracts cannot be enforced, cannot be a state of legal commerce. If the parties who are to contract have no right to compel the performance of the contract, nor even to appear in a court of justice for that purpose, can there be a stronger proof that the law imposes a legal inability to contract? To such transactions it gives no sanction; they have no legal existence; and the whole of such commerce is attempted without its protection and against its authority. Bynkershoek expresses himself with great force upon this argument in his first book, chapter 7, where he lays down that the legality of commerce, and the mutual use of courts of justice are inseparable: he says, that cases of commerce are undistinguishable from cases of any other species in this respect—*Si hosti semel permittas actiones exercere, difficile est distinguere ex quâ causâ oriantur, nec potui animadvertere illam distinctionem unquam usu fuisse servatam.*

Upon these and similar grounds it has been the established rule of the high court of admiralty in England, confirmed by the judgment of the supreme court, that a trading with the enemy, except under a royal license, subjects the property to confiscation:—and the most eminent persons of the law sitting in the supreme court have uniformly sustained such judgments.

Their decisions prove that the rule has been rigidly enforced:—where acts of parliament have on different occasions been made to relax the navigation law and other revenue acts; where the government has authorised, under the sanction of an act of parliament, a homeward trade from the enemy's possessions, but has not specifically protected an outward trade to the same, though intimately connected with that homeward trade, and almost necessary to its existence: that it has been enforced, where strong claims, not merely of convenience, but of necessity excused it on the part of the individual; that it has been enforced where cargoes have been laden before the war, but where the parties have not used all possible diligence to countermand the voyage after the first notice of hostilities; and that it has been enforced, not only against the subjects of the crown, but likewise against those of its allies in the war, upon the supposition that the rule was founded on a strong and universal principle, which states allied in war had a right to notice and apply mutually to each other's subjects.(d)

And such has been immemorially the English maritime law: for trading with the enemy is laid down in the black book of the admiralty, as an offence enquirable in the court of admiralty, *Soit enquis de ceulx qui* ENTRE COMMUNENT, *vendent, ou achatent avec aucun des Ennemys de nostre seigneur le Roy sans license especiale du Roy ou de son admiral.*(e)

It is also expressly laid down by Lord Mansfield, that such is the maritime law of England;(f) and he who for so long a time assisted at the decisions of the supreme court of prize, and at that period, could hardly have been ignorant of the rule of decision on this important subject. What is meant by the addition, *but this does not extend to a neutral vessel*, it is extremely difficult to conjecture, because no man was more perfectly apprised that the neutral bottom gives, in no case, any sort of protection to a cargo that is otherwise liable to confiscation; and therefore it cannot but be concluded, that the words of that great person must have been received with some slight degree of misapprehension.(g)

3. As to the common law of England, it is difficult to conceive that it can by any possibility be otherwise; for the rule in no degree arises from the transaction being on the water, but from principles of public policy and of public law, which are just as weighty on the one element as on the other, and of which the cases have happened more frequently upon the water, merely in consequence of the insular situation of the country. But when an enemy existed in the other part of the island, (the only instance in

(d) 1 *Robinson*, 196. The Hoop.

(e) *Rought*, art. 3. and note to *Clerk's Prax*. 105.

(f) 1 T. R. 85. Gist v. Mason.

(g) 1 *Robinson*, 196. The Hoop.

which it would occur upon the land) it appears from the case referred to by that person, to have been deemed equally criminal in the jurisprudence of the country.[h] And the modern law, though it apparently fluctuated for a while, was at last definitively settled on the same basis, in a case where a British subject shipped from the enemy's country, on board a neutral vessel, goods which he had purchased of the enemy during hostilities, and it was adjudged that an insurance upon the cargo was illegal and void.[i]

Such are the general principles of the rule under which the public law of Europe, and the municipal law of its different states, have interdicted all commerce with an enemy. It is thus sanctioned by the double authority of public and of private jurisprudence, and is founded both upon the sound and salutary principle forbidding all intercourse with an enemy, unless by permission of the sovereign or state, and upon the doctrine that he who is *hostis*—who has no *persona standi in judicio*, no means of enforcing contracts, cannot make contracts unless by such permission.

4. This rule has also been adopted and enforced in the courts of the United States.

Thus where the claimant, a citizen of the United States, had purchased a quantity of goods in the enemy's country a long time before the declaration of the late war against Great Britain, and had deposited them on an island near to the boundary line between the two countries, upon the breaking out of hostilities, his agents had hired the vessel to proceed to the place of deposit and bring away these goods; on her return, she was captured, and with the cargo condemned as prize of war, for trading with the enemy. On the argument in this case it was contended for the claimant, that this was not a trading within the meaning of the cases cited to support the condemnation; that, on

(h) 1 *Rolle's Abridgment*, 173.

(i) 8 T. R. 548. Potts v. Bell, in error.

the breaking out of war, every citizen had a right, and it was the interest of the community to permit its citizens, to withdraw property lying in an enemy's country, and purchased before the war. But the court determined, that whatever relaxation of the strict rights of war, the more mitigated and mild practice of modern times might have established, there had been none on this subject. The universal sense of nations had acknowledged the demoralizing effects which would result from the admission of individual intercourse between the states at war. The whole nation are embarked in one common bottom, and must be reconciled to one common fate. Every individual of the one nation must acknowledge every individual of the other nation as his own enemy, because he is the enemy of his country. This being the duty of the citizen, what is the consequence of a breach of that duty?—The law of prize is a part of the law of nations. By it, a hostile character is attached to trade, independent of the character of the trader who pursues or directs it. Condemnation to the captor is equally the fate of the property of the enemy and of property found engaged in an anti-neutral trade. But a citizen or ally may be engaged in a hostile trade, and thereby involve his property in the fate of those in whose cause he embarks. This liability of the property of a citizen to condemnation as prize of war, may likewise be accounted for on other considerations. Every thing that issues from a hostile country is, *prima facie*, the property of the enemy; and it is incumbent upon the claimant to support the negative of the proposition. But if the claimant be a citizen or an ally, at the same time that he makes out his interest he confesses the commission of an offence which, under a well known rule of the municipal law, deprives him of his right to prosecute his claim. Nor does this doctrine rest upon abstract reasoning only. It is supported by the practice of the most enlightened (perhaps we may say of all) commercial nations. And it afforded the court full confidence in their decision in this case, that they found, upon recurring to the records of the court of appeals in prize causes, established during the war of the revolution, that in various cases it was reasoned upon as the acknowledged law of that court. Certain it is, that it was the law of England before the American revolution, and therefore forms a part of the admiralty and maritime jurisdiction conferred on the courts of the United States by their constitution. Whether the trading in this case was such as, in the eye of the prize law, subjects the property to capture and condemnation, depends on the legal force of the term. If by *trading*, in the law of prize, were meant that signification of the term, which consists in negotiation or contract, this case would certainly not come under the penalty of the rule. But the object, policy, and spirit of the rule is to cut off all communication, or actual locomotive intercourse between individuals of the states at war. Negotiation or contract has therefore no necessary connexion with the offence. *Intercourse*, inconsistent with actual *hostility*, is the offence against which the operation of the rule is directed: And by substituting this term for that of *trading with the enemy*, an answer is given to the argument, that this is not a trading within the meaning of the cases cited. Whether, on the breaking out of war, the citizen has a right to remove to his own country with his property, or not; the claimant, certainly, had not a right to leave his own country for the purpose of bringing home his property from an enemy country. As to the claim for the vessel, it was held to be founded upon no pretext whatever; for the undertaking was altogether voluntary and inexcusable.[k]

So where hostilities had broken out, and the vessel in question, with a full knowledge of the war, and unpressed by any peculiar danger, changed her course and sought an

[k] Per JOHNSON, J. The Rapid. Supreme Court of the U. S. February T. 1814. M. S.

enemy's port, where she traded and took in a cargo, it was determined to be a cause of confiscation. If such an act could be justified, it were vain to prohibit trade with the enemy. The subsequent traffic in the enemy's country, by which her return cargo was obtained, connected itself with the voluntary sailing for a hostile port: nor does the circumstance that she was carried by force into one part of the enemy's dominions, when her actual destination was another, break the chain. The conduct of this ship was much less to be defended than that of the vessel last above cited.([1])

In another case, the vessel owned by citizens of the United States, sailed from thence before the war, with a cargo on freight, on a voyage to Liverpool and the north of Europe, and thence back to the United States. She arrived in Liverpool, there discharged her cargo, and took in another at Hull, and sailed for St. Petersburg under a British license, granted the 8th of June, 1812, authorizing the export of mahogany to Russia, and the importation of a return cargo to England. On her arrival at St. Petersburg, she received news of the war, and sailed to London with a Russian cargo consigned to British merchants, wintered in Sweden, and in the spring of 1813 sailed under convoy instructions of a British man of war for England, where she arrived and delivered her cargo; sailed for the United States in ballast under a British license, and was captured near Boston light house. After the decisions above cited, it was not to be contended that the sailing with a cargo, on freight, from Russia to the enemy's country, after a full knowledge of the war, did not amount to such a trading with the enemy, as to subject both vessel and cargo to condemnation as prize of war, had they been captured whilst proceeding on that voyage. The alleged necessity of un-

([1]) Per MARSHALL, C. J. The Alexander. Supreme Court of the U. S. February T. 1814. M. S.

dertaking that voyage to enable the master out of the freight to discharge his expenses at St. Petersburg, countenanced as the master declared by the opinion of the minister of the United States there—that by undertaking such a voyage he would violate no municipal law; although those considerations, if founded in truth, present a case of peculiar hardship, yet they afford no legal excuse which it was competent for the court to admit as the basis of its decision. The counsel for the claimant, seemed to be aware of the insufficiency of this ground, and applied their strength to shew that the vessel was not taken *in delicto,* having finished the offensive voyage, in which she was engaged, in the enemy's country, and being captured on her return home, and in ballast. It was not denied that if she had been taken in the same voyage in which the offence was committed, though after it was committed, she would be considered as still *in delicto*, and subject to confiscation; but it was contended that her voyage terminated at the enemy's port, and that she was, on her return, on a new voyage. But even admit that the outward and homeward voyage could be separated, so as to render them two distinct voyages, still it could not be denied that the *termini* of the homeward voyage were St. Petersburg and the United States. The continuity of such a voyage cannot be broken by a voluntary deviation of the master for the purpose of carrying on an intermediate trade. That the going from the neutral to the enemy's country was not undertaken as a new voyage was admitted by the claimants, who alleged that it was undertaken as subsidiary to the voyage home. It was, in short, a voyage from the neutral country by the way of the enemy country; and, consequently, the vessel, during any part of that voyage, if seized for any conduct subjecting her to confiscation as prize of war, was seized in *delicto*.[m]

[m] Per Washington, J. The Joseph. Supreme Court of the U. S. February T. 1814. M. S.

Where goods were purchased sometime before the late war by the claimant's agent in Great Britain on his sole account, but not shipped for the United States until the month of May, 1813; they were pronounced liable to condemnation. The court expressed no opinion as to the right of a citizen of the belligerent state, on the breaking out of hostilities, to withdraw his property, purchased before the war, from the enemy's country. Admitting such right to exist, it is necessary that it should be exercised with due diligence and within a reasonable time after a knowledge of hostilities. To admit a citizen to withdraw property from an enemy country a long time after the war, under the pretext of its having been purchased before the war, would lead to the most injurious consequences, and hold out temptations to every species of fraudulent and illegal traffic with the enemy. To such an unlimited extent the right cannot exist. This shipment was not made until more than eleven months had elapsed after war was declared; and the court were of opinion that it was then too late for the party to make the shipment, so as to exempt him from the penalty attached to an illegal traffic with the enemy.[n]

5. The same course of decisions which has established that property of a subject or citizen taken trading with the enemy, is forfeited, has decided also that it is forfeited as prize. The ground of the forfeiture is, that it is taken adhering to the enemy, and therefore the proprietor is *pro hac vice* to be considered as an enemy, and his property must be condemned to the captors.[o] But in a case of this description, a claim was interposed by the United States claiming a priority of right over the captors to the property in question, upon the ground of an antecedent forfeiture

([n]) Per STORY, J. The St. Lawrence. Supreme Court of the U. S. February T. 1815 M. S.

([o]) 1 *Robinson*, 219. The Nelly. *In Notis* to the Hoop

to the United States by a violation of the non-intercourse act of March 1, 1809; the goods having been put on board with an intent to import the same into the United States. It was however held that this claim ought not to prevail, and that the municipal forfeiture under the act, was absorbed in the more general operation of the law of war. The property of an enemy seems hardly within the purview of mere municipal laws of trade, but is confiscable under the *jus gentium*.(p)

6. We have seen what is the rule of public and municipal law on this subject, and what are the sanctions by which it is guarded. Various attempts have been made to evade its operation, and to escape its penalties, but its inflexible rigour has defeated all these attempts.

7. Thus where goods were shipped by subjects of the belligerent state to a neutral port, with an ulterior purpose of sending them on to the enemy's country, the goods were condemned as taken in a course of commerce rendering them liable to confiscation. Without the license of government, no communication, direct, or indirect, can be carried on with the enemy. The interposition of a prior port makes no difference; *all* trade with the enemy is illegal; and the circumstance that the goods are to go first to a neutral port, will not make it lawful. The trade is still liable to the same abuse, and to the same political danger, whatever that may be.(q)

8. So where the trade with the enemy was by a house of trade, one of the partners in which resided in the belligerent state, and the other in a neutral country, the share of the former was condemned. And it has been decided that even an inactive or dormant partner cannot receive

(p) Per STORY, J. The Sally. Supreme Court of the U. S. February T. 1814. M. S.

(q) 4 *Robinson*, 79. The Jonge Pieter. *Vide* also 3 *Robinson*, 22. The Indian Chief.

restitution in a transaction, in which he could not be lawfully engaged as a sole trader.(r)

9. All the apparent exceptions which have been supposed to exist to the rule of law we are considering, far from weakening its force, do but confirm and strengthen it.

10. For example, if a belligerent subject employs a neutral to purchase for him in the country of the enemy, the neutral is, in such case, *but the mere agent:* The goods then must be considered to pass immediately from the enemy to the subject; and such a transaction would be illegal. But if a neutral merchant has a ship or goods lying in a port of the enemy, he is at liberty to dispose of them even to a subject of the belligerent state, as freely as if they were on the seas. The locality of the thing will not affect the legality of the sale.(s) The trading here stated is with a neutral in commodities, which though locally situated in the enemy's country, have become incorporated into the stock of neutral trade. It is not the place where the thing is, which decides its neutral or hostile nature, but the national character of the person to whom it belongs.(t) Here is no communication, nor contract with the enemy; nothing forbidden by the policy of cutting off such communication, and by the impossibility of maintaining an action on such contract.

11. So also in the case of a shipment on the part of a person having been resident in Spain, the enemy's country, as consul of Great Britain, the belligerent state, who purchased the articles in question, for the supply of the British

(r) 6 *Robinson,* 127. The Franklin.

(s) 4 *Robinson,* 284. The Samuel, *in notis* to the Countess of Lauderdale.

(t) *Vattel,* L. 3. c. 5. § 75. *Puisque ce n'est point le lieu où une chose se trouve, qui décide de la nature de cette chose là, mais la qualité de la personne a qui elle appartient—les choses appartenantes à des personnes neutres, qui se trouve en pays ennemi, doivent être distinguées de celles qui appartienent à l'ennemi.*

fleet, restitution was decreed. But the court declared that it did not mean to weaken the obligation to obtain licenses for every sort of communication with the enemy's country, in all cases where the measure is practicable; but thought it saw great difficulties in applying for a license, or in using it in this case. The circumstances of this case might be taken as virtually amounting to a license; inasmuch, as if a license had been applied for, it must have been granted.(u) And in the case of a license for raw materials, in which the article of goods in question was not included, restitution was also decreed under favourable circumstances arising from the situation of the parties, and the fact of the orders having been given previous to the war without an opportunity of countermanding. But the court, at the same time wished it to be understood, that by this decree the necessity of obtaining a license was not in any degree relaxed. On the contrary, the court could not sufficiently inculcate the duty of applying in all cases, for the protection of a license, where property is to be withdrawn from the country of the enemy: it was indeed the only safe way in which parties could proceed.(v) In another case of an adventure originating before the war, but not stopt on notice of hostilities, the imputation of trading with the enemy was held to be removed by the *portus ad quem* ceasing to be hostile before the arrival of the vessel. To constitute the offence there must be an *act* of trading to the enemy country, as well as the *intention*. There must be a legal, as well as a moral illegality. If a man fires a gun at sea, intending to kill a *friend*, which would be legal murder, and by accident does not kill a friend, but an *enemy*, the moral guilt is the same, but the legal effect is different. The accident has turned up in his favour—the criminal act intended has not been committed, and the man is innocent of the legal of-

(u) 4 *Robinson*, 195. The Madonna delle Gracie.

(v) 5 *Robinson*, 141. The Jaffrow Catharina.

fence. So, if the intent was to trade with an enemy, but at the time of carrying the design into effect the person has become not an enemy—the intention here wants the *corpus delicti*. No case had been produced, in which a mere intention to trade with the enemy's country has enured to condemnation. Where a country is known to be hostile, the commencement of a voyage towards that country may be a sufficient act of illegality; but where the voyage is undertaken without that knowlege, the subsequent event of hostility will have no such effect.(w)

12. In the above cases the trading was either with a neutral; or the circumstances were considered as implying a license; or the decree of restitution was declared not to relax in any degree the necessity of obtaining a license; or the trading was not consummated until the enemy had ceased to be such. As to other cases and authorities which have been supposed to form exceptions to the rule, such as the Packet de Bilboa and the note appended by Sir C. Robinson to the case of the Ocean, it may be remarked that the first was not a question of trading with the enemy,—but in whom was the risk of the shipment until delivery, which was allowed to be in the shipper, as being made before the war, contrary to the general rule which will not permit such contracts to be made in time of war, so as to defeat belligerent rights.(x) And as to the second authority, the learned reporter is evidently considering the effect of national character on the property, and not the effect of the trade in which the party was engaged.(y)

13. Not only is a trade with the enemy on the part of the citizens or subjects of the belligerent state, prohibited and punished with confiscation in the courts of their own

(w) 5 *Robinson*, 251. The Abby.

(x) *Chitty's Law of Nations*, 17. 21. 2 *Robinson*, 133. *Vide Supra*. c. III. § 17.

(y) 5 *Robinson*, 91. *In notis*.

sovereign, but during a conjoint war, no subject of a co-belligerent can trade with the common enemy without being liable to a forfeiture of his property engaged in such trade, in the prize courts of the ally.(¹) This rule is a corollary of the other, and is founded upon the principle, that such trade is forbidden to the subject of the co-belligerent by the municipal law of his own country, by the universal law of nations, and by the express or implied terms of the treaty of alliance subsisting between the allied powers. And as the former rule can be relaxed only by the permission of the sovereign power of the state, so this can only be relaxed by the analagous permission of the allied nations, according to their mutual agreement. A declaration of war naturally carries with it an interdiction of all commercial intercourse; it leaves the belligerent countries in a state that is inconsistent with the relations of commerce. This is the natural result of a state of war, and it is by no means necessary that there should be a special interdiction of commerce to produce this effect. At the same time it has happened since the world has grown more commercial, that a practice has crept in of admitting particular relaxations; and if one state only is at war, no injury is committed to any other state. It is of no importance to other nations, how much a single belligerent chooses to weaken and dilute his own rights. But it is otherwise when allied nations are pursuing a common cause against a common enemy. Between them it must be taken as an implied, if not an express contract, that one state shall not do any thing to defeat the general object. If one state admits its subjects to carry on an uninterrupted trade with the enemy, the consequence will be that it will supply that aid and comfort to the enemy, especially if it is an enemy depending very materially on the resources of foreign commerce,

(¹) *Bynkershoek*, Q. J. P. L. 10. 1 *Robinson*, 210. The Enigheid, cited in the Hoop. 4 *Robinson*, 251. The Nayade.

which may be very injurious to the prosecution of the common cause, and the interests of its ally. It should seem, that it is not enough, therefore, to say that the one state has allowed this practice to its own subjects; it should appear to be at least desirable that it could be shewn, that either the practice is of such a nature, as can in no manner interfere with the common operations, or that it has the allowance of the confederate state.([a])

14. The property of a citizen or subject of a belligerent state, taken in a trade prohibited by the municipal law of his own country, is liable to confiscation in the prize courts of that country.

It is a good moral and legal principle, that a man must come into a court of justice with clean hands, and that the law will not lend its aid to a person setting up a violation of law, on the face of his claim. It is a sound maxim, to which the courts of municipal law have always attended; and whether the penalty is great or small, or whether there be no penalty at all, yet, if the act is reprobated, a man will not be allowed to claim a right founded on it: But cases had not occurred in which the court of admiralty had met with occasion to apply such a principle, except in cases of property taken in a trade with the enemy; but in such cases the exception is not to be considered as arising from municipal law, but from the principle of allegiance, which is a general principle of the law of nations. It was in the case of the Eliza Worsely,([b]) that it was first decided that the court of admiralty was bound to take notice of an illegal practice evidently appearing in the conduct of a subject of the belligerent state, whose property had found its way into the hands of a captor of his own country, if the transaction in which that property had been employed, was

([a]) 6 *Robinson*, 403. The Neptunus.

([b]) Lords, July 13, 1798.

a transaction contrary to the law of his own country:[c] And in the case of the Etrusco, it was decided, after long deliberation, that property condemned in consequence of the inadmissibility of such a claim, was to be condemned, not to the individual captor, but to the king.[d]

15. Such has been the course of decisions on this matter in the British courts of prize. But the same courts have determined that the principle did not extent to bar, a *neutral* proprietor on account of his property having been taken in the act of violating the British navigation laws. The cases that have been mentioned were not cases in which the courts that decided them took on themselves to exercise the jurisdiction of the revenue court, or to inflict the penalties growing out of that species of law. What they did was only to reject the claim of *British* subjects in a prize court, in a transaction which evidently showed those individuals to be acting in violation of the laws of their country, which they were bound to observe. But there is no instance in which the same principle has been applied to foreigners. It was asked, if you apply such a principle to British subjects, why not to foreigners? Some distinctions are obvious. In the first place, it is to be recollected that the prize court is a court of the law of nations, though sitting under the authority of the king of Great Britain. It belongs to other nations as well as to its own; and what foreigners have a right to demand from it is the administration of the law of nations, simply, and exclusively of the introduction of principles borrowed from the municipal jurisprudence. In the case of a British subject it is different. To him it is a British tribunal, as well as a court of the law of nations; and if he has been trampling on the known laws of his country, it is no injustice to say, that a person coming into any of the courts of his own

[c] 2 *Robinson*, 77. The Walsingham Packet.

[d] 4 *Robinson*, 256. The Carolina. *In Notis.*

country, to which he is naturally amenable, in such a transaction, can receive no protection from them. This difference of situation affords a sound and material distinction. As to foreign nations and their subjects, the breach of prohibitions of trade are merely *mala prohibita;* it is an offence against the peculiar law of the country, which they may justly demand to have tried more directly under that system of law to which it properly belongs. With respect to a subject, the violation of the laws of his own country, carries with it also the *malum in se*; and therefore it is no injustice to him, that his claim should be subject to rules, which the prize court might not think itself at liberty to apply to the subjects of foreign states.[e]

So also enemy property, being liable to condemnation *jure belli*, cannot be confiscated for a breach of municipal law.[f]

16. The trade in slaves has given rise to a peculiar case, which does not arrange itself under the rule, that the pro-

[e] 6 *Robinson*, 341. The Recovery.

[f] *Vide ante*, § 5. The Sally. This principle of the inadmissibility of a claim in the prize court, in violation of municipal law was applied by the supreme court to a case arising under the Registry Act of the 31st December, 1792, which provides, § 4. That in order to the registry of any ship or vessel, an oath shall be taken and subscribed by the owner, or by one of the owners thereof, declaring, if there be another owner or owners, that there is or are such other owner or owners, specifying his, her, or their *place of abode*. And that in case any of the matters of fact in the said oath alleged, which shall be within the knowledge of the party so swearing, shall not be true, there shall be a forfeiture of the ship or vessel, together with her tackle, furniture and apparel, in respect of which the same shall have been made, of the value thereof, to be recovered with costs of suit, of the person, by whom such oath shall have been made. Lenox, one of the claimants, swore that he, together with Maitland, *of the city of New-York*, were the sole owners; when in fact Maitland was domiciled at the time in Great Britain. The ship was captured and proceeded against as prize of war. It was decreed that the claimants should be turned out of court, the ship forfeited, and the question to whom she should be condemned reserved.

perty of a citizen or subject, taken in violation of the laws of his own country, is liable to confiscation in the prize courts of that country, nor under the negative principle, that the property of a neutral foreigner is *not* liable to confiscation for a breach of the municipal law of the belligerent state; but was decided partly under the former rule, partly under an exception to the latter, and under the law of nature and nations. The conjoint operation of all three enured to condemnation in the case of the Amedie.[g] This ship, under American colours, was captured in December, 1807, by a British cruizer, being employed at the time of capture, in carrying slaves from the coast of Africa to a Spanish colony. The claimant, however, who was a citizen of the United States, complained of the capture, and demanded from the British prize court restitution of property, of which he alleged that he had been unjustly dispossessed. In all the former cases of this kind, which had come before the court, the slave trade was liable to considerations very different from those which belonged to it then. It had formerly been prohibited (so far as respected carrying slaves to the colonies of foreign nations) by the United States; but by the British laws it was still allowed. It appeared, therefore, difficult to consider the prohibitory law of America in any other light than as one of those municipal regulations of a foreign state, of which the court could not take any cognizance. But, by the alteration which had since taken place, the question stood on different grounds, and was open to the operation of very different principles. The slave trade had since been totally abolished in Great Britain, and the legislature had pronounced it contrary to the principles of justice and humanity. Whatever they might think as individuals before, they could not, sitting as judges in a British court of justice, regard the trade in that light, while their own laws permitted it.

[g] Lords, 28th July, 1810.

But they might now assert, that this trade could not, abstractedly speaking, have a legitimate existence. When the learned judge,[h] by whom this decision was pronounced, said *abstractedly* speaking, he meant that Great Britain had no right to control any foreign legislature that might think fit to dissent from this doctrine, and to permit to its own subjects the prosecution of this trade; but they had now a right to affirm, that, *prima facie*, the trade is illegal; and thus to throw on claimants the burden of proof, that, in respect of them, by the authority of their own laws, it is otherwise. As the case then stood, they thought they were entitled to say, that a claimant can have no right, upon principles of universal law, to claim the restitution in a prize court, of human beings carried as his slaves. He must show some right that has been violated by the capture, some property of which he has been dispossessed, and to which he ought to be restored. In this case, the laws of the claimant's country allowed of no right of property such as he claimed. There could, therefore, be no right of restitution. The consequence was, that the judgment of the court below, condemning the property, must be affirmed.[i]

Thus we perceive that this decision which does so much honor to the tribunal by which it was made, and to the judge by whom it was pronounced, although it has at the first view an anomalous tendency, is strictly conformable to principle, and flows with irresistible force from the threefold operation of the law of nature, the act of Congress, and of Parliament. The first prohibits the traffic in men; the second prohibited the carrying of slaves from Africa to the West Indian and American colonies; and the latter enabled a British prize court to enforce this double prohibition against an American citizen. *Jure enim naturali*

(h) Sir William Grant.

(i) *Edinburgh Review*, Vol. 16. No. XXI. p. 436.

omnes homines ab initio liberi nascebantur (k)—and, unless expressly permitted by the municipal law of his own country, no person can assert a right of property in human beings. Much less can he do so where that law expressly prohibits the acquisition and transfer of such property. It is refreshing and delightful to the mind in contemplating the law of war, to repose for a moment on a subject over which humanity has so long wept, but at last begins to lift up her head and rejoice. The abolition of this accursed traffic, in which our own country has the honor of taking so distinguished a lead, incorporated into the late treaties of Paris and of Ghent, will, it is to be hoped, soon form a part of the conventional law of nations, and carry down to posterity the fame of the present age, unrivalled in arts and in arms, and what is still more glorious, in philanthropy!

(k) *Justinian's Institutes*, L. 1. tit. 2.

CHAPTER VIII.

Of ransoms, recapture, and claims for salvage.

1. When a ship and cargo, the property of the enemy, is taken on the high seas, it is the duty of the captors to seize the papers found on board, and to send the vessel into some port for adjudication. But where circumstances will not permit this to be done, or render it inconvenient, they may permit the captured to ransom their property for such sum as may be agreed upon between the parties.[a]

2. This contract is unquestionably legal on the part of the *captors* of every country, although the municipal law of Great Britain prohibits it to be entered into in relation to the property of her subjects captured by her enemies. Thus by the Stat. 22d, George III. c. 25. it is enacted, That it shall not be lawful for any of his majesty's subjects to ransom, or to enter into any contract or agreement for ransoming any ship or vessel belonging to any of his majesty's subjects, or any merchandizes or goods on board the same, which shall be captured by the subjects of any state at war with his majesty, or any person committing hostilities against his majesty's subjects; and that all contracts and agreements which shall be entered into, and all bills, notes, and other securities, which shall be given by any person or persons for ransom of any such ship or vessel, or of any merchandize or goods on board the same, shall be absolutely void in law, and of no effect whatever.

[a] *Consolato del Mare*, c. 290.

It therefore follows that no such contract can be enforced against a British subject in the courts of his own country. There is no such prohibition by the municipal laws of other states, and the contract may therefore be enforced in them according to the mode prescribed by the law of nations. For the belligerent state having authorised its public and private vessels of war, to seize and take the ships and merchandize of its enemies, it has equally delegated to them its authority to ransom the same when taken. There are certain *commercia belli;* and good faith is to be observed even towards enemies. *Si quando singuli hosti promiserint, est in eo fides servanda.*[b]

3. The captor obliges himself by the terms of this contract to release the captured vessel and cargo, and to permit her to proceed to the designated port within a certain limited time, giving the master a safe-conduct for her protection against the cruizers of his nation, and its allies, during the same period of time. This is what results from the express terms which are always used in ransom bills.[c]

4. But it may be asked, how the commander who has made this contract of ransom, by the safe-conduct which he gives to the master of the captured vessel, can bind the other cruizers of his nation, and its allies, to permit the vessel to proceed? For it is a principle of law that one cannot bind a third person by a contract to which he is not a party. The answer is, that it is not this contract alone, and *per se,* which binds the commanders of other cruizers, to respect the safe-conduct thus given; but it is the authority of the belligerent state, under the express or implied sanction of which this safe-conduct is given. For as the state cannot possibly execute every thing by its supreme magistrate, it

(b) *Cicero,* De Officiis, L. 1. c. 13. *Grotius,* De J. B. ac P. L. c. 23. § . *Puffendorf,* L. 3. c. 6. § 11. *Loccenius,* De Jure Maritimo, L. 3. tit. 3. No. 6. *Burlimaqui,* Part 4, c. 4. *Vattel,* L. 3. c. 16. § 223.

(c) 2 *Dallas,* 15. Miller et al. v. the Resolution.

is necessary that it should communicate a part of its power to its military and naval officers. Without a special mandate from the sovereign or state, these officers are considered as invested with all the necessary powers for the proper exercise of their functions. As this is the case with the commanders of public armed vessels, so also is it with those of private armed vessels. They are authorised by the state, whose commission they bear, not only to capture the ships and goods of the enemy, but also to ransom them when they judge it more advantageous. As it is on the part of the state and in the name of the state that they capture the enemy's ships and goods, so also it is on the part of the state, and in some sort, in the name of the state, that they ransom them. This contract, and the safe-conduct which is granted in conformity to it, ought therefore to be considered as sanctioned by the authority of the state, to which all cruizers bearing its commission are bound to defer. So also by the implied obligation of the treaties of alliance, the cruizers of the allies of the captor's country are also bound to respect the safe-conduct which he thus grants according to its terms and conditions.[d]

5. This safe conduct is of no avail unless the vessel is found within the course prescribed and the time limited by the contract. Thus by the French Ordinance of 1706, art. 8, it is permitted to the French cruizers to re-capture any ransomed vessel which they may find deviating from the course and time prescribed by the terms of the ransom-bill, and to bring the same into the ports of the kingdom, for condemnation. If, nevertheless, the ransom vessel appeared to have been driven out of her course by storms, and was about to resume it, it would seem to be equitable to allow her the benefit of the safe conduct.

6. If the ransomed vessel is lost by the perils of the seas before her arrival, the obligation to pay the sum stipu-

([d]) *Pothier*, De Propriété, No. 134, 135.

lated for her ransom is not thereby extinguished. The captor has indeed guaranteed the master of the captured vessel against being interrupted in his course, or re-taken by other cruizers of his nation, or its allies, but he has not insured him against losses by the perils of the seas. If, however, it is expressly agreed by the terms of the ransom-bill, that the loss of the vessel, during her voyage, by the perils of the seas, should discharge the master from the payment of the stipulated sum, this contract ought to be observed in practice. But the frauds to which this clause may expose the captor, render it necessary that it should be rigorously restrained to the case of a total loss on the high seas, instead of extending it to shipwreck or stranding, which would afford the master a temptation to cast away his vessel, in order to save the most valuable part of the cargo, and thus avoid the payment of the ransom money.(e)

7. When the ransomed vessel, having deviated from the prescribed course, and exceeded the limited time, is re-taken by another cruizer of the same nation, a question arises whether the debtors of the ransom are in this case discharged from their obligation? For the negative, it may be said, that if the proprietors of the ransomed vessel and goods are not discharged from the payment of the ransom by the loss of the vessel and goods through the perils of the seas, which is a case of inevitable accident, still less ought they to be discharged from this obligation, where the loss is occasioned by the fault of their agent, the master, who by contravening the contract of ransom has voluntarily exposed himself to be captured by another cruizer. Notwithstanding these reasons, the practice is well settled that when a vessel, after having been ransomed, has been retaken on account of a deviation from

(e) *Pothier*. De Propriété, No. 138. *Valin*, Sur l'Ordonnance, L. 3. tit. 9. Des Prises, art. 19.

the terms of the ransom, the debtors of the ransom are discharged from their obligation, which is merged in the prize, and the amount is deducted from the net proceeds thereof, and paid to the first captor, whilst the residue is paid to the second captor. The reason upon which this practice is founded is, that it is in the name and by the authority of the state, that the first captor ransoms the vessel; it is in the name and by the authority of the state that the second captor retakes her, the state having assigned its title both to the ransom and the prize to them: equity and good faith will not then permit that the state, or one and the same person, should take both the vessel and the ransom of the vessel; the amount of the ransom ought therefore to be deducted from the value of the vessel.(f)

8. When the captor, after having ransomed a vessel belonging to the enemy, is himself taken by the enemy, together with the ransom-bill of which he is the bearer, this ransom-bill becomes a part of the capture made by the enemy, and the persons of the enemy nation, who were debtors of the ransom, are thereby discharged from their obligation. This debt, once extinguished, cannot be again revived, even if the vessel which has ransomed that of the enemy, and is afterwards taken by the enemy, is subsequently re-taken from the enemy.(g)

When a captured vessel is ransomed, the papers are not to be taken possession of by the captor, but to be left on board, and one or more hostages are to be taken as security for the faithful performance of the contract on the part of the captured. The death of this hostage does not discharge the contract; for the party trusts to him as a collateral security only, and by losing it does not also lose his

(f) *Pothier*, De Propriété, No. 139. *Valin*, Sur l'Ordonnance, L. 3. tit. 9. Des Prises, art. 19.

(g) *Pothier*, De Propriété, No. 140.

original security, unless there is an express agreement to that effect.(h)

9. It has been determined in the English courts of common law, that an alien enemy cannot, by the municipal laws of England, sue for the recovery of a right claimed to be acquired by him in actual war;(i) and Sir William Scott states, that even in the case of ransoms, which are contracts, but contracts arising *ex jure belli*, and tolerated as such, the enemy was not permitted to sue in his own proper person for the payment of the ransom bill, even before British subjects were prohibited by the abovementioned statute from entering into this contract; but the payment was enforced by an action brought by the imprisoned hostage in the courts of his own country, for the recovery of his freedom.(k) But it seems difficult, except for mere technical objections, to say why a suit should not be brought directly upon the ransom-bill itself, by the alien enemy, who is the holder of it, if it be a lawful contract. The express terms of the contract, as they are usually inserted in ransom-bills, bind the master of the ransomed vessel, as well in his own name, as in that of the owners of the vessel and cargo, to the payment of the stipulated sum. He is the agent of these owners, lawfully authorised to enter into such contracts as are for their benefit, and conducive to the preservation of the vessel and merchandize entrusted to his care. His signature therefore binds them as debtors of the ransom, and to reimburse the expenses of supporting the hostage, who has been given as a surety, in the enemy's country.(l)

(h) *Valin*, Traité des Prises, c. 11. No. 1 et 3. Burrow's Reports, 1734. Ricord vs. Bettenham.

(i) *Douglas' Reports*, 627. Poreau vs. Hartby.

(k) 1 *Robinson*, 201. The Hoop.

(l) *Pothier*, De Propriété, No. 136, 137.

10. A recapture may be made either from a pirate; a captor, clothed with a lawful commission, but not an enemy; or lastly, from an enemy.

11. In the first case, there can be no doubt the property ought to be restored to the owner; for as pirates have no lawful right to make captures, the property has not been divested from him. He has only been deprived of its possession, to which he has been restored by the recapture. For the service rendered to the owner, the retaker is entitled to a remuneration in the nature of salvage.(m)

Thus by the French Ordinance of 1681, *Liv.* 3. *tit.* 9. *des Prises*, *art.* 10, it is provided that, the ships and effects of the subjects or allies of France, retaken from pirates, and claimed within a year and a day after being reported at the admiralty, shall be restored to the owners, upon payment of one third of the value of the vessel and goods, as salvage. And the same is the law of Great-Britain; but the usage of Holland, and of certain other countries, was formerly otherwise, giving the whole of the property to the retakers, as does that of Spain, if the property has been in possession of the pirates twenty-four hours.

Valin, in his Commentary upon the above article of the French ordinance, is of the opinion that if the recapture be made by a foreigner who is a subject of a state, the law of which gives to the recaptors the whole of the property, it could not be restored to the former owner; and he cites in support of this opinion a decree of the parliament of Bordeaux, of the 8th March, 1635, in favour of a subject of Holland, who had retaken a French vessel from pi-

(m) *Grotius*, De J. B ac P L. 3. c 9. § 17. *Loccenius*, De Jure Mar. L. 2. c. 3. No. 4. *Bynkershoek*, Q. J. P. L. 1. c. 17. 2 *Brown's Civ. & Adm. Law*, c. 11. p. 461. *Ea que piratæ nobis eripuerunt, non opus habent postliminio; quia jus gentium illis non concedit, ut jus dominii mutari possint.* Ff. de capt. et postl. revers. *Abbott on Shipping*—Story's edition 12.

rates.(n) To this opinion Pothier objects, that the laws of Holland having no power over Frenchmen and their property within the territory of France, the French subject could not thereby be deprived of the property in his vessel, which was not divested by the piratical capture, and that it ought consequently to be restored to him upon payment of the salvage prescribed by the ordinance.(o)

Under the term *allies*, in this article, are included *neutrals*; and Valin is also of opinion that the property of the subjects of friendly powers retaken from pirates by French captors ought not to be restored to them upon payment of salvage, if the law of their own country gives it wholly to the retakers, otherwise there would be a defect of reciprocity, which would offend against that impartial justice which is due from one state to another.(p)

But a capture by the Barbary powers is not a piratical seizure, which will have the effect of invalidating the conversion of property under it. They were formerly considered as pirates, but have since acquired the rights of legation and of war in form. Consequently recaptures from these states are to be judged by the same rule as those from any other public enemies.(q)

12. If the property be retaken from a captor clothed with a lawful commission, but not an enemy, there would still be as little doubt that it must be restored to the original owner. For the act of taking being in itself a wrongful act could not change the property which must still remain in him.

If the neutral vessel thus recaptured were laden with contraband goods destined to an enemy of the first captor,

(n) *Valin*, Sur l'Ordonnance, L. 3. tit. 9. Des Prises, art. 10.

(o) *Pothier*, De Propriété, No. 101.

(p) Valin, Sur l'Ordonnance, L. 3. tit. 9. des Prises, art. 10.

(q) 4 *Robinson*, 3. The Helena.

it may be doubted whether they should be restored, inasmuch as they were liable to be confiscated to the first captor. But a Dutch ship taken under these circumstances was restored by the French council of prizes, in 1759; and the decision seems to be conformable to principle. Salvage ought, however, in this instance, to be given to the recaptors, as it is to their exertions that the property is indebted for its escape from condemnation.([r])

But, in general, no salvage is due for the recapture of neutral vessels and effects, upon the principle that the liberation of a *bona fide* neutral from the hands of the enemy is no beneficial service to him, inasmuch as the same enemy would be compelled by the tribunal of his own country to make restitution of the property with costs and damages, for the unjust seizure and detention. Such is the rule laid down in the French prize code.([s])

To this general rule, however, an important exception has been made, founded on the principle mentioned in the *Code des Prises* in case the vessel and cargo are liable to be confiscated by the enemy. In that case, it is immaterial whether the property be justly liable to be thus confiscated according to the law of nations, since that can make no difference in the meritorious nature of the service rendered to the original owner by the recaptor. For the ground upon which salvage is refused by the general rule is that the prize courts of the captor's country will duly respect the obligations of the law of nations; a presumption, which in the wars of civilized states, each belligerent is bound to entertain in their respective dealings with neutrals. But if in point of fact those obligations are not duly

([r]) *Martens on Privateers*, § 52.

([s]) *Sa Majesté a jugé pendant la derniere guerre, que la reprise du navire neutre faite par un corsaire Français (lorsque le navire n'etait pas chargé de marchandises prohibées, ni dans le cas d'être confisqué par l'ennemi) était nulle.* Code des Prises, an 1784, tom. 2.

respected by those tribunals, and in consequence neutral property is unjustly subjected to confiscation in them, a substantial benefit is conferred upon the original owner in rescuing his property from this peril, which ought to be remunerated by the payment of salvage. It was upon this principle that the prize courts of England and of the United States, during the war which was terminated by the peace of Amiens, pronounced salvage to be due upon neutral property retaken from French cruisers. During the revolution in France, great irregularity and confusion had arisen in the prize code, and had crept into the tribunals of that country, by which the property of neutrals was rendered liable to be condemned upon grounds both unjust and unknown to the law of nations. The recapture of neutral property which might have been exposed to confiscation by means of this irregularity and confusion was therefore considered by the English and American courts of prize, as a meritorious service, and remunerated by the payment of salvage.[t] The issuing of the French decreee at Berlin, on the 21st November, 1806, occasioned the exception to be revived in the practice of the British prize courts, who again adjudged salvage to be paid for the re-capture of neutral property which was liable to condemnation under that decree.[u] It is true that that the decree had remained inoperative upon American property until the condemnation of the cargo of the *Horizon* by the council of prizes, in October, 1807, and therefore it may be thought, perhaps, in strictness, the English court of admiralty ought not to have decreed salvage in the case of the *Sansom*, more especially as the convention of the thirtieth September, 1800, between

[t] 2 *Robinson*, 299. The War Onskan. 1 *Cranch*, 1, Talbot vs. Seaman, 4 *Robinson*, 156. The Eleonora Catharina. 5 *Robinson*, 54. The Carlotta. 6 *Robinson*, 104. The Huntress.

[u] 6 *Robinson*, 410. The Sansom. 1 *Edwards*, 254. The Acteon. *Vide* Appendix, No. V.

the United States and France, was then subsisting, and the terms of which were wholly inconsistent with the provisions of the Berlin decree. But as the cargo of the *Horizon* was condemned in obedience to the terms of the imperial rescript of the eighteenth September, 1807, having been taken before the *Sansom*, whether that rescript be considered as an interpretation of a doubtful point in the original decree, or as a declaration of an anterior and positive provision, there can be no doubt the *Sansom* would have been condemned under it—consequently a substantial benefit was rendered to the neutral owner by the recapture, and salvage was due of course. And the same principle would apply to the prize proceedings of all the belligerents, in their turn, during the late maritime war in Europe, all of whom, and none more than Great Britain herself, have trampled under foot the antient law of nations, and in many cases rendered the rescue of neutral property from the grasp of either, a valuable service entitling the recaptor to salvage.

13. Lastly, the recapture may be made from an enemy. The *jus postliminii* was a fiction of the Roman law, by which persons or things taken by the enemy were restored to their former state when coming again under the power of the nation to which they formerly belonged. *Postliminium fingit qui captus est, in civitate semper fuisse*—Inst. L. 1. tit. 12. And it is thus defined in the Pandects, *Jus quo perinde omnia restituuntur jura, de si captus ab hostibus non esset*—L. 49. tit. 15. It was applied to free persons or slaves, returning *post liminii;* and to real property, and certain moveables, such as ships of war and private vessels, except fishing and pleasure boats. *Navibus longis atque onerariis, postliminium est, non piscatories, aut voluptatis causa*—Ff. 49. These things, therefore, when retaken, were restored to the original owner, as if they had never been out of his control and possession; and Grotius attests that such was the ancient maritime law of Europe, which

determined that the property could be divested from the owner only by bringing it *infra præsidia* of the capturing power.[v]

But whatever may be the true rule of the law of nations respecting the time when property vests in the captor so as to preclude a restitution to the former owner upon recapture, it is certain that there is at present no rule operating with the force and authority of a general law. It may be fit there should be such a rule, and it might be either the rule of immediate possession, or the rule of pernoctation and twenty-four hours possession, or it might be the rule of bringing *infra præsidia*; or it might be a rule requiring an actual sentence of condemnation: either of these rules might be sufficient for general practical convenience, although in theory perhaps one might appear more just than another: but there is no such rule of practice; nations concur in principle indeed so far as to require firm and secure possession; but their rules of evidence respecting possession are so discordant, and lead to such opposite conclusions, that the mere unity of principle forms no uniform rule to regulate the general practice. If it be asked, under the known diversity of practice on this subject, what is the proper rule for a state to apply to the recaptured property of its allies, or of neutrals? It is answered, that the liberal and rational proceeding would be, to apply in the first instance the rule of that country to which the recaptured property belongs. Such a rule would be both liberal and just: to the recaptured, it presents his own consent, bound up in the legislative wisdom of his own country: to the recaptor it cannot be considered as injurious. Where the rule of the recaptured would condemn, whilst the rule of the recaptor prevailing amongst his own countrymen would restore, it brings an obvious advantage; and even in the case of immediate restitution, under the rules of the recap-

(v) *Grotius*, De J. B. ac P. L. 3. c. 6. § 3. *Consolato del Mare*, c. 2[illegible]. § 1156.

tured, the recapturing country would rest secure in the reliance of receiving reciprocal justice in its turn. It may be said, what if this reliance should be disappointed?—Redress must then be sought from retaliation; which in the disputes of independent states, is not to be considered as vindictive retaliation, but as the just and equal measure of civil retribution.(w) In any other course of proceeding there would be a defect of that reciprocity which, according to Valin, would offend against the impartial justice due from one state to another.

It is upon these grounds that the law of our own country proceeds. By the act of Congress of the third March, 1800, it is enacted, That the vessels or goods of persons permanently resident within the territory, and under the protection of any foreign government in amity with the United States, and retaken by vessels of the United States, shall be restored to the owner, he paying for, and in lieu of salvage, such proportion of the value thereof, as by the law and usage of such goverement, within whose territory such former owner shall be so resident, shall be required of any vessel or goods of the United States under like circumstances of recapture; and where no such law or usage shall be known, the same salvage shall be allowed as is provided by the first section of this act, Provided also, that no such vessel shall be so restored to such former owner, in any case where the same shall have been condemned as prize by competent authority before the recapture, nor in any case, when by the law or usage of the foreign government, the goods or vessels of citizens of the United States in like circumstances would not be restored.

It becomes then of importance to ascertain what is the law and usage of the different maritime nations on the subject of recaptures; and this is to be sought for either in

(w) 1 *Robinson*, 50. The Santa Cruz. *La retorsion de droit, Vattel*, L. 2. c. 18. § 341.

the municipal code of each country, or in the conventional law by which they are bound to one another.

14. By the French Ordinance of 1681, *Liv.* 3. *tit.* 9. *Des Prises*, *art.* 8. it is provided, That if any French vessel is retaken from the enemy, after being in his hands more than twenty-four hours, she shall be good prize to the recaptor; and if retaken before twenty-four hours have elapsed, shall be restored to the owner, with the goods laden on board, upon the payment of one third the value thereof for salvage.

It seems that the above is the rule applied by France to recaptures of the vessels and effects of her allies. For the council of prizes decided on the ninth February, 1801, as to two Spanish vessels recaptured by a French private armed vessel after the twenty-four hours had elapsed, that they should be condemned as good prize to the recaptor. Had the recapture been made by a public armed vessel, whether before or after the twenty-four hours had elapsed, it appears that the property would have been restored without salvage, according to the usage with respect to French subjects, and on account of the intimate relation subsisting between the two powers.[x] For, notwithstanding the express terms of this article of the ordinance make no exception of *public* armed vessels, yet the usage in France has been to restore property retaken by them, whether it had been in the possession of the enemy twenty-four hours or not, and without the payment of salvage.[y]

A question arose in France upon the construction of this article under the following circumstances. A French private armed vessel, during war with England, had taken an English merchantman and kept possession for three days, at the end of which time both vessels were taken by the

(x) *Azuni*, Part 2. c. 4. § 11.

(y) *Valin*, Sur l'Ordonnance, L. 3. tit. 9. Des Prises, art 3. *Pothier*, De Propriété, No. 97. 1 *Code des Prises*, 9.

English, and after being in their possession sixteen hours were re-taken by another French private armed vessel. There was no doubt raised as to the French private armed vessel which had been re-captured that she must be restored upon payment of one third of the value for salvage. The question was respecting the English merchantman, which the first captor maintained ought to be restored to him as well as his own vessel. The grounds upon which he supported his claim, were that he had acquired the domain of property in this prize, it having remained in his possession for three days, and that he must be considered as preserving it, notwithstanding the recapture by the enemy, who had maintained his possession only sixteen hours. On the other hand the French recaptor contended that although the English prize belonged to the first captor whilst it remained in his possession, it was no longer his when retaken from the enemy; that although he preserved the right of property in his own vessel, because it had not remained in the hands of the enemy more than twenty-four hours, it did not therefore follow that the same rule was to be applied to the English prize, for it is of the nature of domain of property which we acquire in things taken from the enemy that we preserve it no longer than those things are in our possession, and lose it the moment we are divested, and they again fall into the enemy's hands, in the same manner as we retain the property of savage animals only so long as they are in our possession, and lose it the moment we part with the possession, and they have returned to their natural state of liberty. Upon these grounds the council of State decided in his favour, and by a decree of the fifth November, 1748, condemned the English prize to his use.([z])

15. The laws of Spain upon this subject are the same with

([z]) *Valin*, Sur l'Ordonnance, L. 3. tit. 9. Des Prises, art. 8. *Pothier*, De Propriété, No. 98.

those of France, except in the single case of recapture from pirates mentioned above.

16. By the Portuguese Ordinance of May, 1797, the rate of salvage on recaptures was established for ships of war at one eighth, and one fifth for privateers.

17. By the laws of Denmark, if a Danish ship be recaptured, before she has been in possession of the enemy for twenty-four hours, the property is equally divided between the original owner and the re-captors; if after being in possession of the enemy twenty four hours, is then condemned to the recaptors.

18. By the Swedish Ordinance of 1667, it is declared, that in case a Swedish vessel taken by the enemy, shall be recaptured, the recaptor shall be entitled to a salvage of two thirds the value, and the remaining third shall be restored to the owner without regard to the length of time the property may have been in the enemy's possession.

19. By the British statutes of the thirty-third George III. c. 66, forty third George III. c. 160, and forty fifth George III. c. 72, it is enacted, that any vessel, and goods laden therein, taken as prize, which shall appear to have belonged to British subjects, or to the British dominions, and which shall be retaken, shall be restored to the former owners, upon payment for salvage of one eighth part, if retaken by any of his majesty's ships, and if retaken by any privateer, or other vessel or boat, of one sixth part of the value. And if the same shall have been retaken by the joint operation or means of one or more of his majesty's, and one or more private ship or ships, then the proper court shall order such salvage to be paid as shall be deemed reasonable. But if the vessel so retaken shall appear to have been set forth as a vessel of war by the enemy, then the same shall not be restored to the former owners, but shall be adjudged lawful prize for the use of the captors. And if the recaptured vessel had not been carried into an enemy's port, it shall be lawful, with the consent of the recaptors, for her to prose-

tute her voyage, and the recaptors need not proceed to adjudication until six months after, or the return of the vessel to the port from whence she sailed: if the vessel does not return to such port directly, or the recaptors have had no opportunity to proceed to adjudication within the time limited on account of the absence of the vessel, the proper court shall decree restitution to the former owners, at the instance of the recaptors, on payment of salvage, and upon reasonable evidence.

20. By the act of the third March, 1800, the Congress of the United States have provided, Sec. 1. That when any vessel, other than a vessel of war or privateer, or goods, which shall be taken as prize, shall appear to have before belonged to any person resident within or under the protection of the United States; and to have been taken by their enemy, the same not having been condemned as prize before the recapture thereof, the same shall be restored to the former owner, upon payment for salvage, if retaken by a public vessel of the United States, of one eighth part, and if by a private vessel, one sixth part, of the value of the vessel or goods so to be restored, excepting all imposts and public duties to which the same may be liable. And if the vessel so retaken shall appear to have been set forth and armed as a vessel of war, before the retaking thereof, the former owner, shall be adjudged to pay for salvage one moiety of the value of the same. Sec. 2. That when any vessel or goods, which shall be taken as prize, shall appear to have before belonged to the United States, and to have been taken by their enemy, the same not having been condemned as prize before the recapture thereof, shall be restored to the United States. And for salvage, there shall be paid from the treasury, of an unarmed vessel or any goods therein, one sixth part of the value, when made by a private vessel, and one twelfth part when made by a public armed vessel of the United States; and for the recapture of a public armed vessel, or any goods therein,

one moiety of the value when made by a private armed vessel, and one fourth part when made by a public armed vessel of the United States.

It will be perceived that there is a material difference between the British and American laws on this subject; the British continuing the *jus postliminii*, as between the original owners and recaptors, forever, unless the vessel retaken appears to have been set forth by the enemy as a ship of war,—whilst the United States' law continues the *jus postliminii* until the property is divested by a sentence of condemnation in a court of competent jurisdiction, and no longer.(a)

Under the first section of the above law of the United States, it has been adjudged that the salvage for recapture of goods, being American property on board an American armed ship, which was fitted out for war, and made resistance, was only one eighth part, if retaken by a public vessel, and if by a private vessel, one sixth part of the value, although the salvage for the *ship* was one moiety. The words of the statute were construed as expressing this distinction.(b)

21. Where a vessel of the belligerent state had been captured, and afterwards sold by the enemy to a neutral at sea, who purchased for the purpose of restoring her to the original owner, salvage was held to be due. If the neutral had purchased the vessel upon his own account, it would have been an illegal transaction; as he could derive no title from the captors without a previous sentence of condemnation. But being a transaction by which, under the form and colour of a sale, he was to recover the property for the owners, he had rendered them a very meritorious

(a) 4 *Cranch*, 293. Hutson vs Guestier. And such was the principle adopted in the English tribunals before it was changed by their statutes. 2. *Burrow*, 694. 1208. 1. *Edwards*, 186. L'Actif.

(b) The Adeline. Supreme Court of the U. S. February T. 1815. M.S.

service, and was justly entitled to salvage. It is not necessary that the recovery of the property should be attended with personal risk to the salvor; in cases where the enemy makes a present of a captured vessel to a stranger, who has encountered no hazard, who has not endangered a hair of his head, or laid out a sixpence of his money, the party is always held entitled to a salvage if he has been the instrument of bringing the vessel back to the possession of its owner.(c) And the *Consolato del Mare* has prescribed that in case a ship or cargo are ransomed from the enemy by a person other than the original owner, the property shall be restored to the original owner upon repayment of the amount of the ransom money for salvage.(d)

22. Where a public ship of war had a number of merchant vessels under her convoy, and one of them was captured by the enemy, and afterwards re-taken by the ship of war, it was determined that she was entitled to the salvage allowed to public vessels on ordinary occasions. The only material question to be considered was, whether there was such a capture made by the enemy as would found a case of re-capture. Many cases might be put of the effects of immediate acts of re-capture, to show that it is by no means necessary that the possession by the enemy should be *long* maintained, or at any particular distance from the convoying ship. The question will always be, whether it was an effectual possession, and such as would suspend the relation of the convoying ship; not, whether it is a complete and firm possessions, which, for some purpose, is, in contemplation of law, not held to be effected, till the prize is carried *infra præsidia*. The rule of *infra præsidia*, however, is cer-

(c) 1 *Edwards*, 192. The Henry.

(d) c. 290. § 1149. But military salvage is not given unless the property has been in the possession, actual or constructive, of the enemy. 2 *Robinson*, 138. The Packet de Bilboa. 4 *Robinson*, 147. The Franklin.

tainly not the measure to be applied to questions of this kind. As little can it be contended that the vessel should have been out of sight, to found a case of re-capture; it will be sufficient if there has been a complete and absolute possession, which supersedes the authority of the convoying ship; and such a possession must have been maintained for some time in this instance. Every act of possession was exercised; the master was taken out; the vessel was completely manned with as many of the captor's crew as were sufficient to overpower all resistance, and the vessel was taken in tow by the enemy. By these acts the former relation subsisting between the merchant vessel and the convoying ship was necessarily suspended. A ship in possession of the enemy can obey no signal, nor support its former duties and subordination to the convoying ship. There might still remain an obligation on the part of the convoying ship to attempt a re-capture, so far as it could be done consistently with the safety of the other vessels under her protection. Such a duty would result from the injunctions of the law, which provides a reward for the re-captor when the service is effected, and cannot, therefore, be intended to preclude the demand of salvage, though the service rendered to the individual by the re-captor, may be no more than a sense of public duty would otherwise require from him.[e]

23. Salvage is due for the ship, cargo, and freight; but it was decided were the ship was captured, and re-captured on her return voyage, that she was entitled to her whole freight, subject to a deduction for salvage. In this case the master was taken out on the first capture, and owing to that circumstance, no claim was immediately given for the cargo. The case of the cargo was therefore litigated—and was the court to say that the ship was to stay and wait the result of the proceedings, when she herself had

(e) 5 *Robinson*, 315. The Wight

been restored, whilst the cargo was contested, and might be condemned, and whilst it was by no means clear, that any cargo would remain to be carried on? This would be an unreasonable expectation. The court did not say that a party is to act in a hasty manner, and to run away immediately on the restitution of his ship. Something is to be conceded in the way of accommodation; a reasonable time is to be allowed, and if it is not allowed, a proportion of the freight may be deducted. So also where a ship was re-taken, brought in, and immediately restored, with some part of the cargo claimed for the owner of the ship; the remainder of the cargo was sometime afterwards claimed and restored upon the original evidence: The cargo had been unloaded, but the ship was not gone away at the time of the restitution, and a demand was made upon the master to take the cargo on board again, and proceed on his original voyage; but he refused, and went away with the ship; and the owners of the cargo were obliged to find another conveyance for their goods. The question as to the freight was brought before the prize court, and it was objected, that it was not due, as the ship had not performed her part of the contract; but the court decreed the whole freight to be a charge on the cargo.(f) But where a ship was captured on her outward voyage, re-captured, and brought back to the port or *quasi* port of her departure, freight *pro rata itineris* was held not to be due.(g) And in giving salvage on freight the prize court makes no separation as to minute portions of the voyage. When the voyage has commenced, and the freight is in the course of being earned, the whole freight is included in the valuation of the property on which salvage is given.(h)

(f) 3 *Robinson*, 101. The Race Horse. The Hamilton, *in notis*.

(g) *Ib.* 180. The Hiram.

(h) 6 *Robinson*, 88. The Dorothy Foster.

24. But besides the case of recapture which we have hitherto considered, a vessel and goods may be recovered from the enemy's possession by the insurrection of prisoners, on board; or by being forced by stress of weather, or by other accident coming into port, or falling into the hands of the subjects of the belligerent state or of friendly powers. These circumstances form the cases of rescue from the enemy, and the finding of property derelict which has been in his possession.

25. In the case of rescue we must distinguish whether it be of property belonging to the citizens or subjects of the belligerent state by other citizens or subjects of the same; of foreign property by foreigners; of foreign property by the citizens or subjects of the belligerent state; or, lastly, of their property by foreigners. In all these instances the property is restored upon salvage: and in the first mentioned the rule adopted in giving salvage is that of recapture; but the right of a tribunal of the belligerent state to entertain a demand for salvage upon *foreign* property rescued by *foreigners* has been questioned. It has been intimated by a high authority that salvage being a question of the *jus gentium,* and materially different from the question of a mariner's contract, which is a creature of the particular institutions of each country, to be applied, and construed, and explained by its own particular rules, there could be no reason why foreign seamen rescuing foreign property might not maintain an action *in rem* before a court of the law of nations, sitting in the country into which the property was brought. In the last mentioned instances, the claim is general upon the general ground of *quantum meruit*, to be governed by a sound discretion acting on general principles, and no reason can be seen why one country should be afraid to trust to the equity of the courts of another on such a question so to be determined. If it be said that different countries may have different proportions of salvage, and therefore, an inconvenience may

arise from such interference : it is answered that there exists no rule on this matter, beyond that which subjects it to a sound discretion, distributing the reward according to the value of the services that have been performed. There is no peculiar rule prescribed in the British and American laws, and none in the codes of other nations applying to the cases of *foreign* property rescued. This consideration, therefore forms no solid objection against the exercise of the jurisdiction, and there is great reason for it, because it is the only way of enforcing the best security—that of the lien on the property itself. ([1])

The French Ordinance of 1681 prescribes that, if the vessel not having been recaptured, is abandoned by the enemy, or by storms or other accidents returns into the possession of subjects of France, before being carried into an enemy's port, she shall be restored to the former owner, if claimed within a year and a day, although the possession of the enemy may have continued more than twenty-four hours—L. 3. tit. 9. art. 9. Des Prises.

Upon the construction of this article, Valin is of the opinion that it should be likened to the case of a shipwreck, and that the salvor is entitled to one third of the value for salvage as provided in the twenty-seventh article of the same ordinance *Tit. des Naufrages.* To which Azuni objects that the ninth article being silent upon the subject of the payment of salvage, this omission cannot be supplied by a reference to the twenty-seventh, which relates wholly to goods lost by shipwreck, found derelict on the sea, or drawn up from its bottom. He who restores to the original owner a vessel found abandoned on the high seas, has rendered a less meritorious service than he who exposes his life and property to rescue a captured vessel from the hands of an enemy. The reward in the first

([1]) 1. *Robinson*, 271. The Two Friends.

33

case, ought, therefore to be less than in the second, though proportioned to the nature and extent of the service performed, yet always less than a third of the value of the articles recovered. (k)

26. In the case of property found derelict which has been in the enemy's possession, as well as in that of a rescue from him, our municipal law has prescribed no positive rule as to the amount of salvage to be paid. In such a case therefore the amount is not limited by the act of Congress, but may be enlarged or diminished, in the discretion of the court, according to the particular merit of the service rendered.(l)

Where an enemy vessel was taken by the other belligerent, and abandoned on the high seas, and afterwards fell into the hands of a neutral, who brought her into a port of his own country, it was determined in the prize court of that country that immediately on the capture the captors acquired such a right as no neutral nation could justly impugn or destroy; and that consequently the abandonment did not revive the right of property in the original proprietor. The prize was therefore restored to the captor upon the payment of salvage to the neutral salvor.(m)

So where Great Britain and France were at open war, and two French frigates captured the ship in question, and after taking out part of the cargo made a present of her to the libellants in the cause, citizens of the United States then neutral (whose vessel the frigates had before taken and burnt) by whom she was navigated into a port of their own country, and pending the suit instituted by them, war was declared between the United States and Great Britain, a

(k) *Valin*, Sur l'Ordonnance, L. 3. tit. 9. art. 9. Des Prises. *Azuni*, part 2. c. 4. § 8.

(l) *Peter's Adm. Decisions*, 84. Clayton et al. vs. the Harmony. 1 *Robinson*, 279. The Two Friends. *Edwards* 79. The Lord Nelson.

(m) 3 *Dallas*, 188. M'Donnough vs. Dannery and the ship Mary Ford.

question arose whether this was a case of salvage. The fact of the gift was established by a writing under the hand of the commander of the squadron of frigates, in these words, *Je donne au capitaine*, &c. in the language of an unqualified donation *inter vivos*. In this case, the most natural mode of acquiring a definite idea of the rights of the parties in the subject matter, would be, to follow it through the successive changes of circumstances by which the nature and extent of those rights were affected. The capture,—the donation,—the arrival in the neutral country,—and the subsequent state of war. As between belligerents, the capture undoubtedly produces a complete divesture of property. Nothing remains to the original proprietor but a mere *scintilla juris* the *spes recuperandi*. The modern and enlightened practice of nations has subjected all such captures to the scrutiny of judicial tribunals, as the only practical means of furnishing documentary evidence to accompany vessels that have been captured, for the purpose of proving that the seizure was the act of sovereign authority, and not of mere individual outrage. In the case of a purchase made by a neutral, Great Britain demands the production of such documentary evidence issuing from a court of competent authority, or will dispossess the purchaser of a ship originally British.(n) Upon the donation, therefore, whatever right, might, in the abstract, have existed in the captor, the donee could acquire no more than what was consistent with his neutral character to take. He could be in no better situation than a prize master navigating the prize, in pursuance of orders from his commander. The vessel remained liable to British recapture on the whole voyage: and, on her arrival in a neutral territory, the donee sunk into a mere bailee for the British claimant, with those rights over the thing in possession

(n) *Robinson*, 114. The Flad Oyer.

which the municipal law (civil and common) gives for care and labour bestowed upon it.

The question then recurs, was this a case of salvage?

On the negative of the proposition it was contended,—that it was a case of forfeiture under the municipal law, and therefore not a case of salvage as against the United States; that it was an unneutral act to assist the French belligerent in bringing the vessel *infra præsidia*, or into any situation, where the rights of recapture would cease, and therefore not a case of salvage as against the British claimant.

But the court entertained an opinion unfavourable to both those objections.

This could not have been a case within the view of the legislature, when passing the non-importation act of March, 1809. The ship was the plank on which the shipwrecked mariners reached the shore; and although it might be urged that bringing in the cargo was not necessarily connected with their own return to their country, yet, upon reflection, it will be found, that this also can be excused upon fair principles. It was their duty to adhere strictly to their neutral character; but to have cast into the sea, the cargo, the property of a belligerent, would have been to do him an injury by taking away that chance of recovery, subject to which, they took it into their possession. Besides, bringing it into the United States did not necessarily presuppose a violation of the non-importation laws. If it came within the description of property, cast, casually on our shores, as the court were of opinion it did, legal provision existed for disposing of it in such a manner as would comport with the policy of those laws. At last, they could but deliver it up to the hands of the government, to be re-shipped by the British claimant, or otherwise appropriated under the sanction of judicial process. And such was the course that they pursued. Far from attempting any violation of the laws of the country, upon their arrival, they delivered it up to the custody of the laws, and left it to be disposed of under judicial authority. The case had no feature of illegal importation, and could not possibly have imputed to it the violation of municipal law.

As to the question arising on the interest of the British claimant, it would, at that time (war having supervened) be a sufficient answer, that they who had no rights in the court, could not urge a violation of their rights against the libellants. But there was still a much more satisfactory answer. To have attempted to carry the vessel *infra præsidia* of the enemy, would, unless it could have been excused on the ground of necessity, have been an unneutral act. But where every exertion is made to bring it into a place of safety, in which the original right of the captured would be revived and might be asserted, instead of aiding his enemy, it is doing an act, exclusively resulting to the benefit of the British claimant.

It being determined to be a case of salvage, the next question was, as to the amount to be allowed. On this subject, there is no precise rule; nor is it, in its nature, reducible to rule—For it must, in every case, depend upon peculiar circumstances such as peril incurred, labour sustained, value saved, &c. all of which must be estimated and weighed by the court that awards the salvage. When a proportion of the thing saved has been awarded, a half has been the *maximum*, and an eighth the *minimum*; below that, it is usual to adjudge a compensation *in numero*. In some cases, indeed, more than a half may have been awarded; but they will be found to be cases of very extraordinary merit, or on articles of very small amount. In this case the proceeds of the sale of the cargo amounted to near six thousand dollars, and the court were of opinion that one half of that sum would be an adequate compensation.(°)

(°) Per JOHNSON. J. The Adventure, Supreme Court of the U. S. February T. 1814. M. S. *Vide Supra*, C. I. § 3.

CHAPTER IX.

Of the jurisdiction and practice of Courts of Prize.

1. The validity of maritime captures is, with certain exceptions, determined in courts of prize established in the country of the captor, and judging by the law of nations.

2. Among these exceptions is included the case of a neutral power, the prize courts of which have the exclusive authority of determining the validity of captures made by the cruisers of the belligerents within its territorial jurisdiction.

Thus by the laws of the United States the district courts are authorized to take cognizance of complaints, by whomsoever instituted, in case of captures made within the waters of the United States, or within a marine league of the coasts or shores thereof.[a]

3. And a neutral state will restore the property of powers in amity with it, or of their subjects or citizens, taken by armed vessels fitted out within the dominions of the neutral state in violation of its neutrality, and which property is brought into its ports.[b]

4. So also, when captured property is brought into a neutral port, the neutral sovereign or state will restore the property of its own subjects or citizens, if the same has been illegally taken from them.[c]

[a] *Vide supra*, Chapter II. § 14.

[b] *Vide supra*, Chapter II. § 7.

[c] *Peters' Admiralty Decisions*, 330. Hollingsworth et al. vs. the Betsey, 3 *Dallas*, 6. Glass et al. vs. the Betsey.

Thus by the French ordinance of 1681, *Liv.* 3, *tit.* 9, *Des Prises*, art. 15, it is provided that, If on board the prizes brought into our ports by ships of war under the commission of a foreign prince or state, there be found goods belonging to our subjects or allies, those of our subjects shall be restored to them, and the others shall not be stored, nor purchased by any person, under any pretext whatsoever. The same provision is contained in the 16th article of the Spanish ordinance of 1718. And by the preceding article of the French ordinance above referred to, prizes taken by ships of war under a foreign commission, are forbidden from remaining more than twenty-four hours in the ports of France, unless they are detained by tempests, or unless *the prize was taken from the enemies of France*. In his commentary upon these articles, Valin expresses an opinion that it is immaterial whether the prize be taken by the cruisers of an ally or confederate of France, or from a common enemy by a co-belligerent with whom there is no subsisting treaty of alliance; for in either case the goods of the prize may be stored, and purchased with safety by any person.

5. But subject to these exceptions, the right of property acquired by capture continues in the captors who have brought their prize into a neutral port, or within the territorial jurisdiction of a neutral power. For, though the *civil* right of property in the prize may not be vested in the captor until a sentence of condemnation, yet the *military* right of property which is evidenced by possession is completely vested in him by the capture. By what right then shall the neutral sovereign who is the friend of the captor, take from him those things which belong to him, *jure belli*, and give them up to another, though he be equally his friend? He cannot do it by his courts of justice, for he cannot lawfully judge between the captor and his enemy, without the consent of both. But the neutral is bound to see *right* wherever he sees possession; he is

bound to take the *fact* for the *law*. If, therefore, a vessel, after capture, should escape, or be brought into a neutral territory by others than the captor, his agents, or those who otherwise lawfully claim under him, as there is no longer any legal evidence of the *military* right, no *fact* which is to be taken for *law*, the *civil* right of the former owner revives, and the property returns to him by the law of *postliminium*. It is however to be understood that in case the property has been regularly condemned in the proper court, such a condemnation converts the *military* into a *civil* right, and precludes the operation of the law of *postliminium* in favour of the original owner.(d)

6. It is the opinion of many writers of authority, that the belligerents have not only a right of asylum in neutral ports, but that they have a right to sell in those ports their prizes, and to recover and appropriate to themselves the proceeds of the same. But unless it is permitted by the municipal law of the neutral country impartially to all the belligerents, or exclusively allowed to one or more by special treaty, there seems to be nothing in the principles of public law which can prevent the neutral from withholding it entirely. Thus by the French law, as we have seen before, the sale of prizes taken from powers in amity with France, and brought into her ports, is expressly forbidden; and Valin remarks upon this prohibition that it is founded upon the laws of neutrality. *Vide* Bee's Adm. Reports, 263. Consul of Spain, vs. consul of Great Britain.

7. Another exception to this general rule, that the validity of maritime captures is determined in courts of prize *established in the country of the captor*, is to be found in the case of prizes carried into a port of an ally in the war, or of a co-belligerent, and adjudicated upon by a consular tribunal of the captor's nation established in the country of the ally or co-belligerent. The exercise of such a jurisdiction on the part of the consul of a foreign, though *friendly* power, is

(d) *Du Ponceau's Bynkershoek*, Q. J. P. L. 1. c. 15.

unquestionably unlawful, unless it be expressly permitted by treaty. But if the ally or co-belligerent chuse to waive his strict rights of sovereignty for this purpose, other parties cannot complain of it, since he thereby violates no duty, as a neutral would do in a like case. ([e])

8. Subject to these exceptions the validity of maritime captures is always determined in courts of prize established in the country of the captor; and that whether the property is carried into his own port or a port of an ally or co-belligerent, or whether it be carried into a neutral port.

9. And respecting the first case there can be no doubt. In the second case (where the property is carried into the port of an ally, or co-belligerent) there is nothing to prevent the government of the country from permitting the exercise of that last, and crowning act of hostility, the condemnation of the property of one belligerent to the other; there is a common interest between the two governments, and both may be presumed to authorize any measures conducing to give effect to their arms, and to consider each others' ports as mutually subservient. Such an adjudication is therefore sufficient in regard to property taken in the course of the operations of a common war. ([f])

10. But where the property is carried into a *neutral* port, it may appear more doubtful whether the validity of the capture can be determined even by a court of prize established in the captor's country. It may be said, that on principle, the security and consummation of the capture is as complete in a neutral port, as in the port of the belligerent himself. On the mere principle of security, it may perhaps, be so; but it is to be remembered, that this is a matter not to be governed by abstract principles alone: The use and practice of nations have intervened, and shifted the matter from its foundations of that species: The expression

([e]) 2 *Robinson*, 210. *In Notis*. 3 *Robinson*, 333. The Cosmopolite.

([f]) 2 *Robinson*, 209. The Christopher.

which Grotius uses on these occasions *placuit gentibus*, is perfectly correct, intimating, that there is a use and practice of nations to which we are now expected to conform. Without entering into a discussion of the various opinions that have been thrown out on this subject, the better opinion and practice may be stated to have been, that a prize should be brought *infra præsidia* of the capturing country, where, by being so brought, it may be considered as incorporated into the mass of national stock. The greatest exceptions that have been allowed, has not carried the rule beyond the ports or places of security, belonging to some friend or ally in the war, who has a common interest in defending the acquisitions of the belligerent, made from the common enemy of both. In latter times, an additional formality has been required, that of a sentence of condemnation in a competent court, decreeing the capture to have been rightly made *jure belli*; it not being thought fit, in civilized society, that property of this sort should be converted without the sentence of a competent court, pronouncing it to have been seized as the property of an enemy, and to be now become *jure belli* the property of the captor. The purposes of justice require, that such exercises of war should be placed under public inspection; and therefore the mere *deductio infra præsidia* has not been deemed sufficient. From the moment that a sentence of condemnation becomes necessary, it imposes an additional obligation for bringing the property, on which it is to pass, into the country of the captor; for a legal sentence must be the result of legal proceedings, in a legitimate court, armed with competent authority upon the subject matter, and upon the parties concerned—a court which has the means of pursuing the proper enquiry, and enforcing its decisions. These are principles of universal jurisprudence applicable to all courts, and more especially to those which by their constitution, in all countries, must act *in rem*, upon the *corpus* or substance of the thing acquired, and upon the parties, one of whom is not subject to other rights than those of war, and is amenable to no jurisdiction, but such as belongs to those who possess the rights of war against him. Upon principle, therefore, it is not to be asserted, that a ship brought into a neutral port, is with effect proceeded against in the belligerent country. The *res ipsa*, the *corpus*, is not within the possession of the court; and possession, in such cases, founds the jurisdiction. What is the authority over the parties? Over the captors it is complete, on account of their personal relation to the belligerent country. The neutral government may be called upon, in the usual mode of requisition known to the law and practice of nations, to enforce upon the captors the orders and decrees of the state to which they belong. But how will it be maintainable over the other parties, who are not subjects either of the neutral or belligerent state, and are, in respect to the point in issue, only subject to the jurisdiction of war? The belligerent state itself has not the means of exercising the rights of war over them directly:—can it call on the neutral state by requisition so to do? Most clearly not. The neutral state has nothing to do with the rights of force, possessed by the one belligerent against the other; it has nothing to do with the enforcement or consummation of such rights; it owes to both parties the simple rights of hospitality, and even these are very limited in the practice of most civilized states. By the regulations of France, foreign ships are forbidden to enter with prizes into the ports of France, except in cases of distress, and then they are permitted to stay no longer than this necessity exists. Valin observes on this article, that such a rule is exactly conformable to the laws of neutrality; and Hubner admits that a wise hospitality will not be exercised beyond this. At any rate the neutral state can have no compulsory jurisdiction, to exercise upon either party, upon questions of war depending between them; nor can any such jurisdiction be conveyed to it by the authority of one of them. Its own duties of neutrality prevent the acceptance of any belligerent rights; it cannot be called upon by requisition to give any facility or convenience to the one party, to the prejudice of the other, much less to apply modes of compulsion to the one, to serve the hostile purposes of the other. In the administration of a jurisdiction of this kind, the enemy who is vanquished, is not only a necessary party, but likewise a necessary witness, according to the proceedings of all countries. Prisoners are necessary witnesses to be examined. How are they liable to be compelled to undergo such examination? No force can be applied in the way of strict or continual imprisonment to compel their answers to interrogatories. Their refusal would carry no consequence of legal contumacy with it; for legal contumacy can only exist, where a legal jurisdiction has demanded a submission. From these considerations it should seem to result, that in the case of a ship lying in a neutral country, there is not only a want of original jurisdiction in the belligerent country, from the want of possession; but that there is likewise a substantial defect of that authority, which is required for the attainment of justice, and which is essentially necessary to give effect to the ceremony of condemnation.[g]

But the conclusiveness of these reasonings has been contested, and the practice of nations sanctions the condemnation of property brought into neutral ports, by courts of prize established in the country of the captor. The regularity of such a proceeding has therefore been maintained in the British prize courts,[h] and in those of the United States.[i] And by the French Ordinance of the eleventh March, 1705, renewed by the regulation of the eighth November, 1779, the cruisers of France were permitted to

(g) 4 *Robinson*, 43. The Henrick and Maria.

(h) *Ib.* 6 *Robinson*, 139. *In Notis.*

(i) 4 *Cranch*, 241, Rose vs. Himely. *Ib.* 293. Hudson at al. vs. Guestier.

carry their prizes into foreign ports, and there to dispose of them, under the superintendence of the French consuls, who were directed to send home the documentary and other evidence necessary for their adjudication.[k] For the sovereign, whose officer has in his name captured a vessel as prize of war, remains in possession of that vessel, and has full power over her, so long as she is in a situation where that possession cannot be rightfully divested. The fact whether she is an enemy vessel or not, ought however, to be judicially enquired into and decided, and therefore the property in a neutral, captured as an enemy, is never changed until condemnation is passed ; and the practice of nations requires that the vessel shall be in a place of safety before such sentence can be rendered.

In the port of a neutral she is in a place of safety, and the possession of the captor cannot be lawfully divested, because the neutral sovereign, by himself or by his courts, cannot take cognizance of the question of prize or no prize. A vessel captured as prize of war is, then, while lying in the port of a neutral, still in the possession of the sovereign of the captor, and that possession cannot be rightfully divested. Nor is the objection, that his courts can take no jurisdiction of a vessel under such circumstances, because they cannot enforce a sentence of restitution, well founded; since the possession of the captor is in principle the possession of his sovereign; he is commissioned to seize in the name of the sovereign, and is as much an officer appointed for that purpose, as one who in the body of a county serves a civil process. He is under the control and direction of the sovereign, and must be considered as ready to obey his commands legally communicated through his courts. It is true that in point of fact cruizers are often commanded by men who do not feel a due respect for the laws, and who are not of sufficient res-

(k) 1 *Code des Prises*, 357.

ponsibility to compensate the injuries their improper conduct may occasion; but in principle they must be considered as officers commissioned by their sovereign to make a seizure in the particular case, and to be ready to obey his legitimate mandate directing a restitution. The property, therefore, may be restored in a neutral port, and whether it may or may not be sold in the neutral port, the condemnation may change the property, if such condemnation be valid. The difficulty of executing the sentence does not, then, seem to afford any conclusive argument against the jurisdiction of the court of the captor over property in possession of the captor, but lying in a neutral port.(l)

11. These courts of prize are established in every country, according to the municipal constitution of each, and there is in all a superior court of review, consisting of the most considerable persons, to which the parties, who think themselves aggrieved, may appeal; and all these courts, whether supreme or inferior, judge by the same rule, which is the law of nations. And it is the duty of those tribunals, though they are established in the belligerent country, to administer with indifference that justice which the law of nations holds out, without distinction, to independent states, some happening to be neutral and some to be belligerent. The seat of judicial authority is indeed, locally *there*, in the belligerent country, according to the known law and practice of nations: but the law itself has no locality. It is the duty of the person, who sits there, to determine the questions that arise exactly as he would determine the same questions if sitting in the neutral country whose rights are to be adjudicated upon.(m)

(l) *Cranch* 4, 295. Hudson et al. vs. Guestier. Vide 1 *Johnson*, 471. Wheelwright v. Depeyster, *Contra*. In that case it was determined that prize courts cannot adjudicate on a prize lying in a foreign neutral port, or out of the jurisdiction of the captor or his ally.

(m) 1 *Robinson*, 340. The Maria.

12. Thus in France, in the year 1659, the power of deciding prize-causes was vested in a council of prizes, composed of counsellors of state and masters of requests, and presided over by the admiral. From the decisions of this tribunal an appeal lay to the king in council. During the revolution, great confusion prevailed in the administration of prize law, until the re-establishment of the council of prizes by a decree of the eighth March, 1800, which is now composed of a counsellor of state, as president, and of eight other members, this court, which sits at Paris, determines all litigated prize causes, upon simple memoirs presented by the parties or their advocates. The delay in bringing a cause to a hearing cannot exceed three months, where the prize has been brought into the ports of the Mediterranean, and two months, if brought into any other of the ports of France; these periods being reckoned from the day on which the papers in the cause are lodged in the secretary's office. An appeal lies from the decisions of this court to the council of state. (n)

At the first session of the council of prizes, M. Portalis, the commissary representing the French government before it, delivered the following address, which for the soundness of its principles and the eloquence of its style merits to be recorded.

" A wise government, which feels the necessity of justice, and is firmly resolved to exercise it, has called us to fulfil, before you, citizens, the delicate and sublime functions of conscience. It has constituted us, as it were, the ministers of a sacred alliance between policy and morality.

" The principles of morality are obligatory as well upon nations, as upon individuals : they form the common law of the universe. But between different nations this law is deficient in those sanctions by which its observance must be secured ; for they are, in relation to each other,

(n) 2 *Code des Prises*, 476.

in a state of nature, in that state, where every individual is the sovereign arbiter of his own actions, and the supreme judge in his own cause. Hence hostilities, reprisals, and frequent wars which shake empires and ravage the world.

" A citizen, besides the care of his own particular interest, is bound to labour for the public good of his country. A state, besides the care of its own interior government, is charged with the duty of contributing to the happiness of the human race. *Do, in peace, the greatest possible good; in war, the least possible evil:* this is the law of nations. The principles of this law are simple: but in barbarous and ignorant times they were trampled under foot by men abandoned to the influence of blind and unregulated passions. In these latter times, those passions have been softened by civilization; but the multitude and contrariety of different interests, which the ideas of money, of commerce, of national wealth, and of the balance of power, have introduced, have become new causes of emulation, of ambition, of jealousy and of enmity. The science of government not being perfected in proportion to the conflicting interests which we have to conciliate, and the difficulties which we have to vanquish, it happens, that notwithstanding the knowledge we have acquired, we as yet enjoy but partially the advantages which that knowledge seems calculated to secure us.

" The law of war is founded upon the principle that one nation, for its own preservation or in self defence, will, can, or ought, to do violence to another. It is a relation of things, and not of persons, which constitutes war: it is the relation of state to state, and not of individual to individual. Between two or more belligerent nations, the individuals of which they are composed, are enemies by accident only: they are not such as men, nor even as citizens, they are such only as soldiers.

" Let us do justice to our philosophy, which according to its fundamental truths, has repeatedly called upon the governments of Europe, to stipulate for the liberty and security of commerce, and for the safety of the productions of the arts and private property, in time of war; but policy, which is not political right, has hitherto resisted the conclusions of philosophy. It must at the same time be acknowledged that a theory, which is apparently the most perfect, is not always adapted to practice. The maxim of the wise man should be, not to aspire after that absolute good, which the nature of things and of man renders inaccessible, but to seek for that relative good which is within our reach, which is indicated by experience, and which flows from rational principles adapted to the wants of society. In the new position in which the invention of the mariners compass and the discovery of America have placed the world, our commercial relations have become the principal source of wars. It is for the interests of commerce, well or ill understood, that the earth is deluged in blood.

"A great revolution must therefore be effected in human affairs and opinions, before we can hope for one in policy.

"It may, in other respects, be thought that the interruption of commerce between belligerent nations, produces the good effect of connecting, in each government, the dangers of the citizen with the dangers of the country; communicates to the public interest all the force and energy of private interest; discourages by anticipating that waste of resources which the desire of conquest and vain glory must occasion; checks projects of aggrandizement by the certain evils which must follow them; places in opposition the inquietude of the citizen who suffers with the extravagance of the magistrate who governs; and, finally, renders governments more careful in commencing wars and more willing to terminate them.

"But whatever may be our opinion of the question, whether commerce should be prohibited, or should remain free between the belligerent powers, there can be no doubt that neutral nations, since they take no part in the war, should continue to enjoy all the advantages of peace.

" In order to diminish the calamities of one of the most terrible scourges which can afflict humanity, the antients established and consecrated free cities, which served as the asylums of commerce, and in which, in the midst of the most bloody hostilities, industry found a safe retreat. Since civilization has, if I may so speak, added new nations to the human race, there are always among the numerous nations that cover the globe, some who are interested by their situation, to preserve a neutral character ; and this neutrality, which is in time of war, the sole ligament of social relations and useful intercourse among men, should be religiously respected as a real public good. The belligerent powers are, undoubtedly, authorized to watch over and guard against the frauds of a feigned neutrality. If a known enemy be always manifest, the neutral may conceal a real enemy under the robe of a friend ; he is then struck by the law of war, and he deserves to be. But let us be careful, in applying this severe law, to respect treaties, the usages consecrated by the uniform practice of nations, and the principles which guarantee the sovereignty and independence of states. Policy may have its plans and its mysteries ; but reason ought to preserve her influence and dignity. When the arbitrary principles of fear and necessity govern the public councils, all is lost ! every species of violence desolates the earth, and blood flows in torrents. By inspiring terror, we may momentarily increase our forces ; but it is by inspiring confidence that we preserve them forever.

" I felicitate myself, in proclaiming these principles, to be more particularly, by my functions at your bar, the depositary and interpreter of the intentions of government, and to be able to join my feeble voice to that of the eloquent and enlightened minister who has already pointed out in so able a manner the standard of our duties and the course of our labours. We have great interests to weigh, and, perhaps, great errors to repair; but your knowledge and your zeal will preserve you above reproach. It is no part of our duty to adhere servilely to litigious forms, or to yield to disgusting subtleties. The French captors who will come before you are the representatives of the government; for the privilege of cruising is only a grant under the law of war from the sovereign to the individuals who devote themselves to these perilous enterprises. On the other hand, the foreigners whose fortunes will be affected by your decisions, cannot separate their cause from that of the nations of whom they form a part. It would, therefore, as the Roman orator formerly observed, be ridiculous to pretend to decide the rights of nations and the world by the same petty standard which we apply to the disputes of individuals concerning the minutest article of property. War is a necessary, lawful, and lamentable right, which always leaves an immense debt to be paid to humanity. But let justice and peace embrace each other, and already the greater part of the calamities of war are repaired.

" The hero of France, now become the first magistrate of the Republic, has just placed his victories and his name above the reach of envy, by making proposals of peace to the belligerent nations, and professing justice to all. Let us associate ourselves to the great and salutary conceptions of his mind. Equity is the virtue of empires. Moderation is the wisdom of great nations, as well as of great men. Let us be mindful that if war destroys the people, a false policy impedes their prosperity, and may even prevent their multiplication. We have astonished and shaken Europe by the fame and strength of our arms: it is time to revive her confidence by our principles, and to console her by our virtues."

Happy would it have been for the world had these principles continued to animate France and the other belligerent powers! We should not have then seen issued those edicts, by which the law of nations was trampled upon, and neutrals compelled to become *belligerents* in order to protect their rights, whilst the calamities of war were extended to every quarter of the globe.

13. The courts of prize in the British empire are the High Court of Admiralty in England, and the Vice Admiralty courts in the colonies, from which appeals lay to the Lords Commissioners of Appeal in prize causes, consisting of the privy counsellors and the judges of the courts of Westminster hall.

14. The courts of prize which were established in the United States, during the war of the revolution were as follows. On the 25th of November, 1775, Congress resolved that it should be recommended to the several legislatures in the United Colonies to erect courts of justice, or to give jurisdiction to the courts then in being, for the purpose of determining concerning the captures of British property which had been authorised, and to provide that all trials in such case be had by a jury, under such qualifications, as to the respective legislatures should seem expedient; and that an appeal should be allowed to Congress, or to such persons as they should appoint for the trial of appeals. On the 30th January, 1777, Congress resolved, that a standing committee, to consist of five members, be appointed to hear and determine upon such appeals. By the articles of confederation dated the 9th of July, 1778, and ratified by all the States on the 1st March, 1781, the United States were vested with the sole and exclusive power of establishing courts for receiving and determining finally appeals in all cases of captures. Such a court was established by the style of the *Court of Appeals in Cases of Capture,* and on the 24th of May, 1780, the cognizance of appeals then pending before Congres, or the

commissioners of appeals consisting of members of Congress, was referred to the court of appeals thus established. The records and proceedings of this court are deposited in the office of the clerk of the supreme court of the United States.

The cognizance of all causes of admiralty and maritime jurisdiction is now vested in the district courts,(o) from which an appeal lies to the circuit court where the subject matter in controversy is of the value of five hundred dollars, and from thence to the supreme court where it is of the value of two thousand dollars.

By the prize act of June 26th 1812, which subsisted during the late war with Great Britain, it was provided, Sec. 6, that in the case of all captured vessels, goods and effects, which shall be brought within the jurisdiction of the United States, the district court of the United States shall have exclusive original cognizance thereof, as in civil causes of admiralty and maritime jurisdiction ; and the said courts, or the courts being the courts of the United States, into which such causes shall be removed, and in which they shall be finally decided, shall and may decree restitution, in whole or in part, when the capture shall have been made without just cause. And if made without probable cause, or otherwise unreasonably, may order and decree damages and costs to the party injured and for which the owners and commanders of the vessels, making such captures, and also the vessels, shall be liable. But these provisions seem to have been superfluous : For by the constitution, the judiciary power is extended to all cases of admiralty and maritime jurisdiction ; the law had already vested the jurisdiction of such cases in the district courts ; and it is clear that prize causes are included in this general term ; whilst courts of prize from their very nature and constitution are cloathed with the above mentioned powers of decreeing restitution and awarding costs and damages.

(o) 3 *Dallas*, 6. Glass et al. vs. The Betsey et al.

15. The judgments or sentences of the courts of prize, thus having authority to determine the validity of maritime captures, are conclusive as to the title of property in the thing which is the subject matter of adjudication in such courts. A legal condemnation is therefore an essential muniment of the title of a neutral purchaser of captured property, without which he is liable to be evicted. (P)

16. Where a vessel had been captured contrary to the letter of the President's instructions of the 28th August, 1812, commanding &c. not to interrupt any vessels belonging to citizens of the United States coming from British ports to the U. S. laden with British merchandize in consequence of the alleged repeal of the British order in council—The *ship* was condemned in the court below for want of a claim: This sentence was relied on by the captors as establishing the fact, and consequently as depriving the *cargo* of the benefit of exemption from capture as not being in a vessel *belonging to citizens of the United States.*

The conclusive effect which the captors would have given to this sentence was founded in part on reasoning which is technical, and in part on the operation which the fact itself ought to have on the human mind in producing a conviction that the claim was not filed because it could not be sustained.

A sentence of a court of admiralty is said not only to bind the subject matter on which it is pronounced, but to prove conclusively the facts which it asserts. This principle has been maintained in the courts of municipal law in England, particularly as applying to cases of insurance,

(P) 1 *Robinson*, 102. Ib. 135. The Flad Oyen. 5 *Robinson*, 294, Nostra de Conceicas. 2 *Burrow*, 694. Goss v. Withers. 2 *Dallas*, l. 5. Miller et al. v. the Resolution. 3 *Dallas*, 86. Penhallow et al. v. Doane's Adm. In this last case it was determined that the district court has jurisdiction to carry into execution a decree of the late congressional Court of Commissioners of Appeal in prize causes. *Vide* 4 *Robinson*, 360. The Picimento.

and has been adopted by the Supreme Court of the United States.(q) Its application to this case was considered.

The *ship* was not condemned by the sentence of a foreign court of admiralty, in a case prior to and distinct from that in which the *cargo* was libelled. She was comprehended in the same libel with the cargo. The whole subject formed but one cause, and the whole came on together for adjudication before the same judge. By the rules of the court the condemnation of the ship was inevitable, not because in fact she was enemy's property, but because the fact was charged, and was not repelled by the owner, he having failed to appear and to put in his claim. The judge could not close his eyes on this circumstance; nor could he, in common justice, subject the cargo, which was claimed according to the course of the court, to the liabilities incurred by being carried in a hostile bottom. In the same cause, a fact not controverted by one party (who does not appear), and therefore as to him taken for confessed, ought not, on that implied admission, to be brought to bear upon another who does appear, does controvert, and does disprove it. The owners of the cargo had no control over the owners of the vessel. The former could not force the latter to file a claim, nor could the latter file a claim for the former. The evidence that the *ship* was the property of a citizen of the United States could not be looked into so far as respected the rights of her owner, because he was in contumacy; but the owner of the *cargo* was not in contumacy. He was not culpable on account of, and therefore ought not to suffer for, the contumacy of the ship owner. That contumacy in reason and in justice ought not to have prevented the court below from looking into the testimony concerning proprietary interest in the ship, so far as the rights of other claimants depended upon that interest. If we reason from analogy, we find no principle adopted by the

(q) Croudson and others, vs. Leonard. *Cranch's Rep.*

municipal courts of law or equity which, in its application to courts of admiralty, would seem to subject one claimant to injury from the contumacy of another. A judgment against one defendant for want of a plea, or a decree against one defendant for want of an answer, does not prevent any other defendant from contesting, so far as respects himself, the very fact which is admitted by the absent party. No reason exists why a different rule should prevail in a court of admiralty.

If the court below was not precluded by the non-claim of the owner of the *ship* from examining the fact of ownership, so far as that fact could affect the *cargo*, it would not be contended that an appelate court might not likewise examine it.

This case is to be distinguished from those which have been decided on policies of insurance, not only by the circumstance that the cause respecting the ship and the cargo came on at the same time, before the same court, but by other differences in reason and in law which appear to be essential.

The decisions of a court of exclusive jurisdiction are necessarily conclusive on all other courts, because the subject matter is not examinable in them. With respect to itself, no reason is perceived for yielding to them a further conclusiveness than is allowed in the judgments and decrees of the municipal courts of common law and equity. They bind the subject matter as between parties and privies.

The whole world, it is said, are parties in a prize cause, and therefore the whole world is bound by the decision.

The reason on which this *dictum* stands will determine the extent of its application. Every person may make himself a party, and appeal from the sentence. But notice of the controversy is necessary in order to become a party, and it is a principle of natural justice, and of universal obligation, that before the rights of an individual be bound by a judicial sentence, he shall have notice, either actual or implied, of the proceedings against him. Where these proceedings are against the person, notice is served personally, or by publication ; there they are *in rem*, notice is served upon the thing itself. This is necessarily notice to all those who have any interest in the thing, and is reasonable because it is necessary, and because it is the part of common prudence for all those who have any interest in it, to guard that interest by persons who are in a situation to protect it. Every person therefore who could assert any title to the vessel, had constructive notice of her seizure, and may be fairly considered as a party to the libel. But those who had no interest in the vessel which could be asserted in the court of admiralty, had no notice of her seizure, and, can on no principle of justice or reason, be considered as parties in the cause, so far as respects the vessel. When such a person is brought before a court in which the fact is examinable, no sufficient reason is perceived for precluding him from re-examining it. The judgment of a court of common law or the decree of a court of equity would, under such circumstances, be re-examinable in a court of common law, or a court of equity ; and no reason is discerned why the sentence of a court of prize, under the same circumstances, should not be re-examinable in a court of prize.

This reasoning is not at variance with the decision that the sentence of a foreign court of admiralty condemning a vessel or cargo as enemy's property, is conclusive in an action against the underwriters or a policy in which the property is warranted neutral. It is not at variance with that decision, because the question of prize is one of which courts of municipal law have no direct cognizance, and because the owners of the ship and cargo were parties to the libel against them.

In he ase above cited, the reasons assigned for the conclusiveness of a foreign sentence were—the propriety of leaving the cognizance of prize questions exclusively to courts of prize jurisdiction; the very great inconvenience, amounting nearly to an impossibility, of fully investigating such cases in courts of common law; and the impropriety of revising the decisions of the maritime courts of other nations whose jurisdiction is coordinate throughout the world. All the world are parties in an admiralty cause. The proceedings are *in rem;* but any person having any interest in the property may interpose a claim and may prosecute an appeal from the sentence. The insured is emphatically a party, and in every instance has an opportunity to controvert the alleged grounds of condemnation by proving if he can the neutrality of the property. The master is his immediate agent, and is also bound to act for the benefit of all concerned, so that in this respect he also represents the insurer.

These reasons, though they undoubtedly support the decision founded on them, are inapplicable to the solution of this question. The very foundation of the opinion that the insured is bound by the sentence of condemnation is, that he was in law a party to the suit, and had a full opportunity to assert his rights. This decision cannot be applicable to one in which the person to be affected by it was not and could not be a party to it.(r)

17. And the jurisdiction of these courts extends as well to goods taken on land by a naval force, or in consequence of the operations of a naval force, as to property captured on the water. As to plunder or booty in a mere continental land war, without the presence or intervention of any ships, it never has given rise to any legal question. It is often given to the soldiers upon the spot, or wrongfully taken by them, contrary to military discipline. If there is any dispute, it is regulated by the commander in chief. But if the jurisdiction of prize courts did not ex-

(r) Per MARSHALL, C. J. The Mary. Supreme Court of the U. S. February T. 1815. M. S.

tend to a capture on shore, by a naval force, or in consequence of the operations of a naval force, the inconvenience would be great, to the captors; to the claimants; and to the state. The captors are in a miserable condition indeed. The prize cannot be condemned, nor shared. Every officer and seaman may be liable to actions without number. The taking cannot be disputed. To disprove the property, they can only have witnesses from abroad, who cannot be compelled to come; and in every action where the plaintiff recovers to the smallest value, the captor must pay the costs. Colourable claimants might easily ruin the captors through their want of the means of defence. It would be equally mischievous to fair claimants. They could not have their property restored instantly, upon their own papers, books, and affidavits. They must make formal proof, and the owners or crew of a privateer might be all the while spending the effects. But to the state, the consequences would be still more mischievous. By the law of nations every nation is answerable to the other for all injuries done by sea or land, or in fresh waters, or in port. Mutual convenience, eternal principles of justice, the wisest regulations of policy, and the consent of nations, have established a system of procedure, a code of law, and courts for the trial of prize. Every country sues in these courts of the others, which are all governed by one and the same law, equally known to each. The claimant is not obliged to sue the captors for damages, and undergo all the delay and vexation to which he will be liable, if he sues by a form of litigation, of which he is totally ignorant, and subjects his property to the rules and authority of a municipal law by which he is not bound. In short, every reason which created prize courts as to things taken *jure belli* upon the high seas, holds equally when they are thus taken at land.(s)

(s) *Douglas*, 591. Lindo v. Rodney et al. It has been held that the jurisdiction of the prize court extends over prize goods although land-

But in the commissions which were issued to private armed vessels during the late war with Great Britain, they were authorised, to subdue, seize, and take any armed or unarmed British vessel public or private, which shall be found within the jurisdictional limits of the United States, or elsewhere on the high seas, or within the waters of the British dominions;—thus excluding them from making captures on land. Independent of such a municipal prohibition, there is nothing to limit the right of capture, or the jurisdiction of courts of prize, to property found on the high seas or water borne.

18. When a capture is made, and the vessel or other thing captured is brought into port, it is the duty of the captors to deliver up to the proper officer all the papers and documents found on board, and to bring in for examination, touching the capture, the master, and one or more of the principal persons belonging to the captured vessel. At the time when the papers found on board are delivered up, an affidavit is to be made that they are delivered as taken, without fraud, addition, subduction, or embezzlement. It is also the duty of the captors to proceed to the adjudication of the property before the lawful court; and if they omit, or unreasonably delay, thus to proceed, any person claiming an interest in the captured property may obtain a monition against them, citing them to proceed to adjudication; which, if they do not do, or shew cause why the property should be condemned, it will be restored to the claimants proving an interest therein. And this process is often resorted to where the property is lost or destroyed, through the fault or negligence of the captors, in order to obtain a compensation in damages for the unjust seizure and deten-

ed, after capture; but not to things landed before capture. 1 *Robinson*, 271. The Two Friends. This is however to be understood of a landing within the territorial limits of the court's jurisdiction; because it has cognizance of captures made on land, within the enemy's territory, or the territory of states permitting the exercise of hostilities.

tion. A libel is to be exhibited by the captors against the captured property, containing proper allegations, the examinations *in preparatorio* of the captured persons are to be taken upon the standing interrogatories, and a monition is to be issued against all persons in general, having, or pretending to have an interest, &c. citing them to shew cause why the property should not be condemned. A claim must be supported upon oath at least as to belief; and briefly states to whom the ship and goods claimed belong, and that the enemy has no right or interest in them. The testimony upon which restitution or condemnation is to be decreed, must in the first instance, proceed from the documentary evidence and the examinations *in preparatorio;* and if no claim is put in, they are, of course, conclusive.([t])

The documentary evidence consists of the papers found on board the captured vessel, or invoked into the cause from some other cause. The general rule of the prize court is, that where there is a repugnance between these two species of evidence, the documents and the depositions, the conviction of the court must be kept in equilibrio till it can receive further proof; but it is a rule by no means inflexible; it is liable to many exceptions; the exceptions may sometimes be in favour of depositions, and sometimes, though more rarely, on the side of the documentary evidence. A case *may* exist, in which the witnesses may appear to speak with such a manifest disregard to truth, that the court may decide in favour of papers bearing upon them all the characters of fairness and veracity. On the other hand it may happen, and does more frequently happen, that the papers may betray such a taint and leaven of suspicion on the face of them, as will give a decided preponderancy to the testimony of the witnesses examined, especially if these witnesses give a natural account of the part they took in the transaction, and in a manner so

([t]) 2 *Dallas,* 23. Miller v. the Resolution.

distinct and clear, as to carry with it every degree of moral probability. The propriety of this practice will be best illustrated by an example: Let us suppose the case of a ship, furnished with documents, before there has arisen any apprehension of a war; there could then be no reason for the introduction of fraudulent papers: fraud is always inconvenient, and seldom adopted as a matter of choice: under such circumstances there is no particular ground of suspicion against the documents. But on the other side, suppose that there is a war, or the apprehension of a war, when the documents are composed: here, in that decided, or in that doubtful state of things, they become subject to some suspicions *in limine;* which suspicion may be increased by their having passed through the enemy's hands. The suspicions will be still further increased, if the property to which they relate, has continued under the management and direction of the enemy. And if in addition to all this, they carry such contradictions or difficulties on the face of them, as cannot be explained, admitting the matter to be a fair transaction; all or any of these circumstances must divest the papers of their natural credit.(u)

It is a general rule that no evidence shall be admitted in opposition to the documentary evidence, and preparatory examinations; and the reason of the rule is, that fraud may be suppressed and discouraged. But the principle of this rule applies to cases arising in time of war. The circumstance of existing hostilities may impose a peculiar obligation on neutral merchants, to keep their titles of property distinct, and free from any intermixture of enemy's interest, even in appearance; but where no such special reason exists, the principle does not apply with equal propriety, to govern cases of an assumed character in time of peace; where the flag and pass have been adopted without

(u) 1 *Robinson*, 1. The Vigilantia.

any contemplation of war, and for reasons arising out of the internal regulations of a foreign country.(v)

Where a claim is interposed, and the court is not satisfied with the original evidence, further proof is ordered.

This privilege of further proof is forfeited by the claimant if he appears to be guilty of fraud, *mala fides*, or unneutral conduct.(w) And the misconduct of one partner in these respects, will affect his co-partners in a *general* partnership, and render their property liable to share the same fate with his. So also, if the general agent of a neutral cargo covers enemy's property in the same vessel, though without the consent or knowledge of his principal, the property of his principal is condemnable, notwithstanding it may be distinguished by the papers.(x)

Further proof is either *general*, and consists of affidavits and documents introduced on the part of the claimants, or by *plea and proof*.

In the former case, affidavits on the part of the captors are not admitted, except under the special direction of the court. It is seldom done except in cases where there has appeared something in the original evidence, which lays a suggestion for prosecuting the enquiry further. But when the matter is foreign, and not connected with the original evidence of the cause, it must be under very particular circumstances indeed, that the court will be induced to accede to such an application; because, if remote suggestions were allowed, the practice of the court would be led away from the simplicity of prize proceedings, and there would be no

(v) 5 *Robinson*, 2. The Vrow Elizabeth. *Ib.* 15. The Vrow Anna Catharina. 6 *Robinson*, 1. La Flora.

(w) 1 *Robinson*, 127. The Juffrouw Anna. *Ib.* 165. The Vrouw. 124. The Welvaart. 2 *Robinson*, 1. The Cenroom. 3 *Robinson*, 111. The Graaf Bernstorff. 4 *Robinson*, 32. The Jemmy. 6 *Robinson*, 79. The Mars. 3 *Robinson*, 343. The Rosalie & Betty.

(x) 2 *Binney*, 308. The Phœnix Ins. Co. v. Pratt & Clarkson.

end to the accumulation of proof that would be introduced, in order to support arbitrary suggestions.[y] But the captors are permitted, on a general order for further proof, to invoke papers from another vessel, not brought in for adjudication.[z] They are also permitted to invoke from other causes depositions of the same claimants.[a]

In the latter case, where the court order plea and proof, instead of admitting affidavits and documents introduced by the claimants only, each party is at liberty to allege in regular pleadings such circumstances as may tend to acquit or condemn the captured property, and to examine witnesses in support of the allegations, to whom the adverse party may administer interrogatories. This species of proof is of the most solemn nature; it admonishes the parties of the difficulties of their situation, and calls for all the proof that their case can supply. Condemnation must necessarily ensue if this evidence is defective. No second reference can be made for further proof, after the cause has undergone a trial of this nature; it is conclusive, and shuts the door against all supplementary evidence.[b]

If the property be liable to perish or subject to deterioration, it may be sold by order of the court, and the proceeds of the sale brought into court there to abide the final decision in the cause. [c]

Upon appeal, the execution of the sentence is not to be suspended, if the party, in favour of whom the same is rendered, enter into a stipulation to restore the ship or goods or the full value thereof, in case the sentence be re-

(y) 1 *Robinson*, 313. The Adriana. 3 *Robinson*, 330. The Sarah.

(z) 6 *Robinson*, 351. The Romeo.

(a) 4 *Robinson*, 166. The Vriendschap.

(b) 1 *Robinson*, 31. The Magnus.

(c) *Valin*, Sur l'Ordonnance, L. 3. tit. 9. Des Prises. art. 28. 3 *Robinson*, 178. The Copenhagen. 2 *Dallas*, 40. Stoddard v. Read and the Squirrel.

versed. If no such stipulation is entered into, the property is to be sold, and the proceeds brought into court to abide the final decision in the cause.[d]

New and further evidence may be introduced in the appellate court, if upon the hearing that court should be of opinion that the cause is of such doubt as that further proof ought to have been ordered by the court below. But it is not a matter of course in this court to make an order for further proof. When the parties are fully apprized of the nature of the proof which their case requires, and have it in their power to produce it, an appellate court should not readily listen to such an application : but when it appears that the parties who ask this indulgence have withheld from the court letters and other documentary testimony, which must be supposed in the particular case, to have been in their possession, they come with a very ill grace to ask for any further time to make out their title. Where the affidavits upon which further proof is asked for, are silent with respect to the papers which must have been in the claimants' possession, and which are deemed to have been in their possession, further proof cannot be allowed. [e]

Costs and damages may in the discretion of the court, be given to the claimants in cases of the unjustifiable seizure and detention of their property ; [f] and they are condemned in costs and damages where they interpose claims manifestly groundless. So also where the seizure is justifiable on account of the misconduct or fault of the claimants, the captors are allowed their expenses, which are to be paid by the claimants, though restitution of the property be decreed.

(d) 2 *Brown's Civ. and Adm. Law*, 454.

(e) Per Livingston J. The St. Lawrence. Supreme Court of the U. S. February T. 1815 M. S.

(f) 1 *Code des Prises*, 143. 308.

19. After a final sentence of condemnation, the duties, costs, charges, and expenditures, on the captured property are to be first deducted, and (in case the capture be made by a private armed vessel) two per centum on the net amount is then to be paid over to the collector or chief officer of the customs at the port of the United States into which the captured vessel is brought for adjudication, or to the consul or other public agent of the United States if the vessel is brought into a foreign port, in order to form a fund for the support of the widows and orphans of such persons as may be slain, and for the support of such persons as may be wounded, on board of private armed vessels in any engagement with the enemy. The remainder of the proceeds is to be distributed among the captors according to any written agreement which shall be made between them; and if there be no such agreement, then one moiety to the owners, and the other moiety to the officers and crews of private armed vessels, to be distributed among the officers and crew, as nearly as may be, according to the rules prescribed for the distribution of prize money by the act of April, 1800, for the better government of the navy of the United States.

The above is the provision contained in the prize act which subsisted during the late war with Great Britain. But by the act for the protection of the commerce of the United States against the Algerine cruisers, of March, 1815, Sec. 4, it is enacted, That any Algerine vessel, goods or effects, which may be so captured and brought into port by any private armed vessel of the United States, duly commissioned as aforesaid, may be adjudged good prize, and thereupon shall accrue to the owners, and officers, and men of the capturing vessel, and shall be distributed according to the agreement which shall have been made between them, or, in failure of such agreement, according to the discretion of the court having cognizance of the capture.

A libel by the crew of a private armed vessel, for their respective proportions of a prize, is the proper and regular mode to compel a distribution: but where the proceeds of a prize are in the marshall's hands, the parties entitled may either institute a supplemental libel in the prize court or an action at common law for money had and received: And if a marshall makes distribution without the orders of the prize court, he does it at his peril, and the court before issuing the order will guard against fraud and imposition, by providing for latent claims.(g)

20. Before we proceed to state the rules for the distribution of prize money it is material to enquire, who are captors? And this brings us to consider the questions arising from allegations of joint capture.

These may be alleged to have been made by public vessels of war, or private armed vessels; or by the assistance and co-operation of land forces.

In the first case, that of public ships of war, they are entitled to share in a prize from the mere circumstance of having been in sight at the time of capture and lending a constructive assistance.

They are under a constant obligation to attack the enemy wherever seen; a neglect of duty is not to be presumed, and therefore from the mere circumstance of being in sight, a presumption is sufficiently raised, that they are there *animo capiendi*.(h) Thus the French ordinance of June, 1757, art. 10, provides with regard to public vessels of war that those shall be considered as joint captors who shall be found together and in sight of the prize at the time of its being captured. And by the act for the better government of the Navy of the United States, Sec. 6. art. No VII. it is enacted that, wherever one or more public ships or vessels are

(g) 2 *Dallas*, 37. Keane et al. v. The Gloucester. *Ib.* 174. Henderson v. Clarkson.

(h) *Bynkershoek*, Q. J. P. L. 1. ç. 18. 1 *Robinson*, 21. The Vryheid. 5 *Robinson*, 268, La Flore.

in sight at the time any one or more ships are taking a prize or prizes, they shall share according to number of men on board each ship in sight. But in the case of private armed vessels the rule of law is different; and with respect to them, it must be shewn, that they were constructively assisting. The being in sight is not sufficient to raise a presumption of co-operation in the capture. They clothe themselves with commissions of war from views of private advantage only. They are not bound to put their commissions in *use* on every discovery of an enemy. Therefore the law does not presume, in their favour, from the mere circumstance of being in sight, that they were there with the design of contributing assistance, and engaging in the contest. There must be the *animus capiendi* demonstrated by some overt act; by some variation of conduct which would not have taken place, but with reference to that particular object, and if the intention of acting against the enemy had not been effectually entertained. Thus the French ordinance of January, 1706, art. 1 and 2, provides with regard to privateers that none shall be entitled to share in a prize taken from the enemy, unless they have contributed to the capture by fighting, or by making such an effort as may have compelled the enemy to surrender, by intimidating him or cutting off his retreat.(i)

As to land forces, they are not considered as entitled to share in a capture, unless they have actually co-operated and assisted in making it. The mere presence and being in sight of different parties of a naval force is, with the exception of privateers, sufficient to entitle them to be considered as joint captors; because they are always considered to have that privity of purpose which may constitute a community of interests; but between land and sea forces acting independently of each other, and for different purposes, there can be no such privity presumed; and there-

(i) *Bynkershoek*, Q. J. P. L. 1. c. 18. *Martens on Captures*, § 32. 6 *Robinson*, 264. L'Amitié. 1 *Dallas*, 95. Talbot &c. v. Three Brigs.

force to establish a claim of joint capture between them, there must be a contribution of actual assistance, and the mere presence, or being in sight, will not be sufficient. And when there is no pre-concert, it must be not a slight service, nor an assistance rendering the capture more easy or convenient, but some very material service, that will be deemed necessary to entitle an army to the benefit of joint capture; where there is a pre-concert, it is not of so much consequence that the service should be material, because then each party performs the service that is previously assigned to him, and whether that is important or not, it is not so material; the part is performed, and that is all that was expected: But where there is no such privity of design, and where one of the parties is of force equal to the work, and does not ask assistance, it is not the interposing of a slight aid, that will entitle another party to share.[k]

In all cases, the *onus probandi* lies on those setting up a capture by construction, because they are not persons strictly within the prize act, but let in only by the interpretation of those acting with a competent authority to interpret it. It lies with the claimants in joint capture, therefore, either to allege some cases in which their construction has been admitted in former instances, or to shew some principle in their favour, so clearly recognized and established, as to have become almost a first principle in cases of this nature. The being in sight is sufficient to entitle parties to be admitted joint captors, and where that fact is alleged, we do not call for particular cases to authorize the claim; but where that circumstance is wanting, it is incumbent on the party to make out his claim by an appeal to decided cases, or at least to principles, which are fairly to be extracted from those cases. And it has been contended that where ships are associated in a *common enterprise*, that circumstance is sufficient to entitle

[k] 2 *Robinson*, 53. The Dordrecht.

them to share equally and alike in the prizes that are made: but certainly this cannot be maintained to the full extent of these terms; many cases might be stated in which ships so associated would *not* share. Suppose a case, that ships going out on the same enterprise, and using all their endeavours to effectuate their purpose, should be separated by storms or otherwise, no one would contend that *they* should share in each other's captures; there is no case in which such persons have been allowed to share after separation, being not in sight at the time of chasing: it cannot be laid down to that extent, and indeed it would be extremely incommodious that it should; nothing is more difficult than to say precisely where a common enterprise begins. In a more enlarged sense, the whole navy may be said to be contributing in the joint enterprise of annoying the enemy. In particular expeditions every service has its divisions and subdivisions; operations are to be begun and conducted at different places; in the attack of an island there may be different ports, and different fortresses, and different ships of the enemy lying before them; it may be necessary to make the attack on the opposite side of the island; or to associate other neighbouring islands as objects of the same attack: The difficulty is to say where the joint enterprise actually begins. Again, Is it every remote contribution, given *with* intention, or *without intention*, that can be sufficient? *That* is not to be maintained; an actual service may be done without intention; or there may be a general intention to assist, and yet no actual assistance given. Can any body say that a mere intention to assist, without actual assistance, though acted upon with the most prompt activity, would in all cases be sufficient? If persons under such claims could share, there would be no end to dispute; no captor would know what he was about, whether in every prize he made, there might not be some one fifty leagues distant, working very hard to come up: in serving his country every captor would be left in uncertainty, whether some person whom he never saw, and whom the enemy never saw, might not be entitled to share with him in the rewards of his labour. The great intent of prize is to stimulate the present contest, and to encourage men to encounter present fatigue and present danger, an effect which would be infinitely weakened, if it were known that there might be those not present, and not concerned in the danger, who could entitle themselves to share. On these considerations it must ever be held, that the principle of mere common enterprise alone will not be sufficient; it is not sufficiently specific, it must be more limited, nor can it be maintained that ships detached from the squadron on views immediately connected with the main enterprise are entitled to share. Many cases might be put, in which that position could not be maintained. Suppose a fleet going to besiege a place, and one ship detached to procure provisions and stores, which does not come up and join the fleet until the place is taken; it would be very wrong to maintain, that such a vessel, neither present at the commencement, nor at the conclusion of the enterprise, could be entitled to share; it has been decided in practice, that she would not; and the distinction taken was this, that if the ship was sent off for common necessaries, after the operations had begun, or if she returned before the object was accomplished, she should be permitted to share, and not otherwise, though her absence was occasioned solely for the purpose of procuring necessaries for the service. Then the limitation ingrafted on the first principle, namely, that the detachment is made for an object immediately connected with the service is not sufficient, something more must be added, and that must be the being in sight.

21. By the act of the 23d April, 1800, for the better government of the navy of the United States, it is enacted,

Sec. 5. That the proceeds of all ships and vessels, and the goods taken on board of them, which shall be adjudged good prize, shall, when of equal or superior force to the vessel or vessels making the capture, be the sole property of the captors: and when of inferior force, shall be divided equally between the United States and the officers and men making the capture.

Sec. 6. That the prize money, belonging to the officers and men shall be distributed in the following manner:

I. To the commanding officers of fleets, squadrons, or single ships, three twentieths, of which the commanding officer of the fleet or squadron shall have one twentieth, if the prize be taken by a ship or vessel acting under his command, and the commander of single ships, two twentieths; but where the prize is taken by a ship acting independently of such superior officer, the three twentieths shall belong to her commander.

II. To sea lieutenants, captains of marines, and sailing masters, two twentieths; but where there is a captain, without a lieutenant of marines, these officers shall be entitled to two twentieths and one third of a twentieth, which third in such case, shall be deducted from the share of the officers mentioned in article No. III. of this section.

III. To chaplains, lieutenants of marines, surgeons, pursers, boatswains, gunners, carpenters, and masters mates two twentieths.

IV. To midshipmen, surgeons mates, captains clerks, schoolmasters, boatswains mates, gunners mates, carpenters mates, ship's stewards, sail makers, masters at arms, armourers, cockswains, and coopers, three twentieths and a half.

V. To gunners yeomen, boatswains yeomen, quarter masters, quarter gunners, sail-makers mates, serjeants and corporals of marines, drummers, fifers, and extra petty officers, two twentieths and a half.

VI. To seamen, ordinary seamen, marines, and all other persons doing duty on board, seven twentieths.

VII. No commander of a fleet or squadron shall be entitled to receive any share of prizes taken by vessels not under his immediate command; nor of such prizes as may have been taken by ships or vessels intended to be placed under his command, before they have acted under his immediate orders; nor shall a commander of a fleet or squadron, leaving the station where he had the command, have any share in the prizes taken by ships left on such station, after he has gone out of the limits of his said command.

22. By the laws of the United States, no regulation has been adopted as to the distribution of prize money between different *private* armed vessels, joint captors; and of course this distribution must be governed by the general rules of the prize jurisdiction. Upon general principle it would seem reasonable in cases of joint capture that the distribution should be according to the relative strength of the capturing ships. In that proportion, the intimidation of the enemy leading to a surrender would ordinarily be supposed to exist where no battle should be actually fought; and in cases of actual battle the degree of injury done to the enemy would be estimated in the same manner. And in a middle class of cases, where one ship was actually engaged and the other only in general co-operation, the ultimate surrender might well be attributed as much to the despair of escape from the combined force, as the immediate injury from the engaging force. And indeed to attempt a discrimination founded upon different degrees of exertion would be very difficult if not wholly impossible in practice. Bynkershoek therefore, (and he alone is great authority) lays down the rule that the parties shall in joint captures share in proportion to their respective strength.(l) And this is apprehended to be the rule established in the prize courts of England and France; and perhaps forms the basis of the rule of distribution among the other maritime powers of Europe (m) In the manner of estimating this rela-

(l) Q. J. P. c. 18.

(m) 2 *Taunton's Rep.* 7. Buckworth v. Tucker.

tive strength a great diversity of regulations exists. Valin statesthat in France the mode varies in three classes of cases of joint capture; 1st. Between a public ship and a privateer the distribution is in proportion to the number of guns; 2d. Between privateers, in proportion to the force and equipments and the calibre of the guns of the respective ships, and the estimate in this case depending upon such heterogenous and complex combinations, is reduced to a unity of denomination by an arbitrary valuation of the component parts; 3d. Between public ships in proportion to the number and calibre of their respective batteries of cannon. In England, no statute regulation exists as to privateers; and therefore their claims are settled by the general law of relative strength. This relative strength is to be measured, as has been settled by solemn adjudications in the common law and prize courts, by the number of men on board each ship.(n) This rule has the advantage of great practical simplicity and general equity. It seems bottomed on the soundest sense, and places the relative force in the power and activity of animated beings, in which it must always ultimately reside, rather than in the mere instruments, which without such power and activity would be useless and unavailing.(o)

23. At least as early as the year 1708, by the British statutes, one eighth of all prizes made by ships under the command of a flag was given, To the flag officer or officers being actually on board or *directing or assisting* in the capture.(p) Upon the construction of this clause it was held that actual direction or assistance was not necessary, and that the mere circumstance of holding a flag commission and the authority in virtue thereof to direct and assist in the operations of a fleet, was such a constructive direction

(n) *Douglas*, 311. Roberts v. Hartley.

(o) Per STORY J. The Castigator and Fame. Circuit Court of the U. S. for the Massachusetts District, October T. 1813. M. S.

(p) *Robinson's Collectanea Maritima*, 200 Note.

or assistance as entitled the commander to share, although he had never joined the fleet, or given any order, or done any other official act in quality of commander. In point of fact therefore the commander claimed his share of all prizes, made from the date of his commission to the termination thereof. This extensive right was deemed injurious to the service, and at length in 1744, was taken from the flag officer in a variety of cases: 1st. Where prizes were made by ships on a station before he arrived within the limits of his command; 2dly. Where prizes were made by reinforcing ships before their arrival within the limits of his command: and 3dly. Where prizes were made by ships on a station, the flag officer of which was returning home, after he had got out of the limits of his command. In all other cases the right stood upon the general clause and extended to all prizes made by ships under his command. In 1756, these restrictions were somewhat varied, and the form then adopted continued in use until the year 1803. In the regulations of 1756 the flag officer is denied a right to share: 1st, In prizes made by ships on a station, where he is sent to command, before he arrives at the place to which he is sent, and actually takes upon him the command; 2dly, In prizes made by a reinforcing squadron, before it shall arrive within the limits of the command of the superior flag officer and actually receive some order from him; and 3dly, In prizes made by ships left behind to act under another command, when a flag officer is returning home from a station.(q)

24. Upon the construction of these regulations it has been held, that a flag officer is not entitled, who has resigned and accepted under another distinct command, or has been superseded at the time of the capture; nor where the capturing ship has been detached by the admiralty upon a

(q) 1 *H. Bl.* 261. Johnstone v. Margetson. 3 *Bos and Pul.* 257. Nelson v. Tucker. 4 *East*, 238.

secret service; nor where the capturing ship has made the capture without the limits of the station without orders; nor where the flag officer has returned home for temporary purposes, leaving his squadron behind on the station; nor where there has been a temporary suspension of the command, as by the ships going into another station for repairs, and acting while there under another command.(r) But in all cases, not within the exceptions of the articles of 1756, the general rule prevails, that the flag officer actually in command, shall receive the flag eighth: And therefore, if he be actually in command, he is entitled, although he has not given any orders, and the capture was made under orders from a former flag officer. And it matters not whether the actual command be by direct appointment or by devolution in the course of the service.(s)

Such are the most important distinctions which have been recognized under the prize acts and proclamations of Great Britain. And it is impossible for the attention not to be forcibly struck with the exact resemblance which the provisions of the act of March 2d, 1799, sec. 6. bear to them. The distinctions which have been made under them, reflect light on this subject, and were obviously in the view of Congress in framing our own statutes.

25. As such they were applied to the decision of the following case. During the late war, the frigate Chesapeake, commanded by Captain Evans, the brig Argus, and the frigate United States, commanded by Commodore Decatur, were attached together as a squadron, under the command of the latter, by orders from the navy department of the 9th September, 1812. On the 6th October, Commodore Decatur gave the captain of the Chesapeake

(r) 1 *H. Bl.* 265. In Notis. 1 *H. Bl.* 261. Johnstone v. Margetson: 3 *Bos. & Pul.* 257. Nelson v. Tucker. 4 *East*, 238. Vide the Ann. 3 *Robinson*, 60. 6 *East*, Harvey v. Cooke. 4 *Robinson*, 362. The Orion. 8 *East*, 502. Holmes v. Rainer.

(s) 4 *East*, 262. Keith v. Pringle.

sailing orders for a cruize, and soon afterwards sailed from Boston, and captured the British frigate Macedonian, in a memorable engagement, returned with his prize to the United States, previous to the sailing of the Chesapeake, and was blockaded by a superior force of the enemy. On the 28th November, the Secretary of the Navy addressed a letter to the Captain of the Chesapeake, directing him to weigh anchor and proceed as he had *been directed by Commodore Decatur to whose squadron* he was *attached*.. The Chesapeake sailed in December, captured the prize in question, and returned from her cruize in April, when Captain Evans immediately reported his cruize to Commodore Decatur as his commanding officer.

It was contended on behalf of the defendant, 1st, That the Chesapeake at the time of the capture was acting independently of a superior officer within art. No. I. of sec. 6. of the act of the 23d April, 1800; or 2d, That Commodore Decatur had left the station, where he had the command at the time of the capture, within art. No. VII. of the same section.

As to the first point, the court thought it extremely clear that in no sense could the Chesapeake be considered at the time of the capture, as acting independently of a superior officer. Actual presence of the superior officer at the time of the capture, is neither supposed nor required by the law. It is sufficient if the ship be not detached on a separate service by the government, but remain under the command, and subject to the orders of the superior officer. In such a case the superior officer is deemed to afford constructive assistance, and is responsible for his squadron, however far he may be removed from the scene of action.

The second question was whether Commodore Decatur had left the station where he had the command at the time of capture. In order to lay a foundation for the argument on this head, it was necessary to shew that he had a station assigned to him; for otherwise it is impossible to conceive how he could have left it. Now in the statute, a *station* necessarily includes the idea of local limits. It presupposes certain boundaries of place and command, beyond which the squadron could not lawfully proceed in their cruize. Such is the uniform meaning of the word in the British naval code, and it would be difficult to assign it another meaning in our own statute, without involving absurdities in construction. In point of fact, no station was assigned to Commodore Decatur. His orders were of the most unlimited nature. He was at liberty to go where he pleased, consistently with the great object of annoying the enemy. The exception then, supposed in the statute, the *casus fœderis*, if the expression may be used, did not arise. The irresistible conclusion was, that as the exceptions of the statute did not apply, the case fell within the general rule, and Commodore Decatur was entitled to the flag twentieth of the proceeds of the captured vessel.[t]

[t] Per STORY, J. Decatur v. Chew. Circuit Court of the U. S. for Massachusetts District, October T. 1813. M. S.

CHAPTER X.

Of the effects of a treaty of peace on questions of prize.

1. An armistice, truce, or other suspension of hostilities, binds the contracting parties from the date of its conclusion; but it cannot have the force of law with regard to citizens or subjects of each, until it is solemnly published: And as an unknown law imposes no obligation, it binds those citizens or subjects only from the time it is notified to them. So that, if before such notification, they should have committed any act of hostility, they are not punishable therefor. But as the sovereign is bound to fulfil his engagements, he is obliged to restore prizes made subsequent to the period when the suspension of hostilities is to take effect.[a]

2. So also of a treaty of peace. It binds the contracting parties from the date of its conclusion, and they are obligated to carry it into immediate execution. Hostilities are immediately to cease, unless there is a stipulation to the contrary. But it binds the citizens or subjects of each party only from the time it is notified to them. They are consequently not responsible for hostilities committed by them before receiving this notice. But the sovereign is bound to compel the restitution of all prizes made subsequent to the time when the pacification is to take effect.[b]

(a) *Vattel,* L. 3. c. 16. § 239.

(b) *Ib.* L. 4. c. 3. § 24. 2 *Dallas,* 40. Bain et al. v. the Speedwell.

3. But those, who by their fault, are ignorant of the conclusion of an armistice or peace, although they may not be liable to punishment, are responsible for the damages occasioned by their own want of diligence. Mere negligence, and above all slight neglect, *levis culpa*, may, to a certain extent, exonerate from penal responsibility, and certainly does not merit the same punishment with fraud; but cannot dispense the party from the obligation of repairing the injury he has committed. If an act of mischief be done by the officers of the sovereign, though through ignorance, in a place where no act of hostility ought to have been exercised, it does not necessarily follow that mere ignorance of that fact would protect the officers from civil responsibility. And it has been held in England, that if by articles a place or district was put under the king's peace, and an act of hostility was afterwards committed therein, the injured party might have a right to resort to a court of prize; to shew that he had been injured by this breach, and was entitled to compensation; and if the officer acted through ignorance, his own government must protect him: for it is the duty of government, if they put a certain district within the king's peace, to take care that due notice shall be given to those persons by whose conduct that peace is to be maintained; and if no such notice has been given, nor due diligence used to give it, and a breach of the peace is committed through the ignorance of those persons, they are to be borne harmless at the expense of that government whose duty it was to have given that notice.[c] But it has likewise been determined, that the actual wrong doer is the only person compellable to proceed to adjudication, or answerable in damages, in the prize court; and that no suit can be commenced against the commander of the station not privy to the fact, on account of hostilities wrongfully committed.[d]

(c) *Vattel*, L. 3. c. 16. § 239. 1 *Robinson*, 179. The Mentor. (d) *Ibid.*

4. In order to avoid these questions it is a frequent practice to stipulate in the preliminary articles of peace for a cessation of hostilities at certain times in different places, and for the restitution of property taken afterwards; and this as well within, as beyond, the period assigned for the ratification of the preliminary articles themselves. The same provision is afterwards inserted in the definitive treaty.(e)

In the case of such a stipulation, there can be no doubt as to captures made in a particular latitude *after* the period stipulated, that they must be restored, whether the captor knew of the peace or not. But as to a capture made *before* that period by a captor having notice of the cessation of hostilities, the authorities are divided upon the question whether the captured property should be restored. Upon principle it would seem that as the periods stipulated are substituted instead of the date of the treaty itself for the cessation of captures, they ought to be considered as if made *flagrante bello* where they take place before the expiration of the time limited in the particular latitude. Such is the opinion of M. Bonnemant, in his commentary on D'Habreu. But on the other hand it may be said that the object of such stipulations is to supply the defect of positive notice by furnishing a rule of presumptive evidence in its stead, and that where the knowledge of the fact that hostilities have actually ceased is brought home to the party, there is no such defect to be supplied. The legal presumption is overthrown by the positive fact. This is the opinion of Valin,(f) which was adopted in practice by the council of Prizes at Paris in deciding upon captures of British and Austrian vessels made after the treaties of Amiens and Luneville, but before the expiration of the periods limited

(e) 5 *Robinson*, 189. The Adolphus Frederick in the Elsebe. 2 *Brown's Civ. & Adm. Law*, 346.

(f) *Valin, Traité des Prises*, c. 3 no. 5.

for captures, in cases where it was positively proved that the French captors had notice of the existence of peace.(g)

5. It has been determined that such a stipulation extends to recaptures as well as to original captures.

Thus by the late treaty of peace between the United States and Great Britain, signed at Ghent on the 24th December, 1814, and ratified on the 18th February, 1815, it was reciprocally agreed that all vessels and effects which should be taken after the space of twelve days from the ratification, upon all parts of the coast of North America, from the latitude 23 N. to 50 N. and as far eastward in the Atlantic ocean as the 36th degree of W. longitude, should be restored on either side. A vessel, originally British, was captured by a private armed vessel of the United States on the 8th January, 1815, and recaptured on the 7th March by a British ship of war.

There were three parties before the court: the officer and crew of the British ship of war claiming salvage as for a recapture of British property; the original owners praying the vessel to be delivered to them on payment of salvage; and the owners, officers and crew of the American privateer pleading the second article of the treaty of peace. It was admitted that this vessel was seized before the time limited for captures had expired, and was recaptured after that period. It was argued therefore on behalf of the owners of the American privateer, that this vessel became theirs by the original capture, and that the subsequent recapture was not lawful under the treaty, and that consequently the vessel ought to be restored to them. The original British owners, on the other hand, contended that the recapture was lawful, and claimed restitution under their former title.

It was argued that the British prize acts directed that if any vessel taken as prize shall appear to have belonged to

(g) *Azuni*, Part 2, c. 4. art. 1. § 12.

any of his majesty's subjects, and to have been before taken by the enemy, and retaken, it shall be restored to the former owner on the payment of salvage. But the court was of the opinion there was no foundation for the argument deduced from that clause, which is merely a domestic regulation to settle the question which arises between the original owner and the recaptor. In general, the British owner receives his property, and the recaptor receives a salvage. In some few cases, as where a vessel has been fitted out as a ship of war, and consequently the danger of the recaptor is the greater, the recaptor is rewarded with the whole. The mere municipal regulation of an act of parliament cannot be intended to affect, nor can it legally affect, the rights of foreign nations. They must be decided by the general law of nations, and by particular treaties.

It had farther been argued, and a great deal of learning had been displayed to support the argument, from civilians, writers upon the law of nations, and the English lawyers, that the first captors had no title or right to this vessel under their seizure, till a legal adjudication; that, till then, either no right whatever accrued, or at least only to the state, and that therefore the owners of the privateer had no interest to entitle them to claim; that as hostilities were extended by the treaty, in some parts of the world to one hundred and twenty days after the ratification, within which period this recapture was made, that the state of war still subsisted, and this very privateer might have been actually employed in capturing British ships at the time when the owners appeared as claimants in a British court of prize; and finally, that the treaty not having specified recaptures, did not extend to them.

The rule as to the precise time when the right of the captor shall vest, and which is understood to be the same in the United States as in Great Britain, is chiefly a regulation as between the state and the captor. As capturing ships, whether belonging to the state or to individuals, act as a part of the public force, it is not a question here merely with the individual captors themselves but with the nation at large, and it is not affected by any such internal regulation. The rule was moreover introduced to prevent the right of recapture from being defeated by transfers to neutrals immediately upon the seizure. To give the original owners the chance of recapture, it was held that such transfers were not valid till after condemnation. In truth the right is complete upon the capture, as has been observed by writers of authority, since there is a just title, that of war, the *animus possidendi* under that title, and the actual possession, which is sufficient to constitute a perfect right, under all general principles of law. The extension of the time was introduced by mutual consent and practice for particular purposes, and is merely arbitrary, as is evident from the fluctuation which has prevailed relating to it, in the varying and successive rules of twenty-four hours, of *infra præsidia*, and other such securities, till it finally settled down into the condemnation.

But, without entering farther into these nice and abstract questions, it is sufficient for the present purpose, that by the capture, the privateer acquired a legal right of *possession*, which is undeniable. It was admitted that the vessel was taken in time of war, from an enemy by a ship of war, regularly commissioned; a lawful possession was therefore admitted. After the time fixed by the treaty, within the respective limits assigned, a state of peace subsisted between the two countries, as absolute and complete as if no farther hostilities could be any where exercised, and as if the treaty had been concluded for a century.

The true question then was, whether a lawful possession can be divested by an hostile force in time of peace? Merely to put this question is sufficient to answer it. Peace is that state in which rights are discussed and claims made amicably, and by the ordinary proceedings of courts of law; to settle them by violence is peculiar to a state of war. The restoration of peace annuls all modes of force; they become unlawful. There can be no lawful fighting in time of peace. The question is not limited to this particular case. Here indeed there was no shedding of blood, but it was a seizure by force, a mere submission to a superior power. If it was lawful so to take a vessel, it would be equally lawful to apply force in case of resistance. A recapture might equally be made by a battle. Any of the British ships of war under the same circumstances, might be retaken from the Americans, or any of theirs might be retaken by the British in the most sanguinary engagements. If nothing short of a sentence of condemnation could extinguish the right of recapture it might exist to a very long and indefinite period. Ships taken in the East Indies might be a twelve-month or more before they could get home to be condemned. Can that be a state of peace in which ships might lawfully engage, or in which scenes of bloodshed between the vessels of two nations might lawfully be exhibited? Can such a state subsist after it has been expressly agreed by a treaty that all hostilities shall cease? Is the forcible capture of a vessel, or is it not, an act of hostility? If it is, it is prohibited by the treaty.

It was said that the treaty does not stipulate that vessels *recaptured* shall be restored. The words are as general as possible. The restitution is not confined to vessels "belonging to the subjects of the United States," expressions to be found in many treaties, and which, or something equivalent, would probably have been introduced, if such had been the meaning of the two governments, but the words are, "all vessels and effects." To say that a recapture is not a capture is a mere finesse and equivocation. Such recaptures, as well as other captures, are literally comprehended under the treaty; they are "vessels and effects which have been taken" since the time limited.

Independent of the hostility of the act of recapture, and of any particular stipulations in the treaty, the right of possession in the captor was completed by the intervention of peace, and all right of recovering in the original owner was barred—The *uti possidetis* is the basis of every treaty of peace, unless so far as it is otherwise agreed. All things continue in the state in which they are found when the treaty takes effect, unless it is declared otherwise---Where the tree falls there it must lie. All the rules to determine when the title by capture is final are founded upon one principle laid down by Grotius, that the capture is complete when all hope of recovery is lost; but all hope of recovery is certainly lost when the recovery becomes unlawful. The conclusion of a peace is therefore as effectual for that purpose, as carrying *infra præsidia*, condemnation, or any other circumstances which have been fixed upon. Martens, and other writers, who had been quoted, admit, that peace gives the final and perfect title to captures. And with respect to a supposed recovery of this vessel to the former owner by a sort of postliminium, it is justly observed by Vattel. (Liv. III. Ch. 14. § 226) that "since the things of which the treaty of peace says nothing, continue in the state in which they were found at the moment when the peace was concluded, and are tacitly ceded to the possessor, the right of *postliminium* has no place after peace is concluded; it relates entirely to the state of war."

An argument had been raised, and much compassion excited, by a supposition, that, if this prize was restored, the British master and crew found on board must be restored likewise to a state of captivity. For this there was no foundation whatever. The treaty provided that from the ratification there shall be an universal peace between the people of the respective countries, and they can no longer hold each other in a state of captivity.

Restitution was therefore decreed to the American privateer.[h]

6. A treaty of peace has the effect of quieting all titles of possession arising from the war.[i] Therefore where a question arose as to the title of a neutral purchaser under consular and other condemnations, it was held that the intervention of peace had the effect of curing whatever defects might otherwise exist in such title. It was admitted that as to the enemy it would have this effect, and that it would not be lawful to look back beyond the general amnesty, to examine the title of *his* possession. But if the vessel, or other thing, has been transferred to the subject of another country, he also will be entitled to the same benefit from the treaty, as the captor himself would have been, if he had continued in possession. For otherwise it could not be said that the intervention of peace would have the effect of quieting the possession of the *enemy*; because if the neutral purchaser was to be dispossessed, he would have a right to resort back to the belligerent seller, and demand compensation from him. Neither will the supervening of a new war disturb the title. It can have no effect on neutral purchasers who stand in the same situation as before. Those purchasers, though no parties to the treaty, are entitled to the full benefit of it; because they derive their title from those who are.[k]

7. We have before seen that in order to induce the confiscation of enemy's property, found within the territory of the belligerent state at the declaration of war, some act of the government, other than the declaration itself, is essential; and that such property might be claimed upon the termination of hostilities, unless previously confiscated. [l]

(h) Per Dr. Croke. The Legal Tender. Vice Admiralty Court at Halifax, April, 20th, 1815.

(i) *Vattel*, L. 4. c. 2. § 22.

(k) 6 *Robinson*, 138. The Schoone Sophie.

(l) Chapter 1; § 8.

It has also been determined that where a vessel had been captured, and restored with costs and damages, but no further proceedings took place at the time in consequence of the breaking out of war with the claimant's country—his rights revived on the return of peace; no step being taken in the interval of war declaratory of the forfeiture of those rights to the government. The intervention of hostilities puts the property of the enemy in such a situation that confiscation may ensue; but unless some step is taken for that purpose, unless there is some legal declaration of the forfeiture, the right of the owner revives on the return of peace.(m)

(m) *Edwards*, 62. The Neustra Senora de Los Dolores.

APPENDIX.

No. I.

LETTER FROM SIR W. SCOTT AND SIR J. NICHOLL, TO MR. JAY.

SIR,

I HAVE the honour of sending the paper drawn up by Dr. Nicholl and myself; it is longer and more particular than perhaps you meant; but it appeared to be an error on the better side, rather to be too minute, than to be too reserved in the information we had to give; and it will be in your excellency's power either to apply the whole or such parts as may appear more immediately pertinent to the objects of your inquiry.

I take the liberty of adding, that I shall at all times think myself much honoured by any communications from you, either during your stay here, or after your return, on any subject in which you may suppose that my situation can give me the power of being at all useful to the joint interests of both countries;—If they should ever turn upon points in which the duties of my official station appear to me to impose upon me an obligation of reserve, I shall have no hesitation in saying, that I feel them to be such: On any other points, on which you may wish to have an opinion of mine, you may depend on receiving one, that is formed with as much care as I can use, and delivered with all possible frankness and sincerity.

I have the honour to be,

With great respect, &c.

WILLIAM SCOTT.

Commons, Sept. 10th, 1794.

Paper inclosed in the foregoing letter.

SIR,

We have the honour of transmitting, agreeably to your excellency's request, a statement of the general principles of proceeding in prize causes, in British courts of admiralty, and of the measures proper to be taken when a ship and cargo are brought in as prize within their jurisdictions.

The general principles of proceeding cannot, in our judgment, be stated more correctly or succinctly, than we find them laid down in the following extract from a report made to his late Majesty in the year 1753, by Sir George Lee, then judge of the prerogative court, Dr. Paul, his majesty's advocate general, Sir Dudley Rider, his majesty's attorney general, and Mr. Murray (afterwards Lord Mansfield) his majesty's solicitor general.

" When two powers are at war, they have a right to make prizes of the ships, goods, and effects of each other, upon the high seas: Whatever is the property of the enemy, may be acquired by capture at sea; but the property of a friend cannot be taken provided he observes his neutrality.

" Hence the law of nations has established,

" That the goods of an enemy, on board the ship of a friend, may be taken.

" That the lawful goods of a friend, on board the ship of an enemy, ought to be restored.

" That contraband goods, going to the enemy, though the property of a friend, may be taken as prize; because supplying the enemy with what enables him better to carry on the war, is a departure from neutrality.

" By the maritime law of nations, universally and immemorially received, there is an established method of determination, whether the capture be, or be not, lawful prize.

Before the ship, or goods, can be disposed of by the captor, there must be a regular judicial proceeding, wherein both parties may be heard; and condemnation thereupon as prize, in a court of admiralty, judging by the law of nations and treaties.

"The proper and regular court, for these condemnations, is the court of that state to whom the captor belongs.

"The evidence to acquit or condemn, with or without, costs or damages, must, in the first instance, come merely from the ship taken, viz. the papers on board, and the examination on *oath*, of the master, and other principal officers; for which purpose there are officers of admiralty in all the considerable sea ports of every maritime power at war, to éxamine the captains, and other principal officers of every ship, brought in as a prize, upon general and impartial interrogatories: If there do not appear from thence ground to condemn, as enemy's property or contraband goods going to the enemy, there must be an acquittal, unless from the aforesaid evidence, the property shall appear so doubtful, that it is reasonable to go into farther proof thereof.

"A claim of ship, or goods, must be supported by the oath of some body, at least as to belief.

"The law of nations requires good faith;—Therefore every ship must be provided with complete and genuine papers; and the master at least should be privy to the truth of the transaction.

"To enforce these rules, if there be false or colourable papers; if any papers be thrown overboard; if the master and officers examined in preparatorio, grossly prevaricate; if proper ship's papers are not on board; or if the master and crew cannot say, whether the ship or cargo be the property of a friend or enemy, the law of nations allows, according to the different degrees of misbehaviour, or suspicion, arising from the fault of the ship taken, and other circumstances of the case, costs to be paid, or not to be received, by the claimant, in case of acquittal and restitution:—On the other hand, if a seizure is made without probable cause, the capture is adjudged to pay costs and damages: For which purpose all privateers are obliged to give security for their good behaviour; and this is referred to, and expressly stipulated by many treaties.

"Though from the ship's papers, and the preparatory examinations, the property does not sufficiently appear to be neutral, the claimant is often indulged with time to send over affidavits to supply that defect; if he will not shew the property by sufficient affidavits, to be neutral, it is presumed to belong to the enemy. Where the property appears from evidence not on board the ship, the captor is justified in bringing her in, and excused paying costs, because he is not in fault; or, according to the circumstances of the case, may be justly entitled to receive his costs.

"If the sentence of the court of admiralty is thought to be erroneous, there is in every maritime country, a superior court of review, consisting of the most considerable persons, to which the parties who think themselves aggrieved, may appeal; and this superior court judges by the same rule which governs the court of admiralty, viz. the law of nations, and the treaties subsisting with that neutral power, whose subject is a party before them.

"If no appeal is offered, it is an acknowledgment of the justice of the sentence by the parties themselves, and conclusive.

"This manner of trial and adjudication is supported, alluded to, and enforced, by many treaties.

"In this method, all captures at sea were tried, during the last war, by Great Britain, France, and Spain, and submitted to by the neutral powers;—In this method, by courts of admiralty acting according to the law of nations, and particular treaties, all captures at sea have immemorially been judged of in every country of Europe. Any other method of trial would be manifestly unjust, absurd and impracticable."

Such are the principles which govern the proceedings of the prize courts.

The following are the measures which ought to be taken by the captor, and by the neutral claimant upon a ship and cargo being brought in as prize.

The captor immediately upon bringing his prize into port, sends up or delivers upon oath to the registry of the court of admiralty all papers found on board the captured ship. In the course of a few days, the examinations in preparatory of the captain and some of the crew, of the captured ship, are taken upon a set of standing interrogatories, before the commissioners of the port to which the prize is brought, and which are also forwarded to the registry of the admiralty as soon as taken. A monition is extracted by the captor from the registry, and served upon the royal exchange, notifying the capture, and calling upon all persons interested to appear and shew cause, why the ship and goods should not be condemned. At the expiration of twenty days, the monition is returned into the registry with a certificate of its service, and if any claim has been given, the cause is then ready for hearing, upon the evidence arising out of the ship's papers, and preparatory examinations.

The measures taken on the part of the neutral master or proprietor of the cargo, are as follows:

Upon being brought into port, the master usually makes a protest, which he forwards to London, as instructions (or with such further directions as he thinks proper) either to the correspondent of his owners, or to the consul of his nation, in order to claim the ship, and such parts of the cargo as belong to his owners, or with which he was particularly entrusted: Or the master himself, as soon as he has undergone his examination, goes to London to take the necessary steps.

The master, correspondent, or consul applies to a proctor, who prepares a claim supported by an affidavit of the claimant, stating briefly, to whom as he believes, the ship and goods claimed, belong, and that no enemy has any right or interest in them: Security must be given to the amount of sixty pounds to answer costs, if the case should appear so grossly fraudulent on the part of the claimant as to subject him to be condemned therein.

If the captor has neglected in the mean time, to take the usual steps, (but which seldom happens, as he is strictly enjoined both by his instructions and by the prize act to proceed immediately to adjudication) a process issues against him on the application of the claimant's proctor, to bring in the ship's papers and preparatory examinations, and to proceed in the usual way.

As soon as the claim is given, copies of the ship's papers and examinations are procured from the registry, and upon the return of the monition the cause may be heard. It however seldom happens (owing to the great pressure of business, especially at the commencement of a war) that causes can possibly be prepared for hearing immediately upon the expiration of the time for the return of the monition; In that case, each cause must necessarily take its regular turn: correspondent measures must be taken by the neutral master if carried within the jurisdiction of a vice admiralty court, by giving a claim supported by his affidavit, and offering security for costs, if the claim should be pronounced grossly fraudulent.

If the claimant be dissatisfied with the sentence, his proctor enters an appeal in the registry of the court where the sentence was given, or before a notary public (which regularly should be entered within fourteen days after the sentence) and he afterwards applies at the registry of the lords of appeal in prize causes (which is held at the same place as the registry of the high court of admiralty) for an instrument called an inhibition, and which should be taken out within three months if the sentence be in the high court of admiralty, and within nine months, if in a vice admiralty court, but may be taken out at later periods, if a reasonable cause can be assigned for the delay that has intervened. This instrument directs the judge, whose sentence is appealed from, to proceed no further in the cause; it directs the registrar to transmit a copy of all the proceedings of the inferior court: and it directs the party who has obtained the sentence to appear before the superior tribunal to answer to the appeal. On applying for this inhibition, security is given on the part of the appellant, to the amount of two hundred pounds to answer costs, in case it should appear to the court of appeals, that the appeal is merely vexatious. The inhibition is to be served upon the judge, the registrar, and the adverse party and his proctor, by shewing the instrument under seal, and delivering a note or copy of the contents. If the party cannot be found, and the proctor will not accept the service, the instrument is to be served "*viis et modis*," that is by affixing it to the door of the last place of residence, or by hanging it upon the pillars of the royal exchange. That part of the process above described, which is to be executed abroad, may be performed by any person to whom it is committed, and the formal part at home is executed by the officer of the court. A certificate of the service is endorsed upon the back of the instrument, sworn before a surrogate of the superior court, or before a notary public, if the service is abroad.

If the cause be adjudged in a vice admiralty court, it is usual upon entering an appeal there, to procure a copy of the proceedings which the appellant sends over to his correspondent in England, who carries it to a proctor, and the same steps are taken to procure and serve the inhibition, as where the cause has been adjudged in the high court of admiralty. But if a copy of the proceedings cannot be procured in due time, an inhibition may be obtained, by sending over a copy of the instrument of appeal, or by writing to the correspondent an account only of the time and substance of the sentence.

Upon an appeal, fresh evidence may be introduced if upon hearing the cause the lords of appeal shall be of opinion, that the case is of such doubt, as that farther proof ought to have been ordered by the court below.

Further proof usually consists of affidavits made by the asserted proprietors of the goods, in which they are sometimes joined by their clerks and others acquainted with the transaction and with the real property of the goods claimed. In corroboration of these, affidavits may be annexed, original correspondence, duplicates of bills of lading, invoices, extracts from books, &c. These papers must be proved by the affidavits of persons who can speak to their authenticity. And if copies or extracts, they should be collated and certified by public notaries. The affidavits are sworn before the magistrates or others competent to administer oaths in the country where they are made, and authenticated by a certificate from the British consul.

The degree of proof to be required depends upon the degree of suspicion and doubt, that belongs to the case. In cases of heavy suspicion and great importance, the court may order what is called "plea and proof," that is, instead of admitting affidavits and documents introduced by the claimants only, each party is at liberty to allege in regular pleadings such circumstances as may tend to acquit or to condemn the capture, and to examine witnesses in support of the allegations, to whom the adverse party may admininister interrogatories. The depositions of the witnesses are taken in writing; if the witnesses are to be examined abroad, a commission issues for that purpose,—but in no case is it necessary for them to come to England. These solemn proceedings are not often resorted to.

Standing commissions may be sent to America for the *general* purpose of receiving examinations of witnesses in all cases where the court may find it necessary for the purposes of justice, to decree an enquiry to be conducted in that manner.

With respect to captures and condemnations at Martinico, which are the subjects of another inquiry contained in your note, we can only answer in general, that we are not informed of the particulars of such captures and condemnations, but as we know of no legal court of admiralty established at Martinico, we are clearly of opinion that the legality of any prizes taken there, must be tried in the high court of admiralty of England, upon claims given, in the manner above described, by such persons as may think themselves aggrieved by the said captures.

We have the honor to be, &c.

(Signed) WILLIAM SCOTT.
JOHN NICHOLL.

Commons, September 10*th*, 1794.

Report &c. referred to in the preceding letter.

TO THE KING'S MOST EXCELLENT MAJESTY.

May it please your Majesty,

In obedience to your majesty's commands, signified to us by his grace the duke of Newcastle, we have taken the memorial, sentence of the Prussian commissioners, and lists marked A. and B. which were delivered to his grace by Monsieur Michell, the Prussian secretary here, on the 23d of November last; and also the printed *Exposition des Motifs*, &c. which was delivered to his grace the 13th of December last, into our serious consideration; and we have directed the proper officer to search the registers of the court of admiralty, and inform us how the matter appeared from the proceedings there, in relation to the cases mentioned in the said lists A. and B. which he has accordingly done.

And your majesty having commanded us to report our opinion concerning the nature and regularity of the proceedings under the Prussian commission mentioned in the said memorial, and of the claim or demand pretended to be founded thereupon, and how far the same are consistent with, or contrary to, the law of nations, and any treaties subsisting between your majesty and the king of Prussia, the established rules of admiralty jurisdiction, and the laws of this kingdom.

For the greater perspicuity, we beg leave to submit our thoughts upon the whole matter in the following method:

1st, To state the clear established principles of law.

2dly, To state the fact.

3dly, to apply the law to the fact.

4thly, To observe upon the questions, rules and reasoning alleged in the said memorial, sentence of the Prussian commissioners, and *Exposition des Motifs*, &c. which carry appearances of objections to what we shall advance upon the former heads.

First, as to the LAW.

When two powers are at war, they have a right to make prizes of the ships, goods, and effects of each other upon the high seas; whatever is the property of the enemy may be acquired by capture at sea; but the property of a friend cannot be taken, provided he observed his neutrality.

Hence the law of nations has established,

That the goods of an enemy on board the ship of a friend may be taken.

That the lawful goods of a friend on board the ship of an enemy ought to be restored.

That contraband goods going to the enemy, though the property of a friend, may be taken as prize, because supplying the enemy with what enables him better to carry on the war is a departure from neutrality.

By the maritime law of nations universally and immemorially received, there is an established method of determination, whether the capture be, or be not, lawful prize.

Before the ship or goods can be disposed of by the captor, there must be a regular judicial proceeding wherein both parties may be heard, and condemnation thereupon as prize in a court of admiralty, judging by the law of nations and treaties.

The proper and regular court for these condemnations, is the court of that state to whom the captor belongs.

The evidence to acquit or condemn, with or without costs or damages, must, in the first instance, come merely from the ship taken, *viz.* the papers on board, and the examination on oath of the master and other principal officers: for which purpose there are officers of admiralty in all the considerable seaports of every maritime power at war, to examine the captains and other principal officers of every ship brought in as prize, upon general and impartial interrogatories. If there do not appear from thence ground to condemn as enemy's property, or contraband goods going to the enemy, there must be an acquittal: unless from the aforesaid evidence the property shall appear so doubtful, that it is reasonable to go into the further proof thereof.

A claim of ships or goods must be supported by the oath of somebody, at least as to belief.

The law of nations requires good faith; therefore every ship must be provided with complete and genuine papers, and the master at least should be privy to the truth of the transaction.

To enforce these rules, if there be false or colourable papers, if any papers be thrown overboard, if the master and officers examined *in præparatorio* grossly prevaricate, if proper ship's papers are not on board, or if the master and crew cannot say whether the ship or cargo be the property of a friend or enemy, the law of nations allows, according to the different degrees of misbehaviour or suspicion arising from the fault of the ship taken, and other circumstances of the case, costs to be paid, or not to be received, by the claimant in case of acquittal and restitution. On the other hand, if a seizure is made without probable cause, the captor is adjudged to pay costs and damages; for which purpose all privateers are obliged to give security for their good behaviour; and this is referred to, and expressly stipulated by, many treaties.*

Though, from the ship's papers, and the preparatory examinations, the property do not sufficiently appear to be neutral, the claimant is often indulged with time to send over affidavits, to supply that defect; if he will not shew the property by sufficient affidavits to be neutral, it is presumed to belong to the enemy. Where the property appears from evidence not on board the ship, the captor is justified in bringing her in, and excused paying costs, because he is not in fault; or, according to the circumstances of the case, may be justly entitled to receive his costs.

If the sentence of the court of admiralty is thought to be erroneous, there is in every maritime country a superior court of review, consisting of the most considerable persons, to which the parties, who think themselves aggrieved, may appeal; and this superior court judges by the same rule which governs the court of admiralty, *viz.* the law of

* Treaty between England and Holland, 17 Feb. 1668. Art. 13.—Treaty 1 Dec. 1674. Art. 10—Treaty between England and France at St. Germains, 24th of Feb. 1677. Art. 10.—Treaty of Commerce at Ryswick, Sept. 20, 1697, between France and Holland, Art. 30.—Treaty of Commerce at Utrecht, 31 March, 1713, between Great Britain and France, Art. 29.

nations, and the treaties subsisting with that neutral power whose subject is a party before them.

If no appeal is offered, it is an acknowledgment of the justice of the sentence by the parties themselves, and conclusive.

This manner of trial and adjudication is supported, alluded to, and enforced by many treaties.*

In this method all captures at sea were tried, during the last war, by Great Britain, France, and Spain, and submitted to by the neutral powers. In this method, by courts of admiralty acting according to the law of nations and particular treaties, all captures at sea have immemorially been judged of in every country of Europe. Any other method of trial would be manifestly unjust, absurd, and impraticable.

* As appears with respect to courts of admiralty adjudging the prizes taken by those of their own nation, and with respect to the witnesses to be examined in those cases, from the following treaties:—Treaty between England and Holland, 17 Feb. 1668. Art. 9 and 14.—Treaty 1 Dec. 1674. Art. 11.—Treaty 29th of April, 1689. Art. 12, 13.---Treaty between England and Spain, 23 May, 1667. Art. 23.—Treaty of Commerce at Ryswick, 20 Sept. 1697, between France and Holland, Art. 26 and 31.—Treaty between England and France, 3 Nov. 1655. Art. 17 and 18.—Treaty of Commerce between England and France at St. Germain's, 29 March, 1632. Art. 5 and 6.—Treaty at St. Germain's, 24 Feb. 1677. Art. 7.—Treaty of Commerce between Great Britain and France, at Utrecht, 31 March, 1713. Art. 26 and 30.—Treaty between England and Denmark, 29 Nov. 1669. Art. 23 and 34.—*Heineccius*, who was privy counsellor to the king of Prussia, and held in the greatest esteem, in his Treatise *de Navibus ob vecturam vetitarum mercium commissis*, cap. 2. sect. 17 and 18, speaks of this method of trial.

With respect to appeals or reviews,--from treaty between England and Holland, 1 Dec. 1674. Art 12, as it is explained by Article 2. of the Treaty at Westminster, 6 Feb. 1715-16.—Treaty between England and France, at St. Germain's, 24 Feb. 1677. Art. 12—Treaty of Commerce at Ryswick, 20. Sept. 1697, between France and Holland, Art. 23.—Treaty of Commerce at Utrecht. 31 March, 1713, between Great Britain and France, Art. 31 and 32, and other Treaties.

Though the law of nations be the general rule, yet it may, by mutual agreement between two powers, be varied or departed from; and where there is an alteration or exception introduced by particular treaties, that is the law between the parties to the treaty; and the law of nations only governs so far as is not derogated from by the treaty.

Thus by the law of nations, where two powers are at war, all ships are liable to be stopped and examined to whom they belong, and whether they are carrying contraband goods to the enemy; but particular treaties have enjoined a less degree of search, on the faith of producing solemn passports and formal evidences of property duly attested.

Particular treaties too have inverted the rule of the law of nations, and by agreement declared the goods of a friend on board the ship of an enemy to be prize, and the goods of an enemy on board the ship of a friend to be free, as appears from the treaties already mentioned, and many others.*

So likewise, by particular treaties, some goods reputed contraband by the law of nations are declared to be free.]

If a subject of the king of Prussia is injured by, or has a demand upon any person here, he ought to apply to your majesty's courts of justice, which are equally open and indifferent to foreigner or native; so, *vice versâ*, if a subject here is wronged by a person living in the dominions of his Prussian majesty, he ought to apply for redress in the king of Prussia's courts of justice.

If the matter of complaint be a capture at sea during war, and the question relative to prize, he ought to apply to the judicatures established to try these questions.

The law of nations, founded upon justice, equity, convenience, and the reason of the thing, and confirmed by long usage, does not allow of reprisals, except in case of violent

* Particularly by the aforesaid Treaty between England and Holland, 1 Dec. 1674, and the Treaty of Utrecht between Great Britain and France.

injuries directed or supported by the state, and justice absolutely denied *in re minimè dubiâ* by all the tribunals, and afterwards by the prince.*

Where the judges are left free, and give sentence according to their conscience, though it should be erroneous, that would be no ground for reprisals. Upon doubtful questions different men think and judge differently; and all a friend can desire is, that justice should be impartially administered to him, as it is to the subjects of that prince in whose courts the matter is tried.

Secondly as to the FACT.

We have subjoined hereto two lists tallying with those marked A. and B. which were delivered to his grace the duke of Newcastle by Mons. Michell, with the said memorial, the 23d of November last; and also printed at the end of the said *Exposition des Motifs*, &c. from whence it will appear, that as to the list A. which contains 18 ships and their cargoes.

Four, if ever taken, were restored by the captors themselves, to the satisfaction of the Prussians, who never have complained in any court of justice here.

One was restored by sentence, with full costs and damages, which were liquidated at 2801*l.* 12*s* 1*d.* sterling.

Three ships were restored by sentence, with freight, for such of the goods as manifestly belonged to the enemy, and were condemned.

Four ships were restored by sentence, but the cargoes, or part of them, condemned as prize or contraband, and are

* *Grotius de Jure Belli ac Pacis*, lib. 3. cap. 2. sect. 4, 5.

Treaty between England and Holland, 31 July, 1667, Art. 31. Reprisals shall not be granted till justice has been demanded according to the ordinary course of law.

Treaty of Commerce at Ryswick, 20 Sept. 1697, between France and Holland, Art. 4. Reprisals shall not be granted but on manifest denial of justice.

not now alleged in the lists A. or B. to have been Prussian property.

Five ships and cargoes were restored by sentence, but the claiment subjected to pay costs, because, from the ship-papers and preparatory examinations, there was ground to have condemned, and the restitution was decreed merely on the faith of affidavits afterwards allowed.

One ship and cargo was restored by sentence upon an appeal, but from the circumstances of the capture, without costs on either side.

There need no observations upon this list. As to the eight cases first above mentioned, there cannot be the colour of complaint.

As to the four next, the goods must be admitted to have been rightly condemned, either as enemy's property or contraband, for they are not now mentioned in the lists A. or B.

If contraband, the ship could have neither freight nor costs, and the sentences were favourable in restoring the ships, upon presumption that the owners of the ships were not acquainted with the nature of the cargo or the owners thereof. If enemy's property, the ships could not be entitled to freight, because the bills of lading were false, and purported the property to belong to Prussians.

The ships could not be entitled to costs, because the cargoes, or part of them, being lawful prize, the ships were rightly brought in.

As the six remaining ships and cargoes were restored, the only question must be upon paying or not receiving costs, which depends upon the circumstances of the capture, the fairness of the ship's documents, and conduct of her crew; and neither the Prussian commissioners, the said memorial, or said *Exposition des Motifs*, &c. allege a single reason why, upon the particular circumstances of these cases, the sentences were wrong.

As to the list B.

Every ship, on board which the subjects of Prussia claim to have had property, was bound to or from a port of the enemy; and many of them appeared to be, in part, laden with the goods of the enemy, either under their own or fictitious names.

In every instance where it is suggested that any part of the cargo belonged to a Prussian subject, though his property did not appear from the ship's papers, or preparatory examinations, which it ought to have done, sufficient time was indulged to that Prussian subject to make an affidavit that the property was *bonâ fide* in him; and the affidavit of the party himself has been received as proof of the property of the Prussian, so as to entitle him to restitution.

Where the party will not swear at all, or swears evasively, it is plain he only lends his name to cover the enemy's property, as often came out to be the case beyond the possibility of doubt.

It appears by a letter 29th of May and 9th of June, 1747, from Mons. Andrié to his Prussian Majesty, exhibited in a cause, and certified to be a true extract by Mons. Michell, under his hand, that this colourable manner of screening the goods of the enemy was stated in the following words:

"Your majesty's subjects ought not to load on board neutral ships any goods really belonging to the enemies of England, but to load them for their own account, whereby they may safely send them to any country they shall think proper, without any risk. Then, if privateers commit any damage to the ships belonging to your majesty's subjects, you may depend on full justice being done here, as in all the like cases hath been done."

List B. contains thirty-three cases.

Two of them never came before a court of justice in England, but (if taken) were restored by the captors themselves, to the entire satisfaction of the owners.

In sixteen of them the goods claimed by the Prussian

subjects appear to have been actually restored, by sentence, to the masters of ships in which they were laden; and by the customs of the sea the master is in the place of the lader, and answerable to him.

In fourteen of the cases the Prussian property was not verified by the ship's papers, or preparatory examinations, or claimant's own affidavit, which he was allowed to make.

And the other cause, with respect to part of the goods, is still depending, neither party having moved for judgment.* And so conscious were the claimants that the court of admiralty did right, there is not an appeal, in a single instance, in list B.; and but one in list A.

Thirdly, to apply the law to the FACT.

The sixth question in the said *Exposition des Motifs*, &c. states the right of reprisals to be, "*puisqu'on leur a si long tems denié toute la justice, qu'ils étoient fondés de demander.*"

The said memorial founds the justice and propriety of his Prussian Majesty's having recourse to reprisals, because his subjects, "*n'ont pu obtenir jusqu'à present aucune justice des tribunaux Anglois qu'ils ont reclamés ou du gouvernement auquel ils ont porté les plaintes.*" And in another part of the memorial it is put, "*apres avoir en vain demandé des reparations de ceux qui seuls pouvoient les faire.*"

The contrary of all which is manifested from the above state and lists hereto annexed.

In six of the cases specified, if such captures ever were made, the Prussian subjects were so well satified with the restitution made by the captors, that they never complained in any court whatsoever of this kingdom.

The rest were judged of by a court of admiralty, the only proper court to decide of captures at sea, both with respect to the restitution and the damages and costs; acting according to the law of nations, the only proper rule to de-

* The Prussian has since applied for judgment on the 29th of January, and obtained restitution.

cide by; and justice has been done by the court of admiralty so impartially, that all the ships alleged in list A. to have been Prussian were restored, and all the cargoes mentioned in either list A. or B. were restored, excepting fifteen, one of which is still undetermined.

And, in all the cases in both lists, justice was done so entirely to the conviction of the private conscience of the Prussian claimants, that they have acquiesced under the sentences without appealing, except in one single instance, where the part of the sentence complained of was reversed;

Though the Prussian claimants must know that, by the law of nations, they ought not to complain to their own sovereign till injustice *in re minimè dubiâ* was finally done them, past redress; and though they must know that rule of the law of nations held more strongly upon this occasion, because the property of prize was given to the captors, and ought therefore to be litigated with them. The Prussian who, by his own acquiescence, submits to the captors having the prize, cannot afterwards with justice make a demand upon the state. If the sentence was wrong, it is owing to the fault of the Prussian that it was not redressed. But it is not attempted to be shewn, even now, that these sentences were unjust in any part of them, according to the evidence and circumstances appearing before the court of admiralty; and that is the criterion.

For as to the Prussian commission to examine these cases, *ex parte*, upon new suggestions, it never was attempted in any country of the world before; prize or not prize, must be determined by courts of admiralty belonging to the power whose subjects make the capture. Every foreign prince in amity has a right to demand that justice shall be done his subjects in these courts, according to the law of nations, or particular treaties, where any are subsisting. If *in re minimè dubiâ* these courts proceed upon foundations directly opposite to the law of nations, or subsisting treaties, the neutral state has a right to complain of such determination.

But there never was, nor never can be, any other equitable method of trial. All the maritime nations of Europe have, when at war, from the earliest times, uniformly proceeded in this way, with the approbation of all the powers at peace. Nay, the persons acting under this extraordinary and unheard-of commission from his Prussian majesty, do not pretend to say, that in the four cases of goods condemned here, for which satisfaction is demanded in list A. the property really belonged to Prussian subjects; but they profess to proceed upon this principle, evidently false, that though these cargoes belonged to the enemy, yet, being on board any neutral ships, they were not liable to inquiry, seizure, or condemnation.

Fourthly, from the questions, rules, reasonings, and matters alleged in the said memorial, sentences of the Prussian commissioners, and *Exposition des Motifs*, &c. the following propositions may be drawn as carrying the appearance of objections to what has been above laid down:

FIRST PROPOSITION.

"That by the law of nations the goods of an enemy cannot be taken on board the ship of a friend; and this the Prussian commissioners lay down as the basis of all they have pretended to do."

ANSWER. The contrary is too clear to admit of being disputed. It may be proved by the authorities of every writer of the law of nations; some of different countries are referred to.* It may be proved by the constant practice,

* *Il Consolato del Mare*, cap. 273, expressly says, "The enemy's goods, found on board a friend's ship, shall be confiscated." And this is a book of great authority.

ancient and modern; but the general rule cannot be more strongly proved than by the exception which particular treaties have made to it.*

SECOND PROPOSITION.

"It is alleged that Lord Carteret, in 1744, by two verbal declarations, gave assurances in your majesty's name that nothing on board a Prussian ship should be seized, except contraband; consequently, that all effects not contraband, belonging to the enemy, should be free; and that these assurances were afterwards confirmed in writing by Lord Chesterfield, the 5th of January, 1747."

ANSWER. The fact makes this question not very material, because there are but four instances in lists A. or B. where any goods on board a Prussian ship have been con-

Grotius del Jure Belli ac Pacis, lib. iii. cap. 1, section 5, numero 4, in the notes, cites this passage, in the *Il Consolato*, and in his notes, lib. iii. cap. 6. sect. 6.

Loccenius de Jure Maritimo, lib. ii. cap. 4, sect. 12.

Voet de Jure Militari, cap. 5, nu. 21.

Heineccius, the learned Prussian before quoted, *de Navibus ob Vecturam vetitarum Mercium commissis*, cap. 2. sect. 9. is clear and explicit upon this point.

Bynkershoeck Quæstiones Juris Publici, lib. i. cap. 14, per totum.

Zouch (an Englishman) in his book *de Judicio inter Gentes*, pars 2. sect. 8, numero 6.

Treaty between Great Britain and Sweden, 23 Oct. 1661. Art. 12, and 13; Treaty between Great Britain and Denmark, 19 Nov. 1669. Art. 2; and the passport or certificate, settled by that treaty, are material as to this point.

* Treaty between France and England, 24 Feb. 1677. Art. 8.
Treaty of Utrecht between France and England, 1713. Art. 17.
Treaty between England and Holland, 17 Feb. 1668. Art. 10.
Treaty between England and Holland, 1 Dec. 1674. Art. 8.
Treaty between England and Portugal, 10 July, 1654. Art. 23.
Treaty between France and the States General at Utrecht, 11 April, 1713. Art. 26.

demned; and no satisfaction is pretended to be demanded for any of those four cargoes in lists A. and B. However, it may be proper to shew how groundless this pretence is.

Taking the words alleged to have been said by Lord Carteret as they are stated, they do not warrant the inferences endeavoured to be drawn from them. They import no new stipulation different from the law of nations, but expressly profess to treat the Prussians upon the same foot with the subjects of other neutral powers under the like circumstances; *i. e.* with whom there was no particular treaty. For the reference to neutral powers cannot be understood to communicate the terms of any particular treaty. It is not so said. The treaties with Holland, Sweden, Russia, Portugal, Denmark, &c. all differ. Who can say which was communicated? There would be no reciprocity: the King of Prussia does not agree to be bound by the clauses to which other powers have, by their respective treaties, agreed. No Prussian goods on board an enemy's ship have ever been condemned here, and yet they ought, if the treaties with Holland were to be the rule between Great Britain and Prussia; nay, if these treaties were to be the rule, all now contended for, on the part of Prussia, is clearly wrong; because, by treaty, the Dutch, in the last resort, are to apply to the court of appeal here.

Treaty of Alliance between Great Britain and Holland, at Westminster, the 6th of Feb. 1715-16, Article II.

"Whereas some disputes have happened touching the explanation of the 12th article of the treaty marine in 1674, it is agreed and concluded for deciding any difficulty upon that matter, to declare by these presents, that by the provisions mentioned in the said article, are meant those which are received by custom in Great Britain and the United Provinces, and always have been received, which have been granted, and always are granted, in the like case, to the inhabitants of the said countries, and to every foreign nation."

Lord Carteret is said twice to have refused, in which Monsieur Andrié acquiesces, to give any thing in writing, as not usual in England.

Supposing the conversations to mean no more than a declaration of course that justice should be done to the Prussians in like manner as to any other neutral power with whom there was no treaty, there was no occasion for instruments in writing; because in England the crown never interferes with the course of justice. No order or intimation is ever given to any judge. Lord Carteret therefore knew that it was the duty of the court of admiralty to do equal justice, and that they would, of themselves, do what he said to Monsieur Andrié.

Had it been intended, by agreement, to introduce between Prussia and England a variation in any particular from the law of nations, and consequently a new rule for the court of admiralty to decide by, it could only be done by a solemn treaty, in writing, properly authorized and authenticated. The memory of it could not otherwise be preserved; the parties interested and the courts of admiralty could not otherwise take notice of it.

But Lord Chesterfield's confirmation, in a letter of the 5th of January, 1747, being relied upon, the books of the secretary's office have been searched, and the letter to Monsieur Michell is found, which is *verbatim* as follows:

A WHITEHALL, *le* 5 *Janv.* 1747-8.

"MONSIEUR,

"*Ayant eu l'honneur de recevoir les ordres du roy sur ce qui a formé le sujet du memoire que vous m'avez remis du* 8 *de ce mois, N. S. Je n'ai pas voulu tarder à vous informer, que sa majesté, pour ne rien omettre par où elle peut temoigner ses attentions envers le roy votre maitre, ne fait nulle difficulté de declarer, qu'elle n'a jamais eu l'intention, ni ne l'aura jamais, de donner le moindre empechement à la navigation des sujets Prussiens, tant qu'ils auront soin d'exercer leur commerce d'une maniere licite, et conformément à l'ancien usage établi et reconnu parmi les puissances neutres.*

" *Que sa majesté Prussienne ne peut pas ignorer, qu'il y a des traités de commerce qui subsistent actuellement entre la Grande Bretagne et certaines etats neutres, et qu'au moyen des engagemens formellement contractés de part et d'autre par ces mêmes traités, tout ce qui regarde la maniere d'exercer leur commerce reciproquement, a été finalement constaté et reglé.*

" *Qu'en même tems il ne paroit point qu'aucun traité de la nature susdite existe à present, ou a jamais existé, entre sa majesté et le roy de Prusse; mais que pourtant cela n'a jamais empeché que les sujets Prussiens n'ayent été favorisés par l'Angleterre, par raport à leur navigation, autaut que les autres nations neutres: et cela étant, sa majesté ne presuppose pas, que l'idée du roy votre maitre seroit d'exiger d'elle des distinctions, encore moins des preferences, en faveur de ses sujets à cet égard.*

" *Que de plus sa majesté Prussienne est trop eclairée pour ne pas connoitre, qu'il y a des loix fixes et etablies dans ce gouvernement, dont on ne peut nullement s'écarter; et que s'il arrivoit que la marine Angloise s'avisât de faire la moindre injustice aux sujets commerçans du roy votre maitre, il y a un tribunal ici, savoir, la haute cour de l'amirauté, à laquelle ils se trouvent en droit de s'adresser et de porter leurs plaintes; assurés d'avance, en pareil cas, qu'on leur y rendra bonne justice; les procedés juridiques de ladite cour étant et ayant été de tout tems hors d'atteinte et irreprochables; temoin, nombre, d'exemples, où des vaisseaux neutres, pris illicitement, ont été restitués avec fraix et dommages aux proprietaires.*

" *Voici ce que le roy m'a ordonne de vous repondre sur le contenu de votre dit memoire; et sa majesté ne sauroit que se flatter, qu'en consequence de ce que je viens d'avancer; il ne restera plus rien à desirer au roy votre maitre relativement à l'objet dont il est question; et le roy s'en croit d'autant plus assuré, qu'il est persuadé que sa majesté Prussienne ne voudroit rien demander que ne fut équitable.*

"*Je suis, avec bien de la consideration,*
"*Monsieur,*
"*Votre très humble et très*
"*Obeissant serviteur,*
"*CHESTERFIELD.*"

There need no observations; it is explicit, and in express terms puts Prussia upon the foot of other neutral powers with whom there was no treaty, and points out the proper way of applying for redress.

The verbal declarations made by Lord Carteret in 1744, which are said to have been confirmed by this letter from Lord Chesterfield, cannot have meant more than the letter expresses.

And it is manifest by the above extract from Monsieur Andrié's letter to his Prussian majesty, that in May 1747, Monsieur Andrié himself understood that goods of the enemy taken on board neutral ships ought to be condemned as prize.

It is evident from authentic acts, that the subjects of Prussia never understood that any new right was communicated to them.

Before the year 1746 the Prussians do not appear to have openly engaged in covering the enemy's property.

The men of war and privateers could not abstain from captures in consequence of Lord Carteret's verbal assurances in 1744, because they never were nor could be known; and there was no occasion to notify them, supposing them only to promise impartial justice. For all ships of war were bound to act, and courts of admiralty to judge, according to the law of nations and treaties.

Till 1746 the Prussian documents were, a certificate of the admiralty, upon the oath of the builder, that the ship was Prussian built; and a certificate of the admiralty, upon the oath of the owner, that the ship was Prussian property.

From 1746 the Prussians engaged in the gainful practice of covering the enemy's goods, but were at a loss in what shape and upon what pretences it might best be done.

On board the ship the Trois Soeurs was found a pass bearing date at Stettin the 6th of October 1746, under the royal seal of the Prussian regency of Pomerania, &c. alleging the cargo, which was ship timber, bound for Port L'Orient, to be Prussian property, and in consequence thereof, claiming freedom of the ship.

Claiming freedom to the ship from the property of the cargo being quite new, the proposition was afterwards reversed. And on board a ship called the Jumeaux, was found a pass bearing date at Stettin the 27th of June, 1747, under the royal seal, &c. alleging the ship to be Prussian property, and, in consequence thereof, claiming freedom to the goods.

But this pass was not solely relied on, for there was also found on board the same ship another pass, bearing date at Stettin the 14th of June, 1747, under the royal seal, &c. alleging the cargo to be Prussian property.

And it is remarkable that the oaths upon which these passes were granted, appeared manifestly to be false; and neither of the cargoes to which they relate are now so much as alleged to have been Prussian property in said list A. or B.

It being mentioned in the said *Exposition des Motifs*, &c. that Mons. Michell, in September, 1747, made verbal representations to Lord Chesterfield in respect to the cargo taken on board the said ship called the Trois Soeurs, which was claimed as Prussian property, and no mention being made in the lists A. and B. of the said cargo, we directed the proceedings in that cause to be laid before us; where it appears in the fullest and clearest manner, from the ship-papers and depositions, that the cargo was timber, laden on the account and at the risk of Frenchmen, to whom it was to be delivered at Port L'Orient, they paying freight according to charter party; that the Prussian claimant was neither freighter, lader, or consignee; and had no other interest or concern in the matter than to lend his name and conscience; for he swore that the cargo was his property, and laden on or before the 6th of October, 1746, and yet the ship was then in ballast, and the whole of the cargo in question was not laden before May 1747.

Several other Prussian claims had, in like manner, come out so clearly to be merely colourable, that Mons. Andrié, from his said letter the 29th of May and 9th of June 1747, appears to have been ashamed of them.

THIRD PROPOSITION.

"That Lord Carteret, in his said two conversations, specified in your Majesty's name, what goods should be deemed contraband."

Answer. The fact makes this question totally immaterial, because no goods condemned as contraband, or which were alleged to be so, are so much as now suggested to have been Prussian property in the said lists A. and B; and therefore, whether as enemy's property or contraband, they were either way rightly condemned; and, the bills of lading being false, the ships could not be entitled to freight.

But if the question was material, the verbal declarations of a minister in conversation might shew what he thought contraband by the law of nations, but never could be understood to be equivalent to a treaty derogating from that law.

All the observations upon the other parts of these verbal declarations hold equally as to this.

FOURTH PROPOSITION.

" That the British ministers have said that these questions were decided according to the laws of England."

Answer. They must have been misunderstood; for the law of England says, that all captures at sea, as prize, in time of war, must be judged of in a court of admiralty, according to the law of nations and particular treaties, where there are any.

There never existed a case where a court, judging according to the laws of England only, ever took cognizance of prize.

The property of prizes being given during the last war to the captors, your majesty could not arbitrarily release the capture, but left all cases to the decision of the proper courts, judging by law of nations and treaties where there were any; and it never was imagined that the property of a foreign subject, taken as prize on the high seas, could be affected by laws peculiar to England.

FIFTH PROPOSITION.

" That your majesty could no more erect tribunals for trying these matters than the king of Prussia."

Answer. Each crown has, no doubt, an equal right to erect admiralty courts for the trial of prizes taken by virtue of their respective commissions; but neither has a right to try the prizes taken by the other, or to reverse the sentences given by the other's tribunal. The only regular method of rectifying their errors is, by appeal to the superior court.

This is the clear law of nations; and by this method prizes have always been determined in every other maritime country of Europe as well as England.

SIXTH PROPOSITION.

"That the sea is free."

Answer. They who maintain that proposition in its utmost extent, do not dispute but that when two powers are at war they may seize the effects of each other upon the high seas, and on board the ships of friends; therefore that controversy is not in the least applicable upon the present occasion.*

SEVENTH PROPOSITION.

"Great Britain issued reprisals against Spain, on account of captures at sea."

Answer. These captures were not made in time of war with any power.

They were not judged of by courts of admiralty, according to the law of nations and treaties, but by rules, which were themselves complained of in revenue courts; the damages were afterwards admitted, liquidated at a certain sum, and agreed to be paid by a convention, which was not performed; therefore reprisals issued, but they were general. No debts due here to Spaniards were stopped; no Spanish effects here were seized; which leads to one observation more.

The king of Prussia has engaged his royal word to pay the Silesia debt to private men.

It is negotiable, and many parts may have been assigned to the subjects of other powers. It will not be easy to find

* This appears from Grotius in the passages above cited, lib. 3. cap. 1. sect. 5. nu. 4. in his notes; and lib. 3. cap. 6. sect. 6. in his notes.

an instance where a prince has thought fit to make reprisals upon a debt due from himself to private men. There is a confidence that this will not be done. A private man lends money to a prince upon the faith of an engagement of honor, because a prince cannot be compelled, like other men, in an adverse way, by a court of justice. So scrupulously did England, France, and Spain adhere to this public faith, that even during the war they suffered no inquiry to be made whether any part of the public debts was due to subjects of the enemy, though it is certain many English had money in the French funds, and many French had money in ours.

This loan to the late Emperor of Germany, Charles the VIth, in January 1734-5, was not a state transaction, but a mere private contract with the lenders, who advanced their money upon the emperor's obliging himself, his heirs and posterity, to repay the principal, with interest, at the rate, in the manner, and at the times in the contract mentioned, without any delay, demur, deduction or abatement whatsoever; and, lest the words and instruments made use of should not be strong enough, he promises to secure the performance of his contract in and by such other instruments, method, manner, form, and words, as should be most effectual and valid to bind the said emperor, his heirs, successors, and posterity, or as the lenders should reasonably desire.

As a specific real security, he mortgaged his revenues arising from the duchies of Upper and Lower Silesia for payment of principal and interest; and the whole debt, principal and interest, was to be discharged in the year 1745. If the money could not be paid out of the revenues of Silesia, the emperor, his heirs and posterity, still remained debtors, and were bound to pay. The eviction or destruction of a thing mortgaged, does not extinguish the debt or discharge the debtor.

Therefore the empress queen, without the consent of the lenders, made it a condition of her yielding the duchies of Silesia to his Prussian majesty, that he should stand in the place of the late emperor in respect of this debt.

The seventh of the preliminary articles between the Queen of Hungary and the King of Prussia, signed at Breslau the 11th of June 1742, is in these words: "*Sa majesté le roi de Prusse se charge du seul payment de la somme hypothéquée sur la Silesie, aux marchands Anglois, selon le contract signé à Londres le 7me de Janvier* 1734-5."

This stipulation is confirmed by the ninth article of the treaty between their said majesties, signed at Berlin the 28th of July 1742.

Also renewed and confirmed by the second article of the treaty between their said majesties, signed at Dresden at 25th of December 1745.

In consideration of the empress queen's cession, his Prussian majesty has engaged to her that he will pay this money *selon le contract*, and consequently has bound himself to stand in the place of the late emperor in respect of this money, to all intents and purposes.

The late emperor could not have seized this money as reprisals, or even in case of open war between the two nations, because his faith was engaged to pay it without any delay, demur, deduction, or abatement whatsoever. If these words should not extend to all possible cases, he hath plighted his honor to bind himself by any other form of words more effectually to pay the money; and therefore was liable at any time to be called upon to declare expressly that it should not be seized as reprisals, or in case of war; which is very commonly expressed when sovereign princes or states borrow money from foreigners. Therefore, supposing for a moment that his Prussian majesty's complaint was founded in justice and the law of nations, and that he had a right to make reprisals in general, he could not, consistent with his engagement to the empress queen, seize this money as reprisals. Beside, this whole debt, according to the contract, ought to have been discharged in 1745. It should, in respect of the private creditors, in justice and equity, be considered as if the contract had been performed; and the Prussian complaints do not begin till 1746, after the whole debt ought to have been paid.

Upon this principle of natural justice, French ships and effects wrongfully taken after the Spanish war, and before the French war, have, during the heat of the war with France, and since, been restored by sentence of your majesty's courts to the French owners. No such ships or effects ever were attempted to be confiscated as enemy's property here during the war; because, had it not been for the wrong first done, these effects would not have been in your majesty's dominions. So, had not the contract been first broke by non-payment of the whole loan in 1745, this money would not have been in his Prussian majesty's hands.

Your majesty's guaranty of these treaties is entire, and must therefore depend upon the same conditions upon which the cession was made by the empress queen.

But this reasoning is, in some measure, superfluous; because, if the making any reprisals upon this occasion be unjustifiable, which we apprehend we have shewn, then it is not disputed but that the non-payment of this money would be a breach of his Prussian majesty's engagements, and a renunciation, on his part, of those treaties.

All which is most humbly submitted to your majesty's royal wisdom.

GEO. LEE.
G. PAUL.
D. RYDER.
W. MURRAY.

January 18, 1753.

NO. II.

PRESIDENT'S INSTRUCTIONS TO PRIVATE ARMED VESSELS.

1. The tenor of your commission under the act of Congress, entitled "an act concerning letters of marque, prizes and prize goods," a copy of which is hereto annexed, will be kept constantly in your view. The high seas, referred to in your commission, you will understand generally, to refer to low-water mark; but with the exception of the space within one league, or three miles, from the shore of countries at peace both with Great Britain and with the United States. You may nevertheless execute your commission within that distance of the shore of a nation at war with Great Britain, and even on the waters within the jurisdiction of such nation, if permitted so to do.

2. You are to pay the strictest regard to the rights of neutral powers, and the usages of civilized nations; and in all your proceedings towards neutral vessels, you are to give them as little molestation or interruption as will consist with the right of ascertaining their neutral character, and of detaining and bringing them in for regular adjudication, in the proper cases. You are particularly to avoid even the appearance of using force or seduction, with a view to deprive such vessels of their crews, or of their passengers, other than persons in the military service of the enemy.

3. Towards enemy vessels and their crews, you are to proceed, in exercising the rights of war, with all the justice and humanity which characterize the nation of which you are members.

4. The master and one or more of the principal persons belonging to captured vessels, are to be sent, as soon after the capture as may be, to the judge or judges of the proper court in the United States, to be examined upon oath, touching the interest or property of the captured vessel and

her lading: and at the same time, are to be delivered to the judge or judges, all passes, charter parties, bills of lading, invoices, letters and other documents, and writings found on board; the said papers to be proved by the affidavit of the commander of the capturing vessel, or some other person present at the capture, to be produced as they were received, without fraud, addition, subduction or embezzlement.

By command of the President of the U. States.
JAMES MONROE, *Secretary of State.*

NO. III.

DOCUMENTS RELATING TO THE BLOCKADE OF MARTINIQUE AND GUADALOUPE.

(Copy.)

Mr Merry to Mr. Madison.

WASHINGTON, April 12, 1804.

SIR,

Mr. Thornton not having failed to transmit to his majesty's government an account of the representation which you were pleased to address to him, under date of the 27th October last year, respecting the blockade of the islands of Martinique and Guadaloupe, it is with great satisfaction, Sir, that I have just received his majesty's commands signified to me by his principal secretary of state for foreign affairs, under date of the 6th of January last, to communicate to you the instructions which have, in consequence of your representation, been sent to commodore Hood, and to the judges of the vice admiralty courts in the West Indies.

I have, accordingly, the honour to transmit to you, Sir, enclosed, the copy of a letter from Sir Evean Nepean, secretary to the board of admiralty, to Mr. Hammond, his majesty's under secretary of state for foreign affairs, specifying the nature of the instructions which have been given.

His majesty's government doubt not that the promptitude which has been manifested in redressing the grievance complained of by the government of the United States will be considered by the latter as an additional evidence of his majesty's constant and sincere desire to remove any ground of misunderstanding that could have a tendency to interrupt the harmony which so happily subsists between his government and that of the United States,

I have the honour to be,
With high respect and consideration,
Your most obedient humble servant,
(Signed) ANTH. MERRY.

(COPY.)

ADMIRALTY OFFICE, 5th January, 1804.

SIR,

HAVING communicated to the lords of the admiralty, lord Hawkesbury's letters of the 23d ultimo, inclosing the copy of a dispatch which his lordship had received from Mr. Thornton, his majesty's charge d'affairs in America, on the subject of the blockade of the islands of Martinique and Guadaloupe, together with the report of the advocate general.

Thereupon, I have their lordship's commands to acquaint you for his lordship's information, that they have sent orders to commodore Hood, not to consider any blockade of those islands as existing, unless in respect of particular ports which may be actually invested, and then not to capture vessels bound to such ports unless they shall previously have been warned not to enter them, and that they have also sent the necessary directions on the subject to the judges of the vice admiralty courts in the West Indies and America.

I am, &c.

(Signed) EVEAN NEPEAN.

George Hammond, esq.

MR. MERRY TO MR. MADISON.

WASHINGTON, April 12, 1804.

SIR,

I HAVE the honour to acquaint you that I have just received a letter from rear admiral sir John Duckworth, commander in chief of his majesty's squadron at Jamaica, dated the second of last month, in which he desires me to communicate to the government of the United States, that he has found it expedient for his majesty's service, to convert the siege, which he lately attempted, of Curacoa, into a blockade of that island.

I cannot doubt, sir, that this blockade will be conducted conformably to the instructions which, as I have had the honour to acquaint you in another letter of this date, have been recently sent on this subject to the commander in chief of his majesty's forces, and to the judges of the vice admiralty courts, in the West Indies, should the smallness of the island of Curacoa still render necessary any distinction of the investment being confined to particular ports.

I have the honour to be, &c.

(Signed) ANT. MERRY.

No. IV.

CORRESPONDENCE BETWEEN MR. PINKNEY AND MARQUIS WELLESLEY ON BLOCKADES.

Notwithstanding the explicit engagement on the part of the British government contained in the above documents, and confirmed by the decisions of their prize courts, blockades continued to be proclaimed without an actual investiture of the particular ports, and neutral vessels bound to such ports were captured without having been previously warned not to enter them. These blockades were defective, inasmuch as they were constructively established and constructively notified. Their unlawfulness had been settled both by diplomatic and judicial authority, in the war which was terminated by the treaty of Amiens; but this did not prevent their revival in the late war. The practice of the former war, on account of the remoteness of the United States from Europe, had justified a conjectural destination from America to Amsterdam, although the blockade of that port had been proclaimed in the usual manner, and the party was proved to have known its commencement. This rule was incorporated into the treaty between the United States and Great Britain, which was concluded *sub spe rati* in 1806, but not ratified. The British negotiators of that treaty, however, declined to insert in it a definition of blockade similar to that of the convention of 1801 between Russia and Great Britain, although they admitted the doctrine of the British prize courts to be conformable to such a definition. That this omission was not without meaning, is rendered evident by the continuance of the blockade of the European coast, from Brest to the Elbe, proclaimed in May, 1806, but which if valid in point of notice, was defective for want of an actual investiture of the ports and places included in its terms. This blockade, and other inhibitions of neutral trade of a like character, having been made by France the ground of issuing the Berlin decree of November, 1806, and that decree having been retaliated by the British orders in council of January and November, 1807, and of April, 1809; it became an object of the diplomatic discussions which ensued respecting the repeal of these edicts to ascertain whether the blockade of May, 1806, was merged in the orders subsequently issued, and (in case the Berlin decree should be revoked) would fall to the ground with these orders; or whether the blockade would revive after the revocation of the decrees and orders. Mr. Pinkney, the minister of the United States in London, after a great deal of discussion, succeeded in obtaining from the British secretary for foreign affairs, an admission, that either the blockade was merged in the orders, and would consequently be involved in their repeal, or if revived, would be enforced in the manner required by the law of nations. In the course of this discussion, the following letters were written, which are here inserted without any other apology than the preceding explanation.

LORD WELLESLEY TO MR. PINKNEY.*

Foreign Office, December 29, 1810.

SIR,

In acknowledging the receipt of your letter of the 10th instant, I must express my regret, that you should have thought it necessary to introduce into that letter any topics, which might tend to interrupt the conciliatory spirit, in which it is the sincere disposition of his majesty's government to conduct every negotiation with the government of the United States.

* This letter was not received till January 3d, 1811, at night.

From an anxious desire to avoid all discussions of that tendency, I shall proceed without any further observation to communicate to you the view which his majesty's government has taken of the principal question which formed the object of my inquiry, during our conference of the 5th instant. The letter of the French minister for foreign affairs to the American minister at Paris, of the 9th August, 1810, did not appear to his majesty's government, to contain such a notification of the repeal of the French decrees of Berlin and Milan, as could justify his majesty's government in repealing the British orders in council. That letter states "that the decrees of Berlin and Milan are revoked, and that from the 1st of November, 1810, they will cease to be in force, it being understood that in consequence of this declaration, the English shall revoke their orders in council and renounce the new principles of blockade which they have attempted to establish." The purport of this declaration appeared to be that the repeal of the decrees of Berlin and Milan would take effect from the 1st of November, provided that Great Britain antecedently to that day, and in consequence of this declaration, should revoke the orders in council and should renounce those principles of blockade, which the French government alleged to be new. A separate condition relating to America, seemed also to be contained in this declaration, by which America might understand, that the decrees of Berlin and Milan would be actually repealed on the 1st of November, 1810, provided that America should resent any refusal of the British government to renounce the new principles of blockade, and to revoke the orders in council.

By your explanation it appears, that the American government understands the letter of the French minister as announcing an absolute repeal, on the 1st of November, 1810, of the French decrees of Berlin and Milan; which repeal, however, is not to continue in force unless the British government, within a reasonable time after the 1st of November, 1810, shall fulfil the two conditions stated distinctly in the letter of the French minister. Under this explanation, if nothing more had been required from Great Britain, for the purpose of securing the continuance of the repeal of the French decrees, than the repeal of our orders in council, I should not have hesitated to declare the perfect readiness of this government to fulfil that condition. On these terms, the British government has always been sincerely disposed to repeal the orders in council. It appears, however, not only by the letter of the French minister, but by your explanation, that the repeal of the orders in council will not satisfy either the French or the American government. The British government is further required, by the letter of the French minister, to renounce those principles of blockade which the French government alleges to be new. A reference to the terms of the Berlin decree will serve to explain the extent of this requisition. The Berlin decree states, that Great Britain "extends the right of blockade to commercial unfortified towns, and to ports, harbors, and mouths of rivers, which, according to the principles and practice of all civilized nations, is only applicable to fortified places. On the part of the American government, I understand you to require that Great Britain should revoke her order of blockade of May, 1806. Combining your requisition with that of the French minister, I must conclude, that America demands the revocation of that order of blockade as a practical instance of our renunciation of those principles of blockade which are condemned by the French government. Those principles of blockade Great Britain has asserted to be ancient and established by the laws of maritime war, acknowledged by all civilized nations, and on which depend the most valuable rights and interests of this nation. If the Berlin and Milan decrees are to be considered as still in force, unless Great Britain shall renounce these established foundations of her maritime rights and interests, the period of time is not yet arrived, when the repeal of her orders in council can be claimed from her, either with reference to the promise of this government, or to the safety and honor of the nation. I trust that the justice of the American government will not consider, that France, by the repeal of her obnoxious decrees under such a condition, has placed the question in that state which can warrant America in enforcing the non-intercourse act against Great Britain and not against France. In reviewing the actual state of this question, America cannot fail to observe the situation in which the commerce of neutral nations has been placed by many recent acts of the French government; nor can America reasonably expect that the system of violence and injustice, now pursued by France with unremitted activity (while it serves to illustrate the true spirit of her intentions) should not require some precautions of defence on the part of Great Britain.

Having thus stated my view of the several considerations, arising from the letter of the French minister, and from that with which you have honored me; it remains only to express my solicitude that you should correct any interpretation of either which you may deem erroneous. If either by the terms of the original decree to which the French minister's letter refers, or by any other authentic document, you can prove that the decrees of Berlin and Milan are absolutely repealed, and that no further condition is required of Great Britain than the repeal of her orders in council, I shall receive any such information with most sincere satisfaction, desiring you to understand, that the British government retains an anxious solicitude to revoke the *orders in council*, as soon as the Berlin and Milan decrees shall be effectually repealed without conditions injurious to the maritime rights and honor of the united kingdom. I have the honor to be, with great respect and consideration, sir, your most obedient, and humble servant,

(Signed) WELLESLEY.

William Pinkney, Esquire, &c.

MR. PINKNEY TO LORD WELLESLEY.

Great Cumberland Place, January 14, 1811.

MY LORD,

I have received the letter which you did me the honor to address to me on the 29th of last month, and will not fail to transmit a copy of it to my government. In the mean time I take the liberty to trouble you with the following reply, which a severe indisposition has prevented me from preparing sooner.

The first paragraph seems to make it proper for me to begin by saying, that the topics introduced into my letter of the 10th of December, were intimately connected with its principal subject, and fairly used to illustrate and explain it; and consequently, that if they had not the good fortune to be acceptable to your lordship, the fault was not mine.

It was scarcely possible to speak with more moderation than my paper exhibits, of that portion of a long list of invasions of the rights of the United States, which it necessarily reviewed, and of the apparent reluctance of the British government to forbear those invasions in future. I do not know that I could more carefully have abstained from whatever might tend to disturb the spirit which your lordship ascribes to his majesty's government, if, instead of being utterly barren and unproductive, it had occasionally been visible in some practical result, in some concession either to friendship or to justice. It would not have been very surprising, nor very culpable perhaps, if I had wholly forgotten to address myself to a spirit of conciliation, which had met the most equitable claims with steady and unceasing repulsion; which had yielded nothing that could be denied; and had answered complaints of injury by multiplying their causes. With this forgetfulness, however, I am not chargeable; for, against all the discouragements suggested by the past, I have acted still upon a presumption that the disposition to conciliate, so often professed, would finally be proved by some better evidence than a perseverance in oppressive novelties, as obviously incompatible with such a disposition in those who enforce them, as in those whose patience they continue to exercise.

Upon the commencement of the second paragraph, I must observe, that the forbearance which it announces might have afforded some gratification, if it had been followed by such admissions as my government is entitled to expect, instead of further manifestation of that disregard of its demands, by which it has so long been wearied. It has never been my practice to seek discussions, of which the tendency is merely to irritate; but I beg your lordship to be assured, that I feel no desire to avoid them, whatever may be their tendency, when the rights of my country require to be vindicated against pretensions that deny, and conduct that infringes them.

If I comprehend the other parts of your lordship's letter, they declare in effect, that the British government will repeal nothing but the *orders in council*, and that it cannot at present repeal even them, because in the first place, the French government has required, in the letter of the Duke of Cadore to General Armstrong, of the 5th of August, not only that Great Britain shall revoke those orders, but that she shall renounce certain principles of blockade (supposed to be explained in the preamble to the Berlin decree) which France alleges to be new; and, in the second place, because the American government has (as you conclude) demanded the revocation of the British order of blockade of May, 1806, *as a practical instance of that same renunciation*, or, in other words, has made itself a party, not openly indeed, but indirectly and covertly, to the entire requisition of France, as you understand that requisition.

It is certainly true that the American government has required, as indispensible in the view of its acts of intercourse and non-intercourse, the annulment of the British blockade of May, 1806; and further, that it has through me declared its confident expectation that other blockades of a similar character (including that of the island of Zealand) will be discontinued. But by what process of reason your lordship has arrived at the conclusion, that the government of the United States intended by this requisition to become the champion of the edict of Berlin, to fashion its principles by those of France, while it affected to adhere to its own, and to act upon some partnership in doctrines, which it would fain induce you to acknowledge, but could not prevail upon itself to avow, I am not able to conjecture. The frank and honorable character of the American government justifies me in saying that, if it had meant to demand of Great Britain an abjuration of all such principles as the French government may think fit to disapprove, it would not have put your lordship to the trouble of discovering that meaning by the aid of combinations and inferences discountenanced by the language of its minister, but would have told you so in explicit terms. What I have to request of your lordship, therefore, is that you will take our views and principles from our own mouths, and that neither the Berlin decree, nor any other act of any foreign state, may be made to speak for us what we have not spoken for ourselves.

The principles of blockade which the American government professes, and upon the foundation of which it has repeatedly protested against the order of May, 1806, and the other kindred innovations of those extraordinary times, have already been so clearly explained to your lordship, in my letter of the 21st of September, that it is hardly possible to read that letter and misunderstand them. Recommended by the plainest considerations of universal equity, you will find them supported with a strength of argument and a weight of authority, of which they scarcely stand in need, in the papers which will accompany this letter, or were transmitted in that of September. I will not recapitulate what I cannot improve; but I must avail myself of this opportunity to call your lordship's attention a second time, in a particular manner, to one of the papers to which my letter of September refers. I allude to the copy of an official note of the 12th of April, 1804, from Mr. Merry to Mr. Madison, respecting a pretended blockade of Martinique and Guadaloupe. No comment can add to the value of that manly and perspicuous exposition of the law of blockade, as made by England herself in maintainance of rules which have been respected and upheld in all seasons and on all occasions by the government of the United States. I will leave it, therefore, to your lordship's consideration, with only this remark, that, while that paper exists, it will be superfluous to seek in any *French* document for the opinions of the American government on the matter of it.

The steady fidelity of the government of the United States to its opinions on that interesting subject is known to every body. The same principles which are found in the letter of Mr. Madison to Mr. Thornton, of the 27th of October, 1803, already before you, were asserted in 1799, by the American minister at this court, in his correspondence with Lord Grenville, respecting the blockade of some of the ports of Holland; were sanctioned in a letter of the 20th of September, 1800, from the secretary of state of the United States to Mr. King, of which an extract is enclosed; were insisted upon in repeated instructions to Mr. Monroe and the special mission of 1806; have been maintained by the United States against *others* as well as against England, as will appear by the inclosed copy of instructions, dated the 21st of October, 1801, from Mr. Secretary Madison to Mr. Charles Pinkney then American minister at Madrid; and finally, were adhered to by the United States, when belligerent, in the case of the blockade of Tripoli.

A few words will give a summary of those principles; and when recalled to your remembrance, I am not without hopes, that the strong grounds of law and right, on which they stand, will be as apparent to your lordship as they are to me.

It is by no means clear that it may not fairly be contended, on principle and early usage, that a maritime blockade is incomplete with regard to states at peace, unless the place which it would affect is invested by land as well as by sea. The United States, however, have called for the recognition of no such rule. They appear to have contented themselves with urging in substance, that ports not actually blockaded by a present, adequate, stationary force, employed by the power which attacks them, shall not be considered as shut to neutral trade in articles not contraband of war; that, though it is usual for a belligerent to give notice to neutral nations when he intends to institute a blockade, it is possible that he may not act upon his intention at all, or that he may execute it insufficiently, or that he may discontinue his blockade of which it is not customary to give any notice: that consequently the presence of the blockading force, is the natural criterion by which the neutral is enabled to ascertain the existence of the blockade at any given period, in like manner as the actual investment of a besieged place, is the evidence by which we decide whether the siege, which may be commenced, raised, recommenced and raised again, is continued or not; that of course a mere notification to a neutral minister shall not be relied upon, as affecting, with knowledge of the actual existence of a blockade, either his government or its citizens; that a vessel cleared or bound to a blockaded port, shall not be considered as violating in any manner the blockade, unless, on her approach towards such port, she shall have been previously warned not to enter it; that this view of the law, in itself perfectly correct, is peculiarly important to nations, situated at a great distance from the belligerent parties, and therefore incapable of obtaining other than tardy information of the actual state of their ports; that whole coasts and countries shall not be declared, (for they can never be more than *declared*) to be in a state of blockade, and thus the right of blockade converted into the means of extinguishing the trade of neutral nations; and lastly, that every blockade shall be impartial in its operation, or, in other words, shall not open and shut for the convenience of the party that institutes it, and at the same time repel the commerce of the rest of the world, so as to become the odious instrument of an unjust monopoly, instead of a measure of honorable war.

These principles are too moderate and just to furnish any motive to the British government for hesitating to revoke its orders in council, and those analogous orders of blockade, which the United States expect to be recalled. It can hardly be doubted that Great Britain will ultimately accede to them in their fullest extent; but if that be a sanguine calculation (as I trust it is not) it is still incontrovertible that a disinclination at this moment to acknowledge them, can suggest no rational inducement for declining to repeal at once what *every* principle disowns, and what must be repealed at last.

With regard to the rules of blockades which the French government expects you to abandon, I do not take upon me to decide whether they are such as your lordship supposes them to be or not. Your view of them may be correct; but it may also be erroneous; and it is wholly immaterial to the case between the United States and Great Britain whether it be the one or the other.

As to such *British blockades* as the United States desire you to relinquish, you will not, I am sure, allege that it is any reason for adhering to *them* that *France* expects you to relinquish *others*. If our demands are suited to the measure of our own rights, and of your obligations as they respect those rights, you cannot think of founding a rejection of them upon any imputed exorbitance in the theories of the French government, for which we are not responsible, and with which we have no concern. If, when you have done justice to the United States, your enemy should call upon you to go further, what shall prevent you from refusing? Your free agency will in no respect have been impaired. Your case will be better, in truth and in the opinion of mankind; and you will be *therefore*, stronger in maintaining it, provided that, in doing so, you resort only to legitimate means, and do not *once more* forget the rights of others while you seek to vindicate your own.

Whether France will be satisfied with what you may do, is not to be known by anticipation, and ought not to be the subject of inquiry. So vague a speculation has nothing to do with your duties to nations at peace, and, if it had, would annihilate them. It cannot serve your interests; for it tends to lessen the number of your friends, without adding to your security against your enemies.

You are required therefore, to do right, and to leave the consequences to the future, when by doing right you have every thing to gain and nothing to lose.

As to the *orders in council*, which professed to be a reluctant departure from all ordinary rules, and to be justified only as a system of retaliation for a pre-existing measure of France, their foundation (such as it was) is gone the moment that measure is no longer in operation. But the Berlin decree is repealed; and even *Milan* decree, the successor of your orders in council, is repealed also. Why is it, then, that your orders have outlived those edicts, and that they are still to oppress and harass as before? Your lordship answers this question explicitly enough, but not satisfactorily. You do not allege that the French decrees are not repealed; but you imagine that the repeal is not to remain in force, unless the British government shall, in addition to the revocation of its orders in council, abandon its system of blockade. I am not conscious of having stated, as your lordship seems to think, that this is so, and I believe in fact that it is otherwise. Even if it were admitted, however, the orders in council ought nevertheless to be revoked. Can "the safety and honour of the British nation" demand that these orders shall continue to outrage the public law of the world, and sport with the indisputed rights of neutral commerce, after the pretext which was at first invented for them is gone? But you are menaced with a *revival* of the French system, and consequently may again be furnished with the same *pretext!* Be it so; yet still, as the system and the pretext are *at present* at an end, so, of course, should be your orders.

According to your mode of reasoning, the situation of neutral trade is hopeless indeed. Whether the Berlin decree exists or not, it is equally to justify your orders in council. You issued them before it was any thing but a shadow, and by doing so gave to it all the substance it could ever claim. It is at this moment nothing. It is revoked and has passed away, according to your own admission. You choose, however, to look for its re-appearance; and you make your own expectation equivalent to the decree itself. Compelled to concede that there is no anti-neutral French edict in operation upon the ocean, you think it sufficient to say that there *will be* such an edict, you know not when; and in the meantime you do all you can to verify your own prediction, by giving to your enemy all the provocation in your power to resume the decrees which he has abandoned.

For my part, my lord, I know not what it is that the British government requires, with a view to what it calls its *safety* and its *honor*, as an inducement to rescind its orders in council. It does not, I presume, imagine that such a system will be suffered to ripen into law. It must intend to relinquish it, sooner or later, as one of those violent experiments for which time can do nothing, and to which submission will be hoped in vain. Yet, even after the professed foundation of this mischievous system is taken away, another and another is industriously procured for it; so that no man can tell at what time, or under what circumstances it is likely to have an end. When realities cannot be found, possibilities supply their place, and that, which was originally said to be retaliation for actual injury, becomes at last (if such a solicism can be endured or imagined) retaliation for *apprehended* injuries, which the future may or may not produce, but which it is certain have no existence *now!*

I do not mean to grant, for I do not think, that the edict of Berlin did at any time lend even a colour of equity to the British orders in council, with reference to the United States: but it might reasonably have been expected that they, who have so much relied upon it as a justification, would have suffered it and them to sink together. How this is forbidden by your *safety* or your *honor* remains to be explained; and I am not willing to believe that either the one or the other is inconsistent with the observance of substantial justice, and with the prosperity and rights of peaceful states.

Although your lordship has slightly remarked upon certain recent acts of the French government, and has spoken in general terms of "the system of violence and injustice now pursued by France," as requiring "some precautions of defence on the part of Great Britain," I do not perceive that you deduce any consequence from these observations, in favour of a perseverance in the orders in council. I am not myself aware of any edicts of France which, now that the Berlin and Milan decrees are repealed, affect the rights of neutral commerce on the seas. And you will yourselves admit that if any of the acts of the French government, resting on territorial sovereignty, have injured, or shall hereafter injure, the United States, it is for them, and for them only, to seek redress. In like manner it is for Great Britain to determine what precautions of defence those measures of France, which you denominate unjust and violent, may render it expedient for her to adopt. The United States have only to insist that a sacrifice of their rights shall not be among the number of those precautions.

In replying to that passage in your letter, which adverts to the American act of non-intercourse, it is only necessary to mention the proclamation of the President of the United States, of the 2d of November last, and the act of congress which my letter of the 21st of September communicated, and to add that it is in the power of the British government to prevent the non-intercourse from being enforced against Great Britain.

Upon the concluding paragraph of your letter I will barely observe, that I am not in possession of any document, which you are likely to consider as *authentic*, showing that the French decrees are " absolutely revoked upon the single condition of the revocation of the British orders in council;" but that the information, which I have lately received from the American legation at Paris, confirms what I have already stated, and I think proved to your lordship, that those decrees are repealed and have ceased to have any effect. I will now trespass on you no further than to suggest that it would have given me sincere pleasure to be enabled to say as much of the British orders in council and of the blockades, from which it is impossible to distinguish them. I have the honor to be, with great respect and consideration, my lord, your lordship's most obedient humble servant,

(Signed) WM. PINKNEY.

The most noble the Marquis Wellesley.

NO V.

PARIS, le 18 Septembre, 1807.

J'ai soumis à sa majesté l'empereur et roi, monsieur, les doutes que s'était formé S. E. le ministre de la marine et des colonies, sur l'éntendue de quelques dispositions du décrét imperial du 21 Novembre, 1806, qui a déclaré les isles Britanniques en état de blocus ; voici quelles sont les intentions de sa majesté sur les points qui avaient mis en question.

1. Les bâtimens armés en guerre peuvent-ils en vertu du décrét imperial du 21 Novembre dernier, *saisir sur les bâtimens neutres*, soit les propriétés Anglaises, soit même toutes marchandises provenant de manufactures ou du territoire Anglais?

Sa majesté m'a fait connaitre, que, puis qu'elle avait jugé à propos de n'exprimer aucune exception dans son décrét, il n'y avait pas lieu d'en faire dans l'execution à l'égard de qui que ce pût être.

2. Sa majesté a sursis à statuer sur la question de savoir si les armeteurs Français doivent s'emparer des bâtimens neutres qui vont en Angleterre, ou qui en sortent, lors même quil n'ont point à bord de marchandises Anglaises.

3. Sur la troisieme question, qui était de savoir si les armemens Français sont passible de la retenue ordonnée par l'article 6, du décrét du 21 Novembre, sa majesté a déclaré que la disposition de cet article n'etait susceptible d'aucune restriction, c'est a dire, que la retenue doit avoir lieu sur le produit de toutes les confiscations de marchandises et propriétés qui ont été ou pourroient être prononcées en exécution du décrét, sans égard au lieu de la saisie ou à la qualité des saisissans.

Vous voudrez bien, Monsieur, notifier ces décisions au conseil des prises, les faire consigner sur les régistres et m'assurer la reception de ma lettre.

Recevez, &c. &c.

Le gd. juge min. de la justice,

(Signé) REGNIER.

Procureur general imperial conseil des prises.

General Armstrong to M. De Champagny.

PARIS, November 12th, 1807.

SIR,

The document to which these observations are prefixed will inform your excellency that an American ship, trading under the protection of the laws of nations, and of particular treaties, and suffering shipwreck on the coast of France, has recently been seized by his majesty's officers, and adjudged by his council of prizes as follows, viz:

" Our council puts at liberty the American vessel, the Horizon, shipwrecked the 30th of May last, near Morlaix, and consequently orders, that the amount arising from the sale legally made of the wreck of the said vessel, together with the merchandize of the cargo, which, according to an estimate made in presence of the overseers of the administrations of marine and custom-house, shall have been acknowledged not to proceed from English manufactures, nor from English territory, shall be restored to captain Mac Clure, without deducting any other expenses than those relative to the sale.

And with regard to the other merchandize of the cargo, which, from the result of the said estimate, shall be acknowledged to come from manufactures or English territory, by virtue of the fifth article of the decree of the 1st November, 1806, they shall be confiscated for the use of the state; the whole to be sold by the forms prescribed in the regulations: and the application of the product to be made in conformity to the arrangements of the said decree, deduction being made for the expense of saving the goods, and that of the support of the crew, until the day that the captain shall receive the notification of the present decision."

The reasons upon which this decision is founded are at once so new and so alarming to the present friendly relations of the two powers, that I cannot but discuss them with a freedom in some degree proportioned to my sense of their novelty and importance.

"Considering," says the council, "1st. That the neutrality of the ship and cargo were sufficiently established, the whole ought to be restored, (agreeably to the provisions of the convention of the 30th of September, 1800,) provided no merchandize of English origin had been found in her, and of course that she had not been brought within the limits of the imperial decree of the 21st of November, 1806."

Here is an open and unqualified admission, that the ship was found within the rules prescribed by the convention of 1800; that according to these rules, her cargo and herself ought to have been restored, and that such would have been the fact, but for the operation of the decree of the 21st of November, 1806.

In the letter your excellency did me the honour to write to me on the 7th of October last, you thought it "easy to reconcile the obligations of this decree with the preservation of those arising from treaties." It was not for me to examine the means by which this reconciliation could be effected; they, no doubt, fully existed, and yet exist in his majesty's good pleasure; and, taking for granted this fact, I saw in the opinion nothing but proofs of friendly dispositions and pledges that these were not to be either wantonly destroyed or diminished. How inauspicious, however, to its authority and the consolations derived from it, is this recent act of the council of prizes? an act which explicitly acknowledges the opposite characters and conflicting injunctions of these two instruments; and which of course draws after it considerations the most serious to the government of the United States.

The second reason of the council is,

"That the decree declaring (British) merchandize good prize, had principally in view captures made on the high seas; but that the question, whether shipwrecked goods ought to be restored or confiscated, having always been judged under the 14th article of the regulation of the 26th of July, 1778, and according to their character, (which might have rendered lawful, or have even commended their seizure at sea,) there is no reason to introduce in this case any new distinction, which, however philanthropic it may appear, has not as yet been adopted as a rule by any maritime nation."

The doctrine resisted in this passage, and which inculcates the duty of extending protection to the unfortunate, is not new to his majesty's council of prizes. They have themselves consecrated it by their decision of the 5th of March, 1800. By that decision they restored an enemy's ship, (the Diana) on the *single reason*, that "*she had been compelled to enter a French port by stress of weather.*" "I should certainly fail," says the attorney general, "in respect to myself and to the council, before whom I have the honour to represent the government, *were I not to maintain a principle consecrated by our laws, and by those of all nations.* In all circumstances let the loyalty of the French government serve as the basis of your decisions. Prove yourselves at once generous and just: your enemies will know and respect your magnanimity." Such was the principle adopted by the council in the year 1800, and in the case of an enemy's ship, yet we are now told, that this very principle, so honourable to the court, to the nation, and to human nature, is utterly unknown to all maritime people. And on what occasion do we hear this? when an enemy's ship is again thrown on the French coast? No, it has been reserved for the wreck of a neutral and friendly vessel! for a ship of the United States! It is not denied, that had this ship escaped the rocks and made the port of Morlaix, the only inhospitality to which she would have been exposed, (under the most rigorous interpretation of the law in question,) would have been that of being ordered again to sea. Has then the misfortune of shipwreck so far altered her condition as to expose her to the injury of confiscation also? and is this among the principles which the defender of maritime rights means to consecrate by his power and his wisdom? It is impossible.

The third reason of the council is, "That the application of the 5th article aforesaid, in as far as it concerns the American and other nations, is the result both of the general expressions of that very article, and of the communication recently made by his excellency, the grand judge, concerning the primitive intention of the sovereign."

This reason will be found to be substantially answered in my reply to reason, No. 5, of the council. It will be seen, that the opinion given here, that "the application of article 5, of the imperial decree, to American commerce, is the result of the general expressions of that very article," was not the opinion of the council, on the 5th of March last, when they judged the case of the Hibernia; they then declared, in totidem verbis, that the decree "said nothing of its own influence on the convention of 1800, between the United States and France.

The fourth reason of the council is, "that the expedition in question having certainly been made with full knowledge of the said decree, no objection can be drawn, with any propriety, from the general rules forbidding a retrospective action, nor even, in this particular case, from the posterior date of the act, in which the sovereign decides the question, since that act sprung from his supreme wisdom, not as an interpetration of a doubtful point, but as a declaration of an anterior and positive disposition."

A distinction is here attempted to be taken, between the interpretation of a doubtful point, and the declaration of an anterior and positive rule. This distinction cannot be maintained; for if the rule had been positive, there would have been no occasion for the declaration. Neither the minister of marine, nor the council of prizes could have had any doubts on the subject; the execution of the decree would have been prompt and peremptory; nor would a *second act,* on the part of his majesty, after the lapse of twelve months, have been necessary to give operation to the *first.* Need I appeal to your excellency's memory, for the facts on which these remarks turn? You know that doubts did exist—you know that there was, under them, *much hesitation* in pronouncing. You know that as late as the 9th of August I sought an explanation of the decree in question, and that even then your excellency, (who was surely a competent and legitimate organ of his majesty,) did not think yourself prepared to give it: the conclusion is inevitable. His majesty's answer, transmitted to the court of prizes on the 18th of September last, through the medium of the grand judge, was in the nature of an *interpretation,* and being so, could not, without possessing a retro-active quality, apply to events many months anterior in date to itself.

The fifth reason of the council, and the last which enters into my present view of the subject, is, "that though one of the principal agents of his majesty had given a contrary opinion, of *which the council had at no period partaken,* this opinion being that of an *individual,* could not, whatever consideration its author may merit, balance the formal declaration given in the name of his majesty himself; and that, if the communication of this opinion had, as is alleged, given room to, and served as a basis for many American shipments, and particularly of the one in question, this circumstance which may call for the iudulgence of his majesty, in a case in which the confiscation is entirely to the advantage of the state, does not prevent a council rigid in its duty, to pronounce in conformity to the decree of the 21st of November, and of the declaration which followed it."

It would appear from this paragraph that not finding it easy to untie the knot, the council had determined to cut it. Pressed by the fact, that an interpretation of the decree had been given by a minister of his majesty, specially charged with its execution, they would now escape from this fact and from the conclusions to which it evidently leads by alleging,

1st. That at no time had the council partaken of the opinion given by the minister: and,

2d. That this opinion being that of an *individual* could not possess either the force or the authority of one truly ministerial.

It appears to me, as I think it will appear to your excellency, that the council have, in these statements, been less correct than is usual to them on similar occasions. If, as they now assert, they have never partaken of the minister's opinion—if they have never even hesitated on the question, whether the decree of November did, or did not, derogate from the treaty of 1800—Why, I ask, suspend the American cases generally? or why decide as they did in the case of the Hibernia? If I mistake not, we find in this case the recognition of the very principle laid down by the minister of marine. That officer says, " in my opinion the November decree does not work any change in the rules at present observed with respect to neutral commerce, and consequently none in the convention of the 8th Vandemaire, year nine." And what says the council, " *admitting* that this part of the cargo, (the rum and ginger) was of *British origin*, the dispositions of the November decree, (*which contain nothing with regard to their own influence over the convention of the 8th Vandemaire, year nine*,) evidently cannot be applied to a ship leaving America on the sixth of the same month of November ; and of course cannot have authorised her capture in the moment she was entering the neutral port of her destination." We have here three distinct grounds of exemption from the effects of the November decree.

1st. The *ent.re silence* of that decree with regard to its own influence over the convention of 1800.

2d. The *early period* at which the ship left the United States. And,

3d. The *neutral character* of the port to which she was destined. If such, Sir, were the principles admitted by the council on the 5th of March last, with what correctness can it be now said, " that at no period have they partaken of the opinion of the minister ?"

The second fact asserted by the council is, that the interpretation of the decree in question, given on the 24th of December, 1806, was *private* not *publ.c*—or in other words, that it was the interpretation of the *man*, not that of the *minister*—and as such, cannot outweigh the more recent declaration coming directly from his majesty himself.

On the comparative weight of these declarations I shall say nothing, nor shall I do more to repel the first part of the insinuation, (*that the minister's declaration was that only of the individual*)—than to submit to your excellency my letter of the 20th of December, 1806, claiming from that minister an *official* interpretation of the decree in question, and his answer of the 24th of the same month, giving to me the interpretation demanded.

To your excellency, who as late as the 21st of August last, considered the minister of marine as the natural organ of his majesty's will, in whatever regarded the decree aforesaid, and who actually applied to him for information relating to it, this allegation of the council of prizes and the reasoning founded upon it, cannot but appear very extraordinary, and will justify me, in requesting that his majesty may be moved to set aside the decision in question, on the ground of error in the opinion of the council.

If in support of this conclusion I have drawn no arguments from the treaty of 1800, nor from the laws of nations, your excellency will not be at a loss to assign to this omission its true cause. It would surely have been a useless formality to appeal to authorities, not only practically, but even professedly extinct. In the letter of the minister of justice of the 18th September, we are told by his majesty himself, that "since *he* had not judged proper to make any exception in the letter of his decree, there was no room to make any in its execution," and in the report of your excellency's predecessor, of the 20th November 1806, we have these memorable words:

"England has declared those places blockaded, before which she had not a single ship of war. She has done more, for she has declared in a state of blockade, places, which all her assembled forces were incapable of blockading—immense coasts, and a vast empire. Afterwards, drawing from a chimerical right and from an assumed fact the consequence that she might justly make her prey of every thing going to the places laid under interdiction, by a simple declaration of the British admiralty, and of every thing arising therefrom, and carrying this doctrine into effect, she has alarmed neutral navigators, and driven them to a distance from ports whither their interests attracted them, and which the law of nations authorised them to frequent. Thus it is, that she has turned to her own profit, and to the detriment of Europe, but more particularly of France, the audacity with which she *mocks at all rights and insults even reason itself*. Against a power which forgets to such a pitch all ideas of justice, and all humane sentiments, *what can be done but to forget them for an instant one's self?*" Words cannot go further to shew the extinguished authority in the one case, of the treaty subsisting between the United States and his imperial majesty, and in the other, of the law of nations: to appeal to them therefore, would be literally appealing to the dead.

Accept, Sir, &c. &c.

(Signed) JOHN ARMSTRONG.

His Excellency, the Minister
of Foreign Affairs.

No. VI.

RULES OF THE DISTRICT COURT FOR THE SOUTHERN DISTRICT OF NEW-YORK IN PRIZE CAUSES.

1st. There shall be issued under the seal and authority of this court, commissions to such persons as the court shall think fit, appointing them commissioners to take the examinations of witnesses in prize causes in preparatory, on the standing interrogatories which have been settled and adopted by this court, and to discharge such other duties in relation to ships or vessels, or property brought into the district of New-York, as prize, as shall be designated, by the said commissions, and the rules and orders of this court.

2d. The captors of any property brought into the district of New-York, as prize, or some one in their behalf, shall without delay, give notice to one of the commissioners aforesaid, of the arrival of such property, and of the place where the same may be found.

3d. That upon the receipt of such notice, the commissioner or commissioners shall repair to the place where the said prize property then is, and if the same be a ship or vessel, or if the property be on board a ship or vessel, he shall cause the said ship or vessel to be safely moored in sufficient depth of water, or in soft ground, so that the ship may receive no damage. The said commissioner or commissioners shall then take from the captors or others, information of the arrival of the captured ship or vessel, or property, and of the time when the same was brought into the district. That the said commissioner or commissioners, in case the prize be a ship or vessel, shall examine whether bulk has been broken, and if it be found that bulk has been broken, the said commissioner or commissioners shall take information upon what occasion, or what cause the same was done. If the property captured be not a ship or vessel, or in a ship or vessel, the commissioner or commissioners shall examine the chests, packages, boxes or casks containing the subject captured, and shall ascertain whether the same has been opened, and upon what occasion the same were opened, and shall in every case, examine whether any of the property originally captured has been secreted or taken away subsequently to the capture. And in every case, the commissioner, before he leaves the captured property, shall secure the same by seals upon the hatches, doors, chests, bales, boxes, casks or packages, as the case may require, so that they cannot be opened without breaking the said seals, and the said seals shall not be broken, or the property removed, much less unladened from any vessel, unless by special order of this court, excepting only in cases of fire or tempest, or of absolute necessity. If the captured property be not a vessel, or on board a vessel, the commissioner or commissioners shall take a detailed account of the particulars thereof, and shall cause the same to be deposited under seals as aforesaid, in a place of safety, there to abide the order or decree of this court.

4th. If no notification shall within reasonable time have been given by the captors, or by any person on their behalf, of any property which may be brought as prize within this district, and the commissioners, or either of them, shall become informed thereof by any means, it shall be the duty of the said commissioners, or one of them, to repair to the place where such property is, and to proceed in respect to the same, as if notice had been given by the captors.

5th. The captors shall deliver up to the commissioner or commissioners, when he or they shall, conformably to the foregoing rule, repair to the place where such captured property is, or at such other time as the said commissioners, or either of them, shall require the same, all such papers, passes, sea-briefs, charters, bills of lading, cockets, letters and other documents and writings as shall have been found on board the captured ship, or which have any reference to or connexion with the captured property, and which are in the possession, custody or power of the captors. The said papers, documents and writings shall be regularly marked and numbered by the said commissioner or commissioners, and the captor, chief officer or some other person who was present at the taking of the prize, and saw that such documents, papers and writings were found with the prize, must make a deposition before the said commissioner or commissioners, who are hereby authorised to take the same, that they are delivered up to the said commissioner or commissioners as they were found or received, without any fraud, subduction or embezzlement. And if any documents, papers or writings relative to or connected with the captured property are missing or wanting, the deponent shall in his said deposition, account for the same according to the best of his knowledge, information and belief. And the deponent must further swear, that if at any time thereafter, and before the final condemnation or acquittal of the said property, any further or other papers relating to the said captued property shall be found or discovered, to the knowledge of the deponent, they shall also be delivered up, on information thereof given to the commissioners or to this court: which deposition shall be reduced to writing by the commissioners, and shall be transmitted to the clerk of the court as herein after mentioned.

6th. That when the said documents, papers and writings are delivered to a commissioner, he shall retain the same till after the examination in preparatorio shall have been made by him, as is hereafter provided, and then he shall transmit the same with the same affidavit in relation thereto, the preparatory examinations, and the information he may have received in regard to the said captured property, under cover and under his seal to this court, addressed to the clerk thereof, and expressing on the said cover to what captured property the documents relate, or who claims to be the captors thereof, or from whom he received the information of the capture, which said cover shall not be opened without the order of this court.

7th. That within three days after the captured property shall have been brought within the jurisdiction of this court, the captor shall produce to the commissioner or commissioners, three or four, if so many there be, of the company or persons who were captured with or who claim the said captured property, and in case the capture be a vessel, the master, mate or supercargo must always be two in order that they may be examined by the said commissioner or commissioners in preparatory upon the standing interrogatories.

8th. That each commissioner appointed or to be p-pointed pursuant to the rules of this court, for taking examinations in preparatorio, shall be furnished with a printed copy of these rules, and of the standing interrogatories certified by the clerk, and in the examination of witnesses in preparatorio, the commissioner or commissioners shall use no other interrogatories but the said standing interrogatories, unless special interrogatories are directed by this court: nevertheless, they may explain at all times to a witness when it may be necessary, any of the said interrogatories. They shall write down the answer of every witness separately to each interrogatory, and not to several interrogatories together. When a witness declares he cannot answer to any interrogatory, the commissioner or commissioners shall admonish the witness, that by virtue of his oath taken to speak the truth, and nothing but the truth, he must answer to the best of his knowledge, or when he does not know absolutely, then to answer to the best of his belief concerning any one fact.

9th. That the examination of every witness shall be begun, continued and finished in the same day, and not at different times. That copies of the standing interrogatories shall not be returned by the commissioner or commissioners with the examinations, but it shall be sufficient for the answers of the witnesses to refer to the standing interrogatories by corresponding numbers: that before any witness shall be examined in the standing interrogatories, the commissioners, or one of them, shall administer to him an oath in the following form: "You shall true answer make to all such questions as shall be asked of you on these interrogatories, and therein you shall speak the whole truth, and nothing but the truth, so help you God." If the witness is conscientiously averse to swearing, an affirmation to the same effect shall be administered to him.

10th. That the examination of each witness on the standing interrogatories, shall be returned according to the following form. Deposition of A. B. a witness produced, sworn and examined in preparatorio on the   day of   in the year   at the house of   situated in the city of   on the standing interrogatories established by the district court of the United States, for the district of New-York. The said witness having been produced for the purpose of such examination by C. D. in behalf of the captors of a certain ship or vessel, called the   (or of certain goods, wares and merchandize as the case may be.)

1st. To the first interrogatory, the deponent answers that he was born at   &c.

2d. To the second interrogatory, the deponent answers that he was present at the time of the taking, &c.

That when the interrogatories have been all answered by a witness, he shall sign his depositions, and the commissioner or commissioners shall put a jurata thereto in the usual form, and subscribe his name to the same.

11th. That no person having or claiming any interest in the captured property, or having any interest in any ship having letters of marque or commissions of war, shall presume to act as a commissioner. Nor shall a commissioner presume to act either as proctor, advocate or counsel either for captors or claimants in any prize cause whatever.

12th. If the captain or prize master neglect or refuse to give up and to deliver to the commissioner or commissioners, the documents, papers and writings relating to the captured property, according to the foregoing rule, or refuse or neglect to produce, or cause to be produced, witnesses to be examined in preparatory, within three days after the arrival of the captured property within the jurisdiction of this court, or shall otherwise unnecessarily delay the production of the said documents, papers or writings, the commissioners, or one of them nearest to the place where the captured property may be, or before whom the examination in preparatorio may have been already begun, shall admonish in writing the delinquent to produce the said documents, papers and writings, and to bring forward his witnesses, and if he shall still neglect, or unnecessarily delay so to do, such commissioner or commissioners shall certify the same to this court, that such proceedings may thereupon be had as justice may require.

13th. If within twenty-four hours after the arrival within this district, of any captured vessel, or of any property taken as a prize, the captors or their agent shall not give notice to a commissioner, pursuant to the provisions herein made, or shall not, two days after such notice given, produce witnesses to be examined in preparatorio, then any person claiming the captured property and restoration thereof, may give notice to the commissioners as aforesaid, of the arrival of the said captured property, and thereupon such proceedings may be had by the commissioners in respect to the said property, and relative to the documents, papers and writings connected with the said capture, which the claimant may have in his possession, custody or power, and relative to the examination of witnesses in preparatorio as near as may be, as is before provided for cases where the captors shall give notice and examine in preparatorio. And the said claimant may in such cases file his libel for restitution, and proceed thereon according to the rules and practice of this court.

14th. That as soon as may be convenient after the captured property shall have been brought within the jurisdiction of this court, a libel may be filed and a monition shall thereupon be issued, and such proceedings shall be had as are provided by the 89th and 90th sections of the act entitled, An act to regulate the collection of duties on imports and tonnage in cases of vessels, goods, wares and merchandize which become forfeited in virtue of said act.

15th. That in all cases by consent of captor and claimant, or upon attestation exhibited upon the part of the claimant only, without consent of the captor, that the cargo or part thereof is perishing or perishable, the claimant specifying the quantity and quality of the cargo, may have the same delivered to him on giving bail to answer the value thereof if condemned, and further to abide the event of the suit, such bail to be approved of by the captor, or otherwise the persons who give security, swearing themselves to be severally and truly worth the sum for which they give security. But if the parties cannot agree upon the value of the cargo, a decree or commission of appraisement may issue from the court to ascertain the value. In cases when there is no claim, an affidavit being exhibited on the part of the captor, of such perishing or perishable cargo, specifying the quantity and quality thereof, the captor may have a decree or commission of appraisement and sale of such cargo, and bring in the proceeds into court in view of any claim, virtually to abide further orders.

16th. That the name of each cause be entered by the clerk upon the list for hearing in their order, according to the dates of the returns of the monitions, and the lists are to be constantly hung up in the court room and clerk's office for public inspection. Proviso : This order of hearing is to be invariably observed, unless in any cause of great national importance, the judge shall find it necessary to direct the hearing of any particular cause immediately.

17th. That in all cases where a decree or commission of appraisement and sale of any ship and cargo, or either of them shall have issued, that no question respecting the adjudication of such ship and goods or either of them, or as to freight or expenses, shall be heard, till the said decree or commission shall be returned with the account of sales, and the proceeds according to such accompt of sales paid into the clerk, to abide the order of the court in respect thereto.

18th. That after the examinations taken in preparatory in the standing interrogatories, are brought into the registry, and the monition has issued, no further or other examinations upon the said interrogatories shall be taken, or affidavits received in the office without the special directions of the judge, upon application made in open court.

19th. That there shall be no invocation of papers from one captured ship to another, without the special permission of the judge, at least two days previous to the cause coming on, in which such papers are intended to be used, founded on an affidavit on the part of the captors, that such papers, in the opinion of his counsel, are material and necessary ; it being understood that the case of the ship from whence the invocation is proposed to be made, shall have been previously heard, and its papers in possession of the court; and that necessary extracts from such papers should only be used. But as the intention of the captor is to discover fraud, the party who hath an interest in confusing evidence and in fraudulently putting different papers on board different ships, the claimants are precluded from invoking, but may argue from the papers invoked by the captors.

20th. That in all motions for commissions and decrees of appraisement and sale, the time shall be specified, within which it is prayed that the commissions or decrees shall be made returnable.

21st. That the commissioner or commissioners make regular returns on the days in which their commission or decrees are returnable, stating the progress that has been made in the execution of the commissions or decrees, and if necessary, praying an enlargement of the time for the completion of the business.

22d. That the commissioner or commissioners bring in the proceeds which have been collected at the same time with their returns; and if the whole proceeds have not been collected, they return only such sums as may be required to answer accruing expenses.

23d. That on the returns of commissions or decrees, the commissioners or the marshal bring in the vouchers.

24th. That all monies brought into court in prize causes, shall be forthwith paid into bank, pursuant to the
of the general rules of this court, and shall only be drawn out on the specific orders of the court in favor of the persons respectively having right, their agents or representatives duly authorized to receive the same.

25th. That each commissioner, for discharging the duties which he is hereby to perform, shall be entitled to the following fees, and the two commissioners resident in the city of New-York shall each be entitled to the like fees in each case.

For receiving and entering a notice of capture, ...

For attending at place where the captured property is, ...

For attending to the safety of a vessel. For inspecting captured property, putting the same under seal, receiving and examining all letters, documents and papers relative to the same, over and above all disbursements that may actually be paid, for moving or transferring a vessel or property to a place of safety, and under all actual disbursements and expenses, . .

For writing an affidavit with respect to papers, and taking an account thereof, and for marking and numbering the same,

For transferring papers and information to the clerk of the court, ...

For drafting and copying the examination of each witness, and for administering the oath to the same, for each folio, . .

For any special services not herein provided for, such compensation as the court under all the circumstances of the case shall think reasonable and just.

No. VII.

FORM OF PRIZE LIBEL.

District Court of the United States of America, for the District of New-York.

At a special district court of the United States of America, for the district of New-York, held at the city of New-York, in the said district, on the second day of January, in the year of our Lord one thousand eight hundred and thirteen, comes Nathan Sanford, attorney of the said United States, for the district of New-York, who prosecutes in this respect for the said United States, and also for the officers and crew of the frigate of the said United States, called the United States, hereinafter mentioned, and being present in this honorable court in his proper person, in the name and on behalf of the said United States, and the officers and crew aforesaid, alleges, propounds and declares, as follows, that is to say—

First—That open and public war did at all the times mentioned in this libel, exist, and does now exist, between the United States of America and their territories, and the united kingdom of Great Britain and Ireland and the dependencies thereof.

Secondly—That Stephen Decatur is, and at all the times mentioned in this libel, was a captain in the navy of the said United States, and is, and at all the times herein mentioned, was commander of the said frigate of the said United States, called the United States.

Thirdly—That the said Stephen Decatur, captain and commander of the said frigate, called the United States, as aforesaid, did, in pursuance of the said state of war, and instructions from the President of the said United States, on the twenty-fifth day of October, in the year of our Lord one thousand eight hundred and twelve, on the high seas, to wit, on the Atlantic ocean, subdue, seize and take as prize of war, a certain ship, vessel or frigate, called the Macedonian, with her tackle, apparel and furniture, and also her arms, ammunition, stores, provisions and appurtenances.

Fourthly—That the said ship, vessel or frigate, called the Macedonian, is, and at all the times hereinafter mentioned, was a public vessel of war, belonging to the king of the united kingdom of Great Britain and Ireland, and was employed in his service.

Fifthly—That the said ship, vessel or frigate, called the Macedonian, having been so seized and taken as aforesaid, has been brought into the port of New-York, for legal adjudication, and is now in the said port, within the jurisdiction of this honorable court.

Sixthly—That by reason of the premises, the said ship, vessel or frigate, called the Macedonian, with her tackle, apparel and furniture, and also, her arms, ammunition, stores, provisions and appurtenances, have become forfeited to the said United States, and to the officers and crew of the said frigate óf the said United States, called the United States, and ought to be considered to their use.

Lastly—That all the premises are and were true, public, and notorious, of which true proof being made, the said attorney prays the usual process and monition of this honorable court in this behalf to be made, and that all persons interested in the said ship, vessel or frigate, called the Macedonian, her tackle, apparel and furniture, arms, ammunition, stores provisions and appurtenances, may be cited in general and special to answer the premises, and all due proceedings being had, that the said ship, vessel or frigate, called the Macedonian, her tackle, apparel and furniture, arms, ammunition, stores, provisions and appurtenances, may for the causes aforesaid and others appearing, be condemned by the definitive sentence and decree of this honorable court, as forfeited and adjudged to be lawful prize as aforesaid, &c.

NATHAN SANFORD,

Attorney of the United States, for the district of New-York.

ALPHABETICAL INDEX.

A.

B.

C.

D.

E.

F.

G.

H

I.

O.

P.

R.

S.

U.

V.

W.